Developing Communication Skills

Developing Communication Skills

A practical handbook for
language teachers, with examples in
English, French and German

Pat Pattison

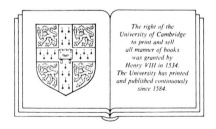

The right of the
University of Cambridge
to print and sell
all manner of books
was granted by
Henry VIII in 1534.
The University has printed
and published continuously
since 1584.

Cambridge University Press

Cambridge
London   New York   New Rochelle
Melbourne   Sydney

To M.P.

Published by the Press Syndicate of the University of Cambridge
The Pitt Building, Trumpington Street, Cambridge CB2 1RP
32 East 57th Street, New York, NY 10022, USA
10 Stamford Road, Oakleigh, Melbourne 3166, Australia

© Cambridge University Press 1987

First published 1987

Printed in Great Britain at the University Press, Cambridge

Library of Congress cataloguing in publication data
Pattison, Pat.
   Developing communication skills.

   Bibliography:
   Includes index.
   1. Languages, Modern – Study and teaching.
2. Communicative competence.   I. Title.
PB36.P34   1987   418'.007   86–12940

British Library Cataloguing in Publication Data

Pattison, Pat
Developing communication skills: a practical
handbook for language teachers with examples in
English, French and German.
1. Language and languages – Study and
teaching   2. Communication
I. Title
400   P51

ISBN 0 521 30177 7 hard covers
ISBN 0 521 31772 X paperback

Contents

Acknowledgements

My thanks go, firstly, to all those learners, teachers and teacher-trainees who, over many years and in many countries, have contributed to the making of this book. One name must stand as representative for so many: Piet Pieterson and his pupils (whose work is quoted in 3.5, 6.5 and 6.7).

My debt is obvious to others who have worked and published in the field of teaching languages for communication. I have also learned from lectures and workshops, and from discussions with many of these writers: their names are included in *Booklists* 2 and 3, and I express my personal thanks to them here.

Very special thanks go to my colleagues at the Education Institute (P.D.I.) of Utrecht University, Leen Don, Heleen de Hondt, Noortje Jacobs, Peter Slagter and Gerard Westoff, for their unfailing interest and in particular for their generosity in giving me time to complete the book.

I am very grateful to Marie-Madeleine Arizcuren, Patricia Clavier and Angela Pfaff, who contributed far more to this book than simply help with translating and correcting the French and German material.

Finally, my thanks to Rosemary Davidson and Amanda Ogden of C.U.P. for their guidance, and to Alison Silver for all her help in discussions and detailed work on the final version of the manuscript.

PAT PATTISON

Some of the texts and pictures in *Teaching material* throughout the book have been collected, translated or adapted over so many years and from so many sources, including learners and generous colleagues, that the originals can no longer be traced. Where such sources should be acknowledged, the author and publishers would welcome information from copyright owners.

Introduction

This book has developed out of my own interest in learning and using languages for communication; and out of my experience as a teacher of modern languages (and English as mother tongue) in state secondary schools, evening classes, private language schools, colleges and universities in Europe and Canada; and most recently in teacher training in Great Britain and the Netherlands.

I discovered that activities designed to develop communication skills could be used in all these situations, adapted to take account of the differences in teaching conditions. The greatest differences, in my experience, lie between classes in private language schools or universities, where many teachers are native speakers, and where it is relatively easy to use communicative activities – and classes in secondary schools, where the motivation, numbers, age of the learners, as well as available time and material, are not likely to be so favourable. These differences are greater than those between average modern language classrooms in Europe, certainly in terms of intrinsic learner motivation and teaching conditions.

In recent years I have been collecting reports from teachers and trainee-teachers – working in primary and secondary schools and evening classes – on which communication activities they found easiest to use, and in what ways. This book, therefore, is based on the experience and opinions of many modern language teachers, and presents communication activities organised in the form found most suitable for general language courses in schools.

In writing it, I have kept in mind the problems most often mentioned by teachers: 'Classes are too large – there isn't enough time – examination pressures – all this is for the future'; and I try to show how communication skills can be developed by often minor adaptations of familiar techniques and textbook material, without far-reaching changes in course-content or organisation, which are beyond the range of practical possibilities for most teachers. In many countries, local and national examinations are beginning to place more emphasis on communication skills, so that 'examination pressures' are likely to work increasingly in favour of a more communicative approach in the classroom.

The description of communication activities assumes the desirability of an eclectic and explorative approach in which teachers can try out a variety of activities and material, techniques and types of classroom organisation, to see which work best for them and their learners. There are examples of teaching material in English, French and German, based on typical material from modern language textbooks (many of these pages can be photocopied). Though the descriptions concentrate on listening and speaking, most activities can be – and have been – used for reading and writing; and there are suggestions for how further material can be found or made by teachers and learners.

The activities in the book are those which were found to be:
– *effective:* that is, they improved learner motivation and performance in practice
– *efficient:* in terms of the time needed to prepare and to use them in class
– *flexible:* in terms of the number of ways in which, or levels at which, the activity could be practised
There are quotations from actual lessons to illustrate how learners and teachers used this material.

The book is not designed to be read from cover to cover: the sections are cross-referenced, and there are detailed indexes and booklists so that readers can find their way to what interests them most.

This is a *handbook* for teachers: it is a guide to possibilities, not a list of prescriptions. It is *for* teachers, offering support and suggestions in those areas where this seems most necessary. But ultimately, it is for both *teachers and learners,* in the hope that both will find pleasure and profit in developing communication skills.

A quote from a thirteen year old British learner of French can stand as the motto for the whole book:

'*It's exciting just learning another language so you can communicate with other people.*'

Using this book

For an overview of all the communicative activities, see the introductions to Sections 1 to 7.

If you are looking for ways of practising particular language items in a more communicative way, turn to the language indexes for examples of given structures, functions, situations or topic areas. Having chosen a suitable activity, see the *Guide to activities* (p. 25) for a description of the layout, the symbols used, and ways of using the activities in the classroom.

The introductory chapter can be consulted at any time for more detailed information on the definition and classroom applications of the communicative approach on which the activities are based.

Developing communication skills

Communication and the four language skills

Communication may involve listening, speaking, reading and writing. This book concentrates on the two primary language skills, listening and speaking, because these, in the opinion of most teachers, are more difficult to practise in classroom conditions; and this applies particularly to speech practice. In reading and writing, learners can take time to reflect on the form and meaning of the language they are dealing with. Oral communication (speaking and listening) does not give unlimited time for consideration or correction of the language being used. Moreover, whereas thirty or more learners can read and write individually and in silence, oral practice with the same number is much more difficult to arrange.

However, such practice cannot be neglected. Questionnaires have repeatedly shown that both learners and teachers feel that being able to speak and understand the foreign language (FL) is an important aim in a general language course. One fifteen year old British learner of Spanish, asked how she would like to use the FL, put this most comprehensively: 'I'd like to use it all over and talk to anyone anywhere and they would be able to talk back!' (This and other quotations in the book are from a questionnaire which I conducted with European schoolchildren between 1982 and 1984.)

Modern textbooks emphasise speech: they contain numerous drills, exercises and dialogues for oral practice, and are often accompanied by tapes of native speakers. Yet many learners still feel that they are not learning the FL as and for communication and that – as their teachers might agree – they would be unable to understand and to express themselves freely in contact with speakers of the FL. This does not mean that language courses should consist mostly of oral practice: it does imply that whatever speech and listening practice there is should have more communicative characteristics.

Oral practice or communication practice?

In acquiring their native language, learners have also acquired experience of how language works as a system of communication. Yet this experience is often ignored or even contradicted in FL lessons. Suddenly, what is said (the content or message) is less important than how it is said (the form). Learners can be trapped into thinking they are being asked for a meaningful response in the FL, when in fact the teacher only wants an example of particular vocabulary or structures.

Examples from practice

1 *A beginners' French class*
   Teacher: Quel temps fait-il?
   Learner 1: Er – il pleut.
   T: Very good.
   L2: But it's not true – it's not raining!
   T: I know it's not true, but it's correct: the French is correct.

It is not hard to comprehend the confusion of young learners confronted with a language that not only differs from their own in its sound and structure, but in the very way it is used. The synonyms 'strange' and 'alien' seem most appropriate for such a 'foreign' language! Of course learners quickly adapt to this sort of language practice, but they can be caught out in the same way at any level:

2 *An intermediate English class*
   T: Where was the parcel thrown?
   L1: On to the road (*teacher shakes head*) – the parcel was thrown on to the road.
   T: Good. (*To L2*) What was thrown on to the road?
   L2: (*hestitating, assuming that the teacher could not be asking for information that had just been given*)
   T: (*helpfully*) The parcel was thrown on to the road.

The learner's assumption was wrong: the teacher was again only interested in form – a sentence in the passive – not in the content of speech.

   This sort of basic language practice has a place in the FL classroom: it can be used whenever teachers simply want to present, and to check if learners can reproduce, new items of language – vocabulary, pronunciation, structures, etc. Problems only arise if learners (and teachers!) do not clearly grasp that they are using the FL at the most basic level of language practice: simple recognition and reproduction of the given items, with attention to the medium, not the message.

However, if their course contains too much of this sort of practice, without any personal interest or involvement in what is being said, learners may well come to feel that they are not learning the FL as and for communication, but learning to repeat more or less meaningless formulae on demand. This cannot be expected to contribute adequately to developing communication skills which the learner can use outside the classroom. It may also be a contributory factor to learner demotivation and high drop-out rates from school FL courses.

Evidence for this – since controlled experiments in genuine classroom conditions are notoriously hard to organise and assess – depends largely on extrapolations from research into learning, on experiments in universities, and the experience reported by individual classroom teachers, who notice a difference, at the very least in learner motivation, when they move from non-communicative to communicative language practice. British schools following communicative objectives in their FL teaching find that drop-out rates are greatly reduced. (See Booklist 3 for sources of more information.)

In working out the differences between non-communicative and communicative use of the FL, I have found it a useful starting point to consider the characteristics of typical oral practice between teachers and learners in the classroom, and the way foreign and native speakers communicate with each other outside the classroom. The characteristics are listed below.

List 1 FL (oral) practice in the classroom	*List 2 FL (oral) communication outside the classroom*
WHAT: *Content of communication*	
Content or topic is decided by teacher, textbook, tape, etc. The meaning of what they say may not always be clear to the speakers. The content is highly predictable.	Speakers express their own ideas, wishes, opinions, attitudes, information, etc. They are fully aware of the meaning they wish to convey. The exact content of any speaker's message is unpredictable.

WHY 1: *Reason for communication*

Learners speak in order to practise speaking; because teacher tells them to; in order to get a good mark, etc.	Speakers have a social or personal reason to speak. There is an information gap to be filled, or an area of uncertainty to be made clear. What is said is potentially interesting or useful to the participants.

WHY 2: *Result of communication*

The FL is spoken; the teacher accepts or corrects what is said; a mark is given, etc. (extrinsic motivation).	Speakers achieve their aims; they get what they wanted, an information gap is filled, a problem is solved, a decision is reached or a social contact is made, etc. The result is of intrinsic interest or value to the participants.

WHO: *Participants in communication*

A large group in which not everyone is facing the speakers or interested in what they say; except for one person, the teacher, who pays less attention to what they say than to how correctly they say it.	Two or more people, usually facing each other, paying attention and responding to what is said, rather than to how correctly it is said.

HOW: *Means of communication*

Language from teacher or tape is very closely adapted to learners' level. All speech is as accurate as possible, and usually in complete sentences. Problems in communicating meaning are often dealt with by trans-lation. Learners are corrected if their speech deviates from standard forms, whether or not their meaning is clear. Teachers help learners to express themselves more correctly.	Native-speaker output is not very closely adjusted to foreigners' level. Meaning is conveyed by any means at the speakers' command: linguistic or para-linguistic (gestures, etc.). Problems are dealt with by negotiation and exchange of feedback between speakers. Trans-lation is not always possible. Errors not affecting com-munication are largely ignored. Native speakers help foreign speakers to express themselves more clearly.

What is possible in the classroom?

There are probably few classrooms where oral practice is always and only as described in List 1 on p. 7–8. On the other hand, no classroom can reproduce completely the conditions described in List 2 on p. 7–8. Organised communication practice in the classroom will always be more or less artificial, particularly where all concerned share the same mother tongue. Moreover, where learners encounter and use the FL for only a few hours a week, they must make optimum use of the time available, and their learning must be structured in some way. This does not mean that it is impossible to develop the learners' communication skills in the FL classroom. It does mean that their classroom practice should have as many characteristics from List 2 as possible.

Oral exercises are sometimes divided into two broad groups. The first contains drills, substitution tables, structure-based dialogues for repetition, etc. These may be variously described as rehearsal, controlled, medium-oriented, pseudo- or pre-communicative practice. The second group includes exercises with functional language, role-play, practice based on situations or themes, language games, free conversations and discussions, etc. These may be described as performance, free, message-oriented or communicative practice. I have found it more useful, however, to employ Lists 1 and 2 as a means of deciding how far any of the above exercise types – from drill to discussion – is or can be made more communicative.

This book is based on the proposition that all the types of oral practice mentioned above can have at least some characteristics drawn from List 2. There is thus a gradation, a difference in the degree or depth of communicative force present in language exercises, depending on how few or how many characteristics from List 2 they contain, rather than a division between types of exercise which are seen as inherently non-communicative or inherently communicative. We can move exercises or activities of any kind closer to the communicative end of the spectrum, so to speak, by increasing the learners' sense of involvement in what they are hearing and saying.

This is exemplified later in this chapter, and in greater practical detail in the introductions and activities in Sections 1 to 7. Within each section, the activities are, in general, arranged in order of increasing communicative depth, though the language used for communication may often be adapted for elementary, intermediate or advanced levels.

How far teachers can move towards a greater depth of communication will depend on themselves, their learners, and their teaching circumstances; but I have found that we are all able to move our classroom practice at least a little way in this direction, and still 'cover the syllabus' – and that there is a very positive response from the learners.

Content, purpose and result of communication (WHAT and WHY)

The characteristics under WHAT in List 2 on p. 7 are important and those under WHY 1 and 2 are essential in any kind of communicative practice. There must be a clear intention behind the learners' speech, with interest in the messages conveyed and the results achieved. As an example, compare the following exercises, from the same textbook unit. Both deal with the simple past at intermediate level. The first exercise has a language frame in the form of a health quiz:

Questions			Answers	
Did you	drink any milk	yesterday?	Yes (1)	No (0)
	eat any sweets		Yes (0)	No (1)
	take any exercise		Yes (1)	No (0)
	etc.		*etc.*	

The points are finally added up to show the 'personal fitness' score. (This exercise can be done in various ways, including oral pair work.)

The second exercise has a language frame for oral pair work beginning:

A: Did you have a good time		last night	
		last weekend? *etc.*	
B: Yes, I did,	I had a	marvellous time	
No, I didn't,		miserable	
A: Oh really? What happened?			

After this learners are free to continue the conversation as they wish. At first sight, the 'health quiz' may seem less communicative because the learners are working with totally controlled language. However, the question 'controlled' or 'free' language is not the essential one. If we look at the two exercises in terms of the characteristics given under WHAT and WHY in list 2, and if we ask in particular: Is there any clear reason and result for their speech which can interest them (in other words, is there any real intention behind their words, other than simply to speak the FL?) – then it appears that the first exercise contains communicative characteristics to a greater degree than the second. The learners exchange genuine personal information, which is potentially interesting, not least because their speech has a clear aim: to find and compare their fitness scores. (See Porter Ladousse 1983 in *Booklist* 2c for further examples of such quizzes.) Learners commonly become far more involved in this kind of practice than in exercises of the second type, which, except with very motivated learners, often lead to desultory and forced conversations: the speakers do not usually provide genuine personal information in the context of such a classroom exercise; what is said is not usually of great interest to either participant; and finally, they have no definite reason or result for their speech – except speech itself.

It is, of course, not always possible to use genuine personal information in classroom practice, so I give one further example of how a simple exercise with given language was gradually adapted in the classroom to add more characteristics from List 2, by letting learners make a personal choice from the language supplied.

A French textbook for beginners had an exercise in which learners answered questions from the teacher or classmates:
Q: *Êtes-vous médecin/architecte/actrice?*
R: *Oui, je suis médecin/architecte/actrice*, etc.
Here, the speakers have no choice in what they say, their speech is totally predictable, and it has no reason or result – except perhaps to hear the teacher say 'Correct' with reference to the form of their questions and answers. The teacher first sought to make this more communicative by letting some learners choose their profession from the list, and giving them flashcards showing their choice. This personal choice of WHAT to say added more interest to the exercise; but it is hardly natural to ask someone with a card saying ACTRICE – *Êtes-vous actrice?* (besides which it cost the teacher too much time to make the flashcards!). The exercise becomes more effective, and more efficient, when learners write down their own secret choices from the list, creating an information gap, and thus giving the learners a reason (WHY) to ask their questions. The answers may be *Oui, je suis actrice* or (adding one word to the basic language frame) *Non, je suis architecte:* so the attention of all the speakers is now on the content, as well as the form, of what is said, and the purpose of the questioners is to make a correct guess (and score a point!). Though the formal language practice remains exactly the same, the drill has in effect become a guessing game, and teachers find their

learners are enthusiastic about the exercise, instead of bored. (See the introduction and first three activities in Section 1 *Questions and answers* for more examples.)

Not all communication practice will consist of this kind of repetition with communicative characteristics; but even totally free speech practice is not fully communicative if it does not answer the question WHY we should communicate – and in the FL? (As is shown by the second example 'Did you have a good time?' on p. 10.) The introduction to Section 7 *Discussions and decisions* covers this point more fully.

Outside the classroom, the exchange of personal information, opinions and ideas has intention and result (not always identical!) – something is done, or the relationship between the speakers is affected in some way. In classroom practice, these effects can be imitated, but not often completely reproduced; learners can be given aims for their speech which are more suited to the classroom context, while resembling those operating outside it: making correct guesses, for which they can score points (this may or may not include points for linguistic accuracy) – see many activities in Sections 1 and 2; finding information that completes or matches their own – see Section 3; creating something, in the form of pictures, stories, role-plays, etc. – Sections 4 and 5; solving puzzles – Section 6; or making plans or decisions – Section 7. The great variety of possibilities is shown in the variety of aims given for the activities in these sections.

Participants in communication (WHO)

Except when introducing new material or a new activity, there are disadvantages in doing communication practice with the whole class. This situation has the fewest characteristics of natural communication (e.g. thirty people all talking to one person and mostly looking at the back of each other's heads). It is also not very efficient since it gives each learner only one minute to speak – even excluding teacher-talk – in a thirty minute session. Each learner can speak for the same time in two minutes of pair work, and in five minutes if they work in groups of four or five.

However, this is one of the areas in which teachers' reports on using communicative activities showed the greatest divergencies. Depending on circumstances, some felt able to move very quickly to group and pair work (stage 3 of most activities in this book), while others organised most communication practice between the teacher and learners in the whole class (represented in stages 1 and 2 of most activities). This applied at all levels. The former often taught in schools where pair and group work was used from the earliest classes, and in several subjects. As teachers and learners gain experience with group work, the easier and more effective this type of practice becomes.

Problems which teachers mentioned in connection with group work in general included: some learners saying nothing while others talked too much; learners speaking their mother tongue or making too many mistakes in the FL; learners wasting time or making too much noise; and difficulty in recalling the attention of the whole class at the end of group work.

Using communicative activities for group work can reduce these problems. Since many tasks depend on learners sharing their information, everyone has to contribute. Language can be controlled by a language frame or model sentences, so that learners are encouraged to use the FL, and do not 'practise mistakes', without this reducing their speech to mere repetition. Moreover, many activities have a game or puzzle element in which the learners are challenged to achieve their objective using only the FL. Speaking the mother tongue therefore counts as breaking the 'rules of the game' – a concept which many learners find more acceptable than speaking the FL simply because their teacher tells them to do so. Where learners are interested and involved in a communicative task, they tend not to waste time! Group work with communicative tasks promotes social interaction skills (which are part of communication) such as turn-taking and paying attention to others; and this includes consideration for others working in the same room. Oral practice can by definition never be silent, but when learners work in small face-to-face groups, they can speak more softly. However, they may need to be frequently reminded of this as the teacher circulates to monitor and help them! Finally, with communicative tasks the learners' speech has a definite aim, which may have to be achieved within a time limit. This makes it easier to recall the attention of the whole class at the given time, in order to report and compare their achievements.

There are more detailed notes on group and pair work in the *Guide to activities*, pp. 29–30.

Means of communication (HOW)

The characteristics under HOW in List 2 on p. 8 should be included in communication practice whenever possible. They can be summarised as the need for *comprehension*, and for *comprehensibility*.

Receptive practice

To prepare them for FL communication outside the classroom, learners need more practice in listening and reading than in speaking and writing, for a variety of reasons:
- as in their mother tongue, they will need to understand far more language than they can produce. In FL communication, they will usually be free to limit or control what they themselves say or write, but they cannot control all they will hear or read. A rich experience of reading and listening, at a level of language rather higher than that which they are expected to produce, prepares them to deal with this.
- this receptive input in itself forms a solid foundation for language development, and ultimately promotes better productive skills, even though it is not immediately used for speech or writing practice in the classroom. Learners should be given more extensive receptive practice to familiarise themselves with new language items, before they are asked to produce them.

The introductory stage of many activities in Sections 1 to 7 can be used to provide purely receptive practice, and production of similar language can be postponed till a later stage (see activities marked 'Receptive' in the *General index*).

'Receptive input' can also include the teacher's use of the FL in the classroom, and this leads to the question of using the mother tongue or FL during oral communication practice.

Using the mother tongue or FL

There are good practical and psychological reasons for using the mother tongue for certain purposes in an FL course. However, using the mother tongue in communication practice has several undesirable consequences, even for such incidental remarks as 'It's your turn now,' or 'Could you repeat that please?':
- the learners receive a subtle message that the FL is not to be used for authentic communication (and the remarks quoted

above are perfect examples of authentic communication in the classroom setting).

- it is artificial to ask learners to speak in the FL if teachers do not do so themselves. The FL becomes rather like numbers in a mathematics lesson, a series of ciphers embedded in normal speech: 'What is 2 plus 2? – 4 – Very good. Now tell me *Où est la plume de ma tante? – Elle est sur le bureau de mon oncle* – Correct!'
- learners miss the opportunity to receive maximum input in the FL.
- the constant switching between languages disturbs the natural learning process of seeking to understand from context, and of gaining confidence that one can express oneself adequately in the FL without need of the mother tongue.

All teachers who have used the Direct Method, taught in a polyglot class, or in any class with learners whose language they do not speak, know that it is possible to conduct whole lessons – whole courses – using the FL alone. In classes where everyone shares the same mother tongue, it requires more careful planning (and if possible preliminary discussion with the learners) to conduct a part or all of a lesson exclusively in the FL – and then self-discipline on both sides! Teachers may judge, for example, that a beginners' class could not follow an explanation of the communication activity in the FL and will use the mother tongue for this, making it clear that as soon as the activity proper begins, the aim is to achieve all communication in the FL.

Some teachers use extra means to ensure that only the FL is spoken during communication practice. One had a kitchen timer which was set for progressively longer (and carefully planned) periods during which only the FL could be used: learners were greatly encouraged at the end of the year to find how long they could continue without using the mother tongue. Some teachers have a fines system: anyone slipping into the mother tongue during communication practice pays a small coin, and the money is given to charity or used to buy a treat at the end of term (one hopes it will be enough for a small bag of toffees rather than a luxury box of chocolates!). Learners, incidentally, delight in fining the teacher who inadvertently exclaims 'Where's the chalk?' instead of 'Où est la craie?'

Psychologically, it is a great help, for both sides, to know that the FL is absolutely the only means of communication they have for a certain period of time. Once this is accepted, it is surprising what can be achieved, even with beginners.

Example from practice

A beginners' class in French was working with an overhead projector when the bulb broke. The teacher gave the broken bulb to a learner and said:

Allez chez Monsieur Smith (the caretaker) *et demandez une autre lampe, s'il vous plaît.*

The context made the meaning perfectly clear to the learners and their faces showed how impressed they were with their own ability to function in the FL, even in an unexpected situation.

Nothing is absolute in teaching: communication activities require far more from the learners than ability to understand and to use the FL more or less correctly. They must develop the ability to communicate using both linguistic and para-linguistic means; they may need logic, imagination, or lateral thinking to complete their communicative tasks, as well as social and discourse skills. Learners are thus under great pressure and may at times drop into the mother tongue. If this threatens to damage the purpose of the exercise, teachers or the learners can call for 'time out' to discuss their problems and then return to the FL activity. It is also useful to provide time at the end of practice for learners to discuss in the mother tongue what they have done, and any problems they still have with the language used.

One form of FL communication in the classroom is very important: talking informally to learners about matters of general interest, for purely receptive practice, or inviting them to talk about their own interests and experiences, in the FL. Some teachers find this difficult in classroom conditions – or with particular classes – but it is worth persisting, and seizing any opportunity to initiate or respond to personal communication. Many activities provide such opportunities, particular those under 'Personal information or values' in the *General index*.

Comprehensibility

The kind of speech described in the previous paragraphs cannot be in the controlled form illustrated in most examples so far. Learners must ultimately be able to communicate independently, and this means they must also have classroom practice with non-controlled language. At all levels, they should be given the chance to experiment and to see how far they can communicate with whatever language they have, and to practise communication strategies such as paraphrase and gesture. (These are dealt with in Section 4 *Communication strategies*.) In such exercises, the teacher often steps back and functions as 'First Aid Post' or 'Last Resort', offering help when communication breaks down and learners cannot help each other further. The emphasis is on how far the learners' speech is comprehensible, rather than on how far it conforms to standard FL speech.

The relation between comprehensibility and conformity (or fluency and accuracy) is not fixed: the emphasis will shift at different times in a lesson or a course. But teachers do need to be aware of their own and their learners' ultimate goals in a language course (and by this I do not mean examinations, which are discussed later in this chapter under *Time for communication practice*). As regards oral skills, I take it that the aim is not to produce learners who can speak, in a restricted area, exactly *like* native speakers of the FL (in terms of accuracy), but learners who can communicate, over a wide area, *with* native speakers (in terms of fluency). Their success, in the world outside the school, will be decided by their ability to understand and to make themselves understood, to express their own meaning, rather than by their ability to produce fault-free sentences which may not reflect what they really want to say. Consider the British schoolgirl in Paris – who shall remain nameless – asking a waiter for *Deux sandwichs au jambon* although she only wanted one, because she was not sure if it was *un* or *une sandwich* in French: full marks for accurate speech, zero for accurate communication!

Nevertheless, teachers feel an important part of their task is to help the learners achieve greater accuracy – as well as fluency – in the FL, and so the problem arises of how to deal with learners' errors.

Dealing with errors

We all know it is impossible for learners to speak totally without errors, and that we cannot correct every single error they make. It is not only impossible, it is unnecessary – even undesirable. A certain amount of trial and error is an indispensable part of learning, and constant correction inhibits learners and discourages them from trying.

In activities with controlled language, we can invite learners to correct careless mistakes with phrases that might occur in normal conversation: 'What? What did you say? Could you say that again?' and by referring them to the correct form on the blackboard, etc. In games or quizzes, learners may lose points for careless mistakes. In team and group work, they usually look out for these deviations themselves, because it may affect the score.

In free communication practice, errors must be dealt with rather differently. Studies of how native speakers react in communication with foreign speakers (or how adults speak with young children) are relevant: they usually ignore formal errors which do not affect comprehensibility, or echo the message using preferred forms (this provides correct input without putting stress on the other speaker). They concentrate on querying errors of content or anything else which makes the message hard to follow. As FL teachers we are working in a different situation, but in free communication practice we can respond in similar ways. In the class, this may involve pretending not to speak the learners' mother tongue, so that they are forced to practise various communication strategies, including explanation and paraphrase, which they will need in communication with FL native speakers.

Examples from practice

Intermediate and advanced levels.

1 *Vocabulary*
   L: In this game, you trick a lot.
   T: I don't understand – you mean you play a lot of tricks?
   L: No – you take a paper, a lot, and it has a number, and this tells if you go first . . .
   T: Oh, you mean you draw lots!

2 *Pronunciation*
   L: And we saw Bernard Shaw's /pleɪs/ in London.
   T: His place in London? You mean his house?
   L: No, his place – 'Devil's Disciple' and . . .
   T: Oh, you mean plays!

3a *Grammar*
   L: (*struggling with English tense system*) My brother was in Paris for two years.
   T: Where is he now?
   L: In Paris.
   T: Oh, you mean he's been in Paris for two years.

3b L: My brother is in Paris since two years.
   T: Oh, he's been there for two years, has he? Does he like it?

1 and 2 show how teachers can re-interpret unclear items – or

simply repeat them with questioning intonation if they are totally incomprehensible. 3a shows how a teacher, aware of the kind of mistakes learners make, picks up a possibly faulty communication which a native speaker might not even recognise. In 3b, the meaning is perfectly clear, so the teacher simply repeats the correct form in response. Compare the last example with a classroom exchange in which the teacher concentrates on the formal rules:

L: We're here since twenty minutes. (*The class had indeed started twenty minutes earlier.*)

T: No, 'since' is always used with the present perfect and a definite time in the past. Repeat 'We have been here since two o'clock.'

This overload of information does not help learners to see whether or not they have communicated any meaning, and may well cause their 'communicative circuits' to fuse – they will prefer to keep silent; or, as I found when I conscientiously embarked on these explanations in the past, they lead to confusion and over-compensation errors as in example 3a.

It takes some practice to let the role of 'helpful native speaker' take precedence over the role of 'teacher as authority and judge', but I have found it a valuable guideline as to when and how to correct learners in communication practice. This technique helps learners to realise the importance of conforming to the 'rules': the penalty for breaking them is not a 'Wrong!' from the teacher or a low mark – it is that their attempts to communicate in the FL may be misunderstood, or not understood at all. It gives them a better sense of the relative importance for communication of the many errors they make. The standard can be raised as the learners progress: maximum explicit help to beginners (as native speakers give most help to someone struggling with just a few basic words in their language), and more resort to queries or invitations to repeat at higher levels: 'I don't understand what you mean by . . .' etc.

Learners may not pick up all the explicit or implicit corrections at once: they will tend to retain those they most need or can use at that point in their language development. If certain errors which affect communication occur regularly and with many learners, they will need further controlled or guided practice with the problem language items.

An important aim in communication practice is to build the learners' confidence in using the FL, and the above approach to dealing with errors helps in this. To quote a sixteen year old Austrian learner of French and English:

'*You must have the necessary knowledge and also the courage to speak even if you make mistakes. If you don't have these in the right measure, neither grammar alone, nor being forced to speak is enough.'*

Time for communication practice (WHEN)

The heading WHEN does not appear in List 2 on p. 7–8, but the question of how much time can be given to communication practice is an important one for teachers. There is never enough time to achieve everything one would like in a language course: priorities have to be determined, taking account of external constraints such as available material and examination demands. However, the learners' basic wish to learn languages for oral communication, and the motivating effects of oral communication practice, should never be ignored in deciding priorities.

Many teachers feel constrained by their textbooks, and the need to cover all their contents in the available time. The approach to developing oral communication skills described here is compatible with almost any textbook; but it is neither possible nor necessary to have communicative oral practice with *all* the contents of a textbook – or indeed *only* with the contents of the book. Dialogues, exercises, etc. can be considered with the following question in mind: is this language useful for oral communication? If the answer is yes, the next question will be: is this exercise communicative to any degree or does it need to be adapted or even replaced? Most books contain some exercises which have many, or very few characteristics from List 2. The introductions to Sections 1, 2, and 5 in particular show how the latter can be adapted to increase their usefulness for communication practice, while the *Language indexes* refer to language items found in most textbooks – structures, functions and topic areas – and to examples of communicative activities with these items in various sections of this book.

Another constraint on teachers is the kind of test or examination that their learners must take. The weighting given by national, local or school examinations to oral skills – or communicative use of language in general – is increasing. However, whatever the system of language testing in general, and oral testing in particular, I believe that communicative oral practice is never wasted. It motivates learners, and it develops their confidence, willingness and ability to express themselves in the FL, thus preparing them for oral examinations biased towards either accurate or fluent language use. Formal speech practice, emphasising accuracy above meaning, is much less motivating, and prepares them only for the former type of examination.

When we look beyond examinations and consider learning as a preparation for life, then there is no doubt that developing communication skills – which automatically involves some accuracy in language use – is more important than developing accuracy alone, which does not automatically involve readiness and ability to communicate fluently in the FL.

Communication practice and the learners

Age Communication practice is suitable for learners of any age though it may be introduced in different ways with different age groups. Younger learners, and many adults, often appreciate an introduction to activities which stresses their game-like qualities. I have avoided using the term 'game' in this book (though many activities are adaptations of well-known games – see introduction to Section 3) because it seems that some learners (and some teachers!) may regard 'games' purely as relaxation or reward after 'serious' work, rather than as ways of learning which are potentially more effective than more conventional exercises.

Adolescent learners may suspect they are being treated as children if asked to take part in a language 'game'. Teachers are advised to see what gives best results with which classes: saying 'Now we're going to have some communication practice' or 'a game' or simply 'a language exercise'. For example, some classes may respond more positively to a communicative task described in these terms: 'We have three minutes to ask questions to find out where the bomb is hidden' while older learners may prefer to be told that they are (also) practising interrogatives and propositions. Learners – and teachers – who are used to a structural syllabus are reassured to know that they are indeed practising structures and vocabulary, but in ways that will help them to use the language more communicatively.

Ability Communicative oral activities have proved suitable for learners of all academic levels, and for mixed ability classes. The stress on ability to communicate allows all kinds of learner to experience success: some can convey their meaning acceptably with a minimum of language and a maximum of gesture, while others will express themselves with more words and correspondingly more formal errors not affecting their comprehensibility; and still others will achieve higher degrees of both comprehensibility and conformity to rules. But all of them will have shown they can communicate in the FL. A further advantage for mixed ability – or any – classes is that much of the work can be done in groups, with or without the help of language frames and word lists, etc. This means, for example, that slower learners can continue with guided language for longer than others. The content or ways of using many activities can be adjusted to suit the needs or abilities of particular groups of learners; this is mentioned with particular activities.

Learning styles   Learners differ not only in age and ability but also in their personalities and learning styles. There are learners who feel more secure with carefully structured activities and material, who fear mistakes and dislike taking risks, and so prefer to work with guided language. Others like to explore and discover for themselves and are natural risk-takers who become impatient with too much guided practice. Some learners learn best through the eye, some through the ear, some by action. You will have learners who excel in tasks demanding careful observation, or logical thinking, or imagination and creativity. Some are willing – even unstoppable – talkers in their own or the FL, others are shy or taciturn. Teachers cannot satisfy all these types simultaneously – which is probably one reason why they have almost always chosen to work eclectically than to apply one method rigidly. The variety of communication activities in Sections 1 to 7 permits teachers to suit different types of learner at different times. It also permits learners to extend their repertoire to some extent: the careful find they can take risks, the careless are required to pay attention to detail; logical thinkers exploit their imagination, dreamers try out step-by-step deduction, etc. – and all by means of the FL.

Using a variety of activities has its rewards for the teacher also. I cannot be the only teacher who has been as bored as her learners with predictable drills and dialogues. The lessons I have most enjoyed have been those in which learners have both entertained and impressed me by their inventiveness and resourcefulness, revealing unexpected talents – in role-play, story-telling, puzzle solving, etc. – which I could not equal, despite my greater knowledge of the FL; creating admiration on my part and a clear improvement in self-esteem and self-confidence on theirs.

FL teachers and teaching departments

Language teaching is sometimes described in terms
suggesting a movement between opposing goals:

A	B
accuracy	fluency
knowledge about language	skill in using language
academic achievement	social and personal develop-ment
cognitive aims	affective aims

Of course these goals are not mutually exclusive but are
complementary: to neglect factors from either side makes for
incompleteness, and there can be few teachers who work
exclusively for A or B. Most of us seek a middle position,
allowing us to encompass both sets of goals to some degree.
Obviously, individual teachers tend to favour one end of the
range more than the other (to be Ab or aB) – just as learners
differ in their needs and abilities. But all teachers can seek to
broaden the range of techniques, of material and of activities
they use, and to vary the emphasis in their lessons: in other
words, to avoid being AA or BB. The broader the range of the
individual teachers, the greater the chance that they can
promote the optimal development of their various learners
and their communication skills.

It helps if the FL teachers within a department or school are
agreed on the broad aims of their teaching and share the same
general approach, so that (to take an extreme example)
learners are not wrenched from lessons exclusively directed to
accuracy with strong emphasis on grammar and written
work, in one year or with one FL, to lessons emphasising
fluent oral communication with little work on accuracy or on
reading and writing, in another year or with another language.
It would of course be equally regrettable, for the general
learner, if all the teaching they received were exclusively of
one type or the other.

With regard to developing communication skills, if all the
teachers in a department use at least some communication
activities of the kind described in Sections 1 to 7 (not
necessarily only for oral work), it becomes progressively
easier to incorporate such activities into lessons, as the learners
become used to them and the various kinds of classroom
organisation that can be used. When one teacher begins to use
a more communicative approach, I find that colleagues are
often interested in adopting similar techniques and activities,
simply because learner response is found to be so positive.

Teachers in the same or different FL departments can discuss what they have done and with what success (if only to avoid classes being asked to solve the same logic problem in two FLs in the same year – it has happened!). Teachers can also help each other in choosing, adapting and devising communicative material on an intra- or inter-departmental basis, and can exchange material their learners have made. In other words, the communicative approach can lead to more communication between teachers, as well as between learners!

Guide to activities

Sections 1 to 7

The introductions to each section give an overview of the contents, and discuss their aims and communicative characteristics. Each section contains a group of five or six basic activities plus variants, with examples of teaching material; the grouping is based in general on the type of language practice or material involved. Broadly speaking there is a progression, in terms of communicative depth, through the sections and through the activities within each section; and from those involving controlled language, most easily used for elementary level (at the beginning of each section), to those at the end of each section giving more opportunities for free language use. The cross-references mean that you read and use the activities in any order, following up cross-references, when, for example, you need more information, or are looking for related activities. All the activities are described in terms of listening or speaking practice, but most can easily be adapted for – or already include – reading and writing. (See *General index* under 'Reading & writing' for the activities most easily adapted for these skills.)

Layout of activities

0.0 Title   Number and title of the activity in English, French and German.

Basic gap   This describes the basic gap in information, ideas, etc., which gives the learners a reason to speak to each other. The terms used are illustrated in the following examples, all based on a picture of an empty room:

a) 'Information gap based on split information'
   Some learners have or make a picture of the room when furnished, which they must describe to the others, who can only see the picture of the empty room. (See 4.6 *Picture dictation*.)

b) 'Opinion gap based on shared information'
   The learners all see the picture and discuss how they would furnish the room for a ten year old boy, a grandmother, themselves, etc. (See 3.4 *People and things*.)

c) 'Ideas gap based on shared information'
   The learners all see the picture and must imagine why the room is empty – what has happened? Who might come into the room? etc. (See 5.8 *Strange pictures*.)

         d) 'Observation gap based on shared information'
            All the learners see two pictures of the room; there are
            slight differences between them which learners try to find.
         e) 'Observation gap based on split information'
            The two different pictures are divided between the learners
            so that they must describe the pictures to each other in
            order to discover the differences. (See 5.6 *Spot the*
            differences.)

Aim   The results which the speakers seek to achieve by their
communication. In the above examples, these results may be
in the form of:
a) drawing pictures;
b) drawing pictures or making reports;
c) making up stories or role-plays;
d) and e) scoring points for all the differences found.

Language   This may be more or less completely *controlled* by a language
frame, such as a substitution table or basic dialogue; *guided*
(semi-controlled) by the teacher or by model phrases, etc.; or
free, with any communication strategies (for details of the latter see
4.1 *Introduction* to *Communication strategies*). Many of the
activities can be used at any level and with various structures
or functions and vocabulary; there are concrete examples in
the *Teaching material* at the end of each activity, and you can
also refer to the *Language indexes*.

Preparation   What preparation and what media, if any, are required or
and material   recommended – blackboard, overhead projector (OHP),
poster, handouts, textbooks, etc. See the *General index* for a
summary of activities requiring little or no preparation.

Stages

Stage 1   The activity is introduced or demonstrated, and tried out by
the learners. This enables you to ensure that they understand
or can use the minimum language necessary to function
successfully (including adequate pronunciation and
intonation). This stage can often be used as an independent
activity in which all communication stems from or is directed
at the teacher. In some activities it can be used for purely
receptive practice (listening or reading) with language which
learners will only use productively (in speech or writing) at a
later date. Such activities are shown in the *General index* under
'Receptive'.

Stage 2   Learners continue to practise with given language or with
your help and guidance, but most speech is now between the
learners themselves. Correction of errors, if and when you feel
it is necessary, can take place most conveniently in stages 1 and

2 (see p. 17 for ways of dealing with errors). In general, you will be able to judge from the learners' performance with controlled or guided language in stages 1 or 2, whether or not they are ready for stage 3.

Stage 3 This gives independent practice between learners, without reliance on language frames, model phrases or constant teacher help. When learners are familiar with the activity, stage 3 can sometimes be used as a filler – to occupy pairs or groups who finish work before others, or who need an alternative activity. Such activities are listed in the *General index* under 'Filler'.

The activities are described in three stages to show how they can be used in different ways, moving from receptive, teacher-centred or controlled practice to productive, learner-centred or independent practice. The stages need not be followed closely. For example, an elementary class may only be able to practise with simple guided language in stages 1 and 2 of some activities, and will not reach stage 3, while an advanced class may move straight from a brief introduction in stage 1 to independent practice in stage 3. Not all learners need move to stage 3 simultaneously: some groups of learners may continue to need your help or to work with given language, while others are ready to work more independently.

The descriptions in each stage are reasonably full because I assume that not all readers will be familiar with all activities, and a step-by-step description, like a step-by-step recipe, is most helpful. It is easier to skip the parts you do not need than to find information which is not there!

I have based the descriptions, and the *Examples from practice*, on my own experience and on reports and comments from other teachers, all of us working with various languages at various levels. For ease of reading, all *Examples from practice* are given in English (with the original language noted in brackets). The selection and description of activities reflects what was found to be most generally usable by teachers working in a variety of situations: individual teachers, therefore, may find that some suggestions go too far for their taste, while others – perhaps in more favourable teaching circumstances – may feel that they do not go far enough! Teachers' reports showed that we all adapted the activities to suit our own situations, and I recommend all readers to do the same.

If you are trying out something new, it is a good idea to do so with your most co-operative class, if necessary explaining that it is an experiment, and asking for their comments afterwards (and I give thanks here to all those learners who have helped me in this way!). At a first trial, you may follow the instructions fairly closely, and later adapt, alter, add to or ignore them according to what seems to work best and in which conditions.

Headings within each stage

E,I,A   These letters give a general indication of the levels for which each stage is suitable: E(lementary), I(ntermediate) or A(dvanced). Broadly speaking, these correspond to the beginning, middle and final stages of a language course; or the lower, middle and upper classes in school.

Obviously these indications are very approximate and you will make your own decisions about what you can use with which classes. Most of the activities can be used from E(lementary) to A(dvanced) levels, by adapting the linguistic content. Therefore, the various stages of an activity may be marked as suitable for two or more levels.

Minutes   Timing for each stage is given in multiples of five minutes, but this can only be very approximate. More or less time may be needed according to the size or level of the class, and how familiar they are with the activity. Many activities can be split into five or ten minute practice sessions over a series of lessons. This is often more effective than one long and exhaustive practice period, since it prevents learners from becoming bored, and keeps them eager for further practice with activities they have enjoyed.

Class/team/   The recommended form of organisation for each stage of the
group/pair   activity. The following descriptions are based on classes of thirty or more, but all activities can be used in larger or smaller groups.

Class   This means one person (teacher or learner) speaking while everyone else listens. However, I find that when learners have to volunteer their ideas and opinions for everyone to hear, they often do this more willingly (and produce better ideas in more fluent language) if they have the chance to consult one or two classmates first. This is sometimes called working in 'buzz-groups', describing the few moments of 'buzz' in the classroom as learners sitting side by side quickly discuss what to say. You may give them this chance several times in the course of whole-class practice (the possibility is mentioned in the appropriate activities).

Team   The class may be divided into two or more teams. Learners turn to face each other across the middle of the room if possible, so that there is some form of face-to-face communication between them. Alternatively, teams may be formed of learners sitting side by side: those on the left in each pair are team A, those on the right are team B. This helps in activities where teams have to check what the others have written down.

An incidental advantage of team work is that it is easier to remember who has and has not had a turn to speak when the class is divided into sections: there is less tendency to forget the learners in the corners or at the back. If the teams are to be permanent, ensure that each contains a fair number of the gifted and slow learners, so that one team does not win or lose too regularly. Team work can be used to encourage co-operation instead of competition between individual learners, since team members are encouraged to help each other to win points for the team. (There are more detailed notes in 6.2 *Quiz organisation*.)

Group   This assumes groups of four or five learners. Extra learners or volunteers may be needed to act as referees (for example, to ensure that everyone in the group speaks the FL). In most classrooms it is simplest to form groups of learners sitting together, but you may also find it useful to put together learners of similar abilities or interests; or to form mixed ability groups; or to let learners choose their own grouping. These possibilities are mentioned with the relevant activities, but, in general, experimentation is recommended to discover what kinds of organisation work best with which activities, or in which classes.

Groups should always report back or show their results in some form: speech, writing or drawing. If no interest is shown in what they have achieved, they soon learn that they can safely waste time or talk in their mother tongue! Equally, if they know they must report back in the FL, they find that it is to their advantage to prepare by using the FL in the group (and to look to you or their books for help), otherwise they will be tongue-tied later. Reporting back does not take much time (or space) when there are only seven or eight groups in a class. The results of all the activities here are designed to be of interest to the whole class, and may lead to further language work as learners go on to compare and discuss their ideas, interpretations, solutions, and decisions.

Many activities work better in groups than in the whole class, where learners may be unwilling to speak. One reason is clear: it is psychologically quite stressful to speak in front of the whole class, particularly in a language which you are not confident in, and perhaps feeling that the teacher is noting every mistake. Speaking in a small group is less stressful, and learners also seem to speak more willingly at the report stage following such group work. Knowing that they speak as 'group representatives', rather than as individuals seems to offer some psychological protection. You may find it advisable to choose some of these 'representatives' yourself, if the same fluent or extrovert speakers volunteer every time. This can help to increase participation and co-operation within the group, since each member knows that he or she has to be prepared to speak on behalf of the others.

For most group and pair activities you can set a time limit within which they try to complete their task. Groups who finish early can begin writing down their results, if appropriate, or begin another task (for example, one of the activities listed under 'Filler' in the *General index*).

The advantages of group work for communicative activities are discussed on pp. 12–13.

Pair   Many of the remarks above also apply to pairs (though reporting back must be briefer when there are fifteen or more pairs in the class). Some activities involve writing: pair work is recommended for this because there is a greater flow of ideas, the learners correct each other's grosser errors, and the hard-worked teacher has only half the number of papers to check!

Changing pairs/   Some activities give learners the opportunity to move round
groups   the classroom speaking to each other: the groups or pairs of speakers are thus not fixed but changing. For this, you need space to move between the desks. If you do not want to have all the learners speaking with each other, you can split them into groups of ten or fifteen, in different parts of the room (for example, using the central aisle, and the space to the right and left of the teacher's desk). None of these activities needs to last very long – two to five minutes is usual – and the refreshing and stimulating effect is striking. There is no other classroom organisation which involves so many learners in speaking so intensively and so naturally, in such a short time. It is excellent for ice-breaking activities in classes where the learners do not know each other very well (see activities under 'Ice-breaking' in the *General index*); and it also develops social skills, minimising inhibitions about approaching people and initiating conversations. To quote a ten year old Austrian learner of English:
'What I like about our lessons is that we can sometimes walk round the classroom and speak English with our classmates.'

Jury panel   Communication activities benefit from being in the hands of the learners as far as possible, and the jury panel is often useful when some verdict or decision has to be given on the reports or results of the various groups. The panel can be composed, for example, of one learner from each group, or those who have been acting as referees during the activity. They can ask about the results, discuss them further with the class and finally 'award the prize'.

There are notes on classroom seating arrangements for communication activities on p. 32.

Variants

These are alternative forms of practice with the same basic material or type of activity: they are described more briefly without the extra headings mentioned above. You, and the learners, can devise other variants to suit your own needs.

Finding and making material

This section describes how you or the learners can collect or prepare material, and/or adapt textbook material for further practice. This is very much part of the whole language-learning process: making material provides useful and purposeful reading and writing practice for the learners, and helps teachers by providing a supply of material which reflects the learners' level and interests very closely. Most importantly, it shows learners that they can make a useful contribution to the content of their lessons, instead of just sitting back and accepting what is given, and thus plays a part in increasing learner involvement and motivation.

This section also contains any notes on the following *Teaching material*, and references to sources of further material and ideas in *Booklists* 2a, b and c.

Teaching material

There are pages of teaching material in the order ENGLISH, FRANÇAIS, DEUTSCH for the majority of the activities and variants, both to give concrete examples of how the activities can be used, and to save preparation time for teachers. Where suitable, these pages may be photocopied for direct use in the classroom. This teaching material is not labelled E(lementary), I(ntermediate) or A(dvanced), since I assume that teachers are in the best position to judge where particular language items fit into their courses.

The examples for each language are not always identical: some are suited to the needs of a particular language; different ways of presenting material are sometimes divided between the three languages; and some texts are different for each language. This has been done in order to provide a greater variety from which to choose – I have assumed that most teachers will be able to translate, or to have translated, any material which they would like to use.

In vocabulary lists for FRANÇAIS, the article is given in full; for DEUTSCH, gender is indicated by *(de)r Mann, (di)e Frau, (da)s Kind,* or *(de)n Mann* for masculine accusative.

Booklists

Booklist 1 gives all the textbooks consulted in preparing this book. *Booklists* 2a, b and c give sources of material and ideas for communication practice. *Booklist* 3 gives books containing further information on the theory and practice of the communicative approach in the classroom.

Indexes

The *Language indexes* refer you to activities which have examples of particular structures (*Language index* 1), functions (*index* 2), and situations or topic areas (*index* 3) either in *Teaching material*, or within the description of the activity itself. They also refer to the activities which can be used to practise various language items, whether or not there are concrete examples in the book. The *General index* shows which activities or variants can be used with minimal preparation; for listening, reading or writing practice; with tape, video or computer; with cultural or literary content; and with personal information or as 'ice-breaking' activities.

Classroom seating arrangements

This is one of the practical considerations facing the teacher who wants to use communication activities including group work and movement in the classroom. The ideal arrangement of desks permits all learners to see each other's faces, the teacher, and the blackboard, with no more than a 90° turn to left or right; it permits easy transition between whole-class, group and pair work; and provides space for learners and teachers to move easily between the desks, for role-plays or other activities. Where classrooms are shared with other teachers, the seating plan must also be acceptable to them, or involve minimum rearrangement. Clearly, no single seating plan can meet all these requirements.

Figures (i), (ii) and (iii), based on a class of thirty-two with movable double desks, provide basic ideas which you may be able to adapt to your own situation. Groups are shown by dotted lines between the numbers; the numbers also show where each desk is moved to in each arrangement.

Figure (i)   The traditional rows provide space for movement and, in most schools, would not need to be rearranged between lessons. The disadvantage for communication practice is that learners are listening or speaking to the backs of heads or to people sitting behind them: face-to-face communication is only possible with immediate neighbours or the teacher. Group work requires half the learners to move their chairs through 180°.

Fig. (i)

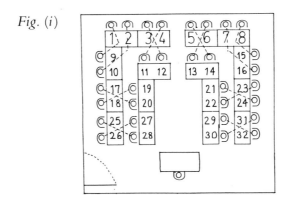

Figure (ii)   The double horseshoe is often acceptable to colleagues who rarely use group work. It allows more eye contact between speakers in whole-class practice, though some learners may have to move their desks or chairs for group work and it is not so easy to move around the classroom. However, there is more central space for role-plays, etc.

Fig. (ii)

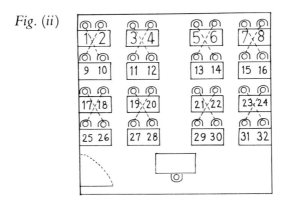

Figure (iii) The grouping of desks allows easy movement between them, good eye contact between speakers and listeners in whole-class practice, and needs no rearrangement for group work. However, colleagues may prefer desks to be moved back to rows for their lessons.

Fig. (iii)

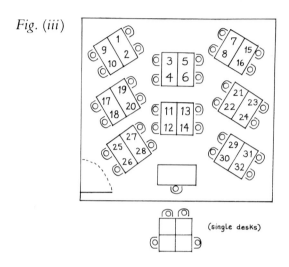

(single desks)

If you have single desks, even more flexible planning is possible; for example, each group can sit in a semi-circle arrangement, as shown under figure (iii).

Most teachers sharing classrooms seem to have variations on figures (i) and (ii), although figure (iii) has the advantage of greater versatility and works well if learners are used to it from the beginning – and in this case, classes quickly learn to rearrange desks for other purposes or other lessons.

1 Questions and answers

1.1 Introduction

Most textbooks have pattern drills and question and answer exercises in which learners follow the book, teacher or tape with little or no choice of what to say. The purpose and result of speech is to produce formally correct sentences. As no important message is being communicated, learners need not think about what they are saying or pay attention to what others say. Teachers have to work hard to overcome the lack of involvement and inattention which often accompanies this type of reproduction and manipulation practice.

Given that repetition of basic language patterns is a necessary part of language learning in school, such practice can easily be made more communicative by letting learners make a personal and secret choice from a list of language items which all fit into a given language frame. This creates an information gap, providing communicative elements in the content of speech and in the purpose and result: to discover their classmates' secret choices – for which points can be scored. Learners write down or otherwise mark their secret choices at the start of each activity: otherwise there is a great temptation to change their choices once the guessing starts!

1.2 *Catch* is a simple example, based on location, which can be used with various language items. 1.3 and 1.4, *Secret choice I and II*, show how the basic principle can be extended to almost every kind of stimulus–response or pattern drill, whether based on structures or on notions and functions. In *Secret choice I* the learners indicate whether their classmates' guesses are right or wrong; in *Secret choice II* they respond to incorrect guesses or suggestions by giving the correct answer: *No, I'm not from London, I'm from Edinburgh*. Both activities can be used from level E, to introduce or to revise language items. At level A they can be used to give extra practice with language items which still cause problems. The variants give opportunities for more complicated language patterns, such as reported speech. Mistakes in following the basic language pattern can be dealt with in any of the ways suggested on pp. 17–20 *Dealing with errors*.

The principle of a secret choice from given language items can be widely used to create communication practice with controlled or guided language, and further examples will be found in almost every section.

Question and answer drills can also be used with authentic personal information. This does not mean simply asking partners about their families, pets, likes and dislikes, etc. Such practice has communicative content, but is weak on the purpose and result of speech. Learners eventually realise that the aim is in fact not to gather information but to practise given language items. With the same teaching aim, one can make the exercises still more communicative. In 1.5 *Hunt the answer* learners aim to find specific information from their classmates. Results are checked: who managed to collect the answers they needed? – and the answers are followed up. 1.6 *Questionnaires* also provides a clear purpose and result: the answers are used to build a class profile, and learners can try to predict the results as closely as possible.

Since the ultimate result of 1.5 and 1.6 is better knowledge of one's classmates, they can both be used as 'ice-breakers' in classes where the learners do not yet know each other very well (see the *General index* for more examples of ice-breaking activities). See Moskowitz 1978 in *Booklist* 2a for more activities based on personal information, opinions and feelings.

I have found that organising question and answer practice in these ways creates greater learner enthusiasm, permitting constant repetition of basic language patterns without loss of interest. Learners have some choice and purpose in what they are saying: the essential success or failure of their interaction depends on what they say and hear, and not only on how they say it. In other words they feel that, however simply, they are using the foreign language to communicate.

1.2   Catch
Prendre au piège
Fangen

Basic gap	Information gap based on secret choice
Aim	To 'catch' someone who has chosen the same location
Language	Controlled
Preparation and material	Minimal – putting simple language frame on display or handouts (optional: visual aids or realia)

Stage 1   E,I (5 minutes)

Class   Choose suitable names for the 'catchers' and 'caught', such as *Cat* and *Mouse*, then ask three or four learners to make and write down a secret choice of location from a list, to show where the mouse is hiding – such as *on, in, under, behind the box*.

Choose a location for the cat yourself and announce this: for example (level E) *The cat's on the box*; asking the learners in turn: *Where's the mouse?* until you find someone who has chosen the same place. This learner – or there may be more than one – is caught, and the others have escaped.

For level E learners, use visual aids or realia to reinforce the meaning of what is said.

Stage 2   E (10 minutes)

Team   Some learners can volunteer to keep the score, or to move any visual aids or realia. The rest divide into teams and all write down a secret choice of location from the frame; each team also chooses its name – *Cat* or *Mouse*, etc. (see examples in *Teaching material*). Members of the 'catching' team take it in turns to declare their own location and ask one member of the other team about theirs, scoring a point if they 'catch' someone. The answerers score a point for every escape (and can be asked to show what they have written down, to prevent cheating; see p. 28 *Team*). The answerers usually get the higher score, so the teams can change roles halfway through the time allowed, or when half the learners have spoken; this does not involve making new secret choices.

You can also give the 'catchers' a second chance from time to time: after every five or six answers, the next person can ask someone who has already answered. This encourages everyone to pay careful attention to all the answers and try to remember them, so that they may be able to catch someone when they have this second chance.

Stage 3   E,I (10 minutes)

Team   As above, without using the language frame.

See 2.3 *Detectives* and 6.4 *Quizzes* for more extensive questioning about place and time; and 1.3 *Secret choice I, Variant 1*, or 3.6 *Find your partners* for more varied practice in finding identical choices.

Finding and making material

The basic activity can be used with any suitable language in the textbook. Learners can suggest other team names and situations, and can help by making visual aids or bringing realia.

The pages of *Teaching material* have slightly different language frames for each language, according to where they offer the most useful language practice. The frames for German include *der*, *die* and *das* words: early practice can, however, be confined to a single gender – *vor dem Tisch, Stuhl, Schrank, Sessel*, etc.

The pictures on p. 40 show simple shapes which can be drawn on the board (or textbook pictures can be used) in association with the language frames. The pictures in boxes represent flashcards which can be moved according to the locations named by the speakers. Real objects or models permit even more realistic practice.

Teaching material

ENGLISH *Catch*

'Cat and mouse'
(*Present (progressive); prepositions*)

Q: The cat's (sitting) →	on the right	of the box
Where's the mouse?	on the left	of the books
A: It's (sitting) →		

(*Present perfect/direct object*)

Q: I've put the cat →	on	
Where've you put	in front of	the box
the mouse?	on the right of	
A: I've put it →	on the left of	

FRANÇAIS *Prendre au piège*

'L'araignée et la mouche (le moustique)'
(Il, elle; *prepositions with* à, au *and* de la)

Q: L'araignée est →	au dessus	
Où est la mouche	au dessous	de la pendule
(le moustique)?	à droite	
R: Elle (il) est →	à gauche	

'Le chat et la souris (le rat)'
(*Perfect participle agreeing with direct object; prepositions with* à *and* du, de la, des)

Q: J'ai mis le chat →	à gauche	du livre
Où as-tu mis la souris (le rat)?	à droite	de la boîte
R: Je l'ai mise (Je l'ai mis)		des livres

'Policiers et voleurs'
(*Perfect of* aller; au, à la)

Q: Les policiers sont allés →	au supermarché, musée
Les voleurs sont allés où?	à la banque
R: Ils sont allés →	à l'hôtel

DEUTSCH *Fangen*

'Die Katze und der Vogel (die Maus, das Mäuschen)'
(Zwischen *with dative, all genders*; er, sie *or* es)

F: Die Katze ist →		dem Stuhl und
Wo ist der Vogel (die		dem Tisch
Maus, das Mäuschen)?	zwischen	dem Buch
		der Kiste
A: Er (sie, es) ist →		den Büchern

(*Perfect*; zwischen *with accusative, all genders*; ihn, sie *or* es)

F: Ich habe die Katze →			
Wo hast du den Vogel (die Maus, das Mäuschen) hingesteckt?	zwischen	den Stuhl und den Tisch die Kiste das Buch die Bücher	gesteckt
A: Ich habe ihn (sie, es) →			

'Die Polizisten und die Diebe'
(Sein; in *with dative, all genders*)

F: Die Polizisten sind →	im Laden
Wo sind die Diebe?	im Hotel
A: Sie sind →	in der Bank

(Gehen, *future tense*; in *with accusative, all genders*)

F: Morgen werden die Polizisten →	in den Laden	
Wohin werden die Diebe gehen?	in die Bank	gehen
A: Sie werden →	ins Hotel	

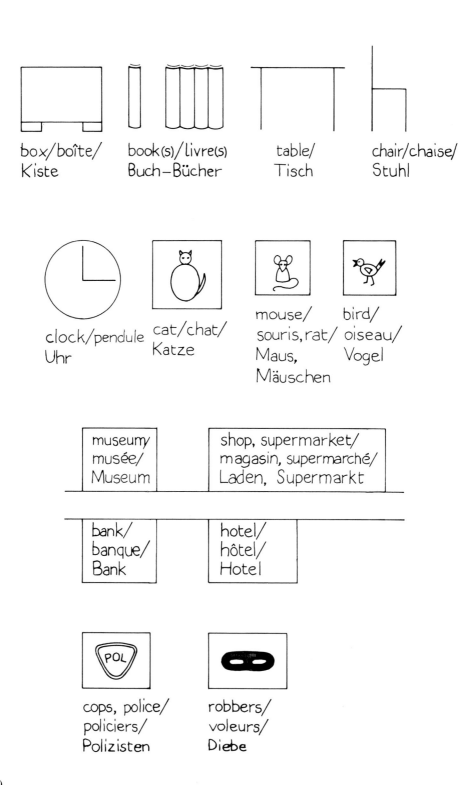

box/boîte/
Kiste

book(s)/livre(s)
Buch—Bücher

table/
Tisch

chair/chaise/
Stuhl

clock/pendule
Uhr

cat/chat/
Katze

mouse/
souris, rat/
Maus,
Mäuschen

bird/
oiseau/
Vogel

museum/
musée/
Museum

shop, supermarket/
magasin, supermarché/
Laden, Supermarkt

bank/
banque/
Bank

hotel/
hôtel/
Hotel

cops, police/
policiers/
Polizisten

robbers/
voleurs/
Diebe

1.3   Secret choice I
Choix secret I
Geheime Wahl I

Basic gap	Information gap based on secret choice
Aim	To discover a secret choice in the fewest possible questions
Language	Controlled
Preparation and material	Minimal – putting simple language frame and list on display or handouts; or using textbook material (optional: visual aids where appropriate)

Stage 1   E,I,A (5 minutes)

Class/team   A learner makes a secret choice from a list (of at least six items), and you ask questions until you discover the choice. Example:

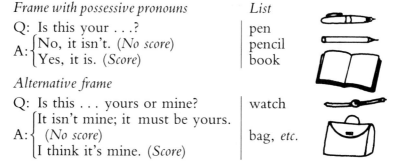

Frame with possessive pronouns

Q: Is this your . . .?
A: {No, it isn't. (*No score*)
   {Yes, it is. (*Score*)

List

pen
pencil
book

Alternative frame

Q: Is this . . . yours or mine?
A: {It isn't mine; it must be yours.
   { (*No score*)
   {I think it's mine. (*Score*)

watch

bag, *etc.*

Make a secret choice yourself and let learners ask you questions until someone discovers your choice (and scores a team point). With the above frame, visual aids or realia may be used instead of a word list.

Stage 2   E,I,A (5 minutes)

Team/group/ pair   Learners make secret choices, which the others try to guess: the 'winner' becomes the next person to be asked.

Stage 3   E,I,A (5 minutes)

Team/group/ pair   As above, without looking at the language frame.

Variant 1 Same choice

Learners ask each other questions to find out who has made the same choice as themselves: the frame includes the question (Q), *yes* or *no* answers (A), and appropriate responses (R). Example:

Frame		*List*
Q: Can you . . . ?		play the guitar
A: Yes, I can	No, I can't	play the piano
R: So can I	But I can	play chess, *etc.*
(*Score*)	(*No score*)	

Alternatively, ask learners to choose one thing from the list for a negative answer, and to question each other to find who has made the same 'negative' choice. Example:

Q: Do you like . . .?		
A: No, I don't	Yes, I do	(List of sports, pop groups,
R: Neither do I	But I don't	food, drinks, *etc.*)
(*Score*)	(*No score*)	

See 1.5 *Hunt the answer, Variant 2*, 3.6 *Find your partners, Variant 1* and 5.6 *Spot the differences, Variant 3*, for similar practice with authentic personal information.

Variant 2 Double secret choice

The frames and lists can allow for a double secret choice to be guessed, to build up a mini-conversation or to practise contrasting language items. (Use lists with only three or four items each for this variant.) Example:

Frame contrasting present perfect and simple past

Q1: Have you ever been to . . .?	Accra
A1: $\begin{cases} \text{No, I haven't. (\textit{Stop!})} \\ \text{Yes, I have. (\textit{Continue}\ldots)} \end{cases}$	Athens Berlin
Q2: Did you go there . . .?	last year
A2: $\begin{cases} \text{No, I didn't. (\textit{No score})} \\ \text{Yes, I did. (\textit{Score})} \end{cases}$	two months ago in September

Finding and making material

Almost all textbooks have exercises or lists which can be used with 'secret choice' to provide more communicative practice, and some textbooks have exercises incorporating this principle. You and the learners can devise other language frames and lists: see notes in *Finding and making material* for 1.4 *Secret choice II*.

Teaching material

ENGLISH *Secret choice I*

(*Talking about breakdowns*)

Q: What's wrong with the . . .?	radio
A: { Nothing, it's OK. (*No score*) It's out of order. (*Score*)	television telephone, *etc.*

Variant 2 Double secret choice
(*Present perfect or present with* for)

Q1: How long have you been here – . . .?	2 days
A1: { No, we've been here for . . . (*Stop!*) Yes, we have. (*Continue . . .*)	3 days 4 days
Q2: And how long are you here for – . . .?	a week
A2: { Yes, we're here for . . . (*Score*) No, we're here for . . . (*No score*)	2 weeks a month

FRANÇAIS *Choix secret 1*

(*Possessive pronouns*)

Q: Il/elle est à Marie, (. . .) . . .?	(ce) sac
R: { Non, ce n'est pas son/sa . . . (*1 point*) Oui, c'est le sien/la sienne. (*0 point*)	(ce) stylo (cette) voiture, *etc.*

Variant 1 Le choix identique
(*Perfect / direct object*)

Q: Vous avez vu . . .?	(*List: film titles*)
R1: Oui, je l'ai déjà vu.	Non, je ne l'ai pas encore vu.
R2: Moi aussi. (*1 point*)	Ah? Moi si. (*0 point*)

(*Se lever / frequency adverbs (negative choice)*)

Q: Tu te lèves à . . .?		6.30
R1: Non, je ne me lève jamais à . . .	Oui, je me lève souvent à . . .	6.45 7.00
R2: Moi non plus! (*Point*)	Mais moi pas! (*0 point*)	7.15 7.30

Variant 2 Double choix secret
(*Suggesting, accepting, rejecting appointments*)

Q1: Tu veux aller . . .?	au cinéma
R1: { Non, j'ai trop de devoirs. (*Stop!*) Bonne idée! (*Continuez . . .*)	au café à la piscine
Q2: On y va . . . alors?	ce soir
R2: { Dommage, . . ., je ne peux pas. (*Stop!*) Oui, . . . je veux bien. (*1 point*)	demain samedi, *etc.*

DEUTSCH   *Geheime Wahl I*

(Offering, accepting, rejecting food and drink)

F:	Möchten Sie noch . . . haben?	ein Stück Brot
A:	{ Ja, danke sehr. (*Punkt*)	eine Tasse Kaffee
	{ Danke, das reicht. (*0 Punkt*)	ein Glas Wein, *usw.*

Gehören *with dative article or pronoun)*

F:	Gehören diese Bücher . . .?	⚲	dem Lehrer (ihm)
A:	{ Ja, sie gehören (. . .). (*Punkt*)	⚲	der Lehrerin (ihr)
	{ Nein, sie gehören (. . .) nicht.	⚲⚲⚲	den Schülern
	(*0 Punkt*)		(ihnen)

Variant 1 Dasselbe wählen
(Possessive pronouns)

F:	Ist dein Wagen . . .?		schnell
A1:	Ja, sehr . . .	Nein, im Gegenteil.	klein
A2:	Meiner auch.	Meiner wohl.	bequem
	(*Punkt*)	(*0 Punkt*)	*usw.*

(Languages (negative choice))

F:	Sprechen Sie . . .?		Holländisch
A1:	Nein, kein Wort.	Ja, gewiß	Italienisch
A2:	Ich auch nicht.	Aber ich nicht.	Schwedisch
	(*Punkt*)	(*0 Punkt*)	Griechisch
			Spanisch

Variant 2 Zweifache geheime Wahl
(Separable verbs)

F1:	Steht Frank um . . . auf?	7.20
A1:	{ Aber nein! (*Halt!*)	7.40
	{ Ja, er steht immer um . . . auf. (*Mach weiter*)	8.10
F2:	Und fängt er seine Arbeit um . . . an?	8.30
A2:	{ Nein. (*Halt!*)	8.45
	{ Ja, er fängt um . . . an.	9.15

1.4 Secret choice II
Choix secret II
Geheime Wahl II

Basic gap	Information gap based on secret choice
Aim	To discover and remember as many secret choices as possible
Language	Controlled
Preparation and material	Minimal – putting simple language frame and list on display or handouts; or using textbook material

Stage 1   E,I (5 minutes)

Class   Invite learners to suggest five or six language items which will fit into a given question and answer frame. Example:

G: Can you speak . . .?   Arabic
A: {Yes, I can.   Russian
    No, (I can't speak . . .) but I can speak . . .   Chinese
    (*The negative may be omitted.*)   Swahili, *etc.*

Learners each make a secret choice from the list and write it down. Ask a few learners about their choices: *Can you speak Arabic?* etc. to see how many you can guess correctly. A few learners can also ask you questions (you will need to change your secret choice each time).

Stage 2   E,I (5 minutes)

Team   Learners ask each other questions in turn, between the teams. One or two learners can keep the score of correct guesses on the board. When several answers have been heard, give one member of each team the chance to ask someone who has already answered. If this 'second chance' is repeated at regular intervals, learners are encouraged to pay attention to all the answers they hear, in case they are given a second chance to score a point in this way. Example:

(*Teams A and B*)

Aline: Barbara, can you speak Chinese?
Barbara: No, I can't speak Chinese, but I can speak Arabic.
             Axel, can you speak Chinese?
Axel: Yes I can. (*Barbara scores a point.*) Robert, can you
             speak Russian?
Robert: No, I can't speak Russian, but I can speak Swahili.
             Anne, can you . . . *etc.*

After several more answers, there is a 'second chance' and the next questioner comes back to Barbara.

Ali: Barbara, can you speak Arabic?

Barbara: Yes I can. (*Ali scores a point. Barbara also has a 'second chance' question*) Anne, can you . . . *etc.*

After this, normal guessing resumes. The second chance provides a natural context for question tags: they can be added to the language frame if necessary. Examples:

E   *You can speak . . ., can't you?*
F   *Vous parlez . . ., n'est-ce pas?*
D   *Sie können . . . sprechen, nicht wahr?*

It is most useful with the great variety of question tags in English.

Stage 3   E,I,A (5 minutes)

Team   As above, without looking at the language frame.

Variant 1 Wh- questions

Some frames can be designed to allow the use of *wh-* questions. Examples:

E   *When did you go to the theatre – on . . .? / Tuesday, etc.*
    (Second chance: *You went to the theatre on . . ., didn't you?*)
F   *Où allez-vous demain – . . .? / à la plage, etc.*
    (Second chance: *Vous allez . . . demain, n'est-ce pas?*)
D   *Was machst du am liebsten – . . .? / schwimmen, usw.*
    (Second chance: *Du . . . am liebsten, nicht wahr?*)

Variant 2 Second chance frames

This is an extension of the 'second chance' mentioned in stage 2. Learners ask questions referring to previous answers in the third person: *Does Barbara speak Arabic?* or in reported speech: *Did Barabara say she spoke Arabic?* The variant can be used for a second round of questions or, in a large class, after several learners have answered using the first frame. Learners can ask questions about members of their own or of the opposing team. The following, based on the example in stage 2, should make the process clear: the learners are now using a second frame, with reported speech, to ask about previous answers. Example:

Frame: Q: *Did x say that s/he could speak . . .?*
          A: *Yes, s/he did.*
             No, s/he said s/he could speak . . .

Amy: Bill – did Axel say that he could speak Chinese?

Bill: Yes, he did. (*No one scores, as this is correct. Bill continues.*)
        Axel – did Barbara say that she could speak Russian?
        (*He has either forgotten Barbara's original answer, or he is
        hoping to trick Axel, a technique which learners quickly learn
        to try out in this variant!*)

Axel: No, she said she could speak Arabic. (*Axel scores a point,
        and asks the next question.*) Bella – did Anne say that she
        could . . . etc.?

If there is any doubt about the quoted answers, the learners
who originally gave them can show the choice which they
wrote down.

Variant 3 Parallel questions

To introduce more variety into the questions and answers, or
to contrast two language patterns, you can work with two
language frames at once. The two frames may also require two
lists, as in the example below. Learners must then make secret
choices from both lists, and pay attention to the questions they
are asked so that they give the appropriate answer. Examples:

Frame and list 1

Q: Are there many . . . in your basket?	apples
A: Yes, there are.	cakes
No, there aren't many . . ., but there are	oranges
lots of . . .	sandwiches

Frame and list 2

Q: Is there much . . . in your basket?	cheese
A: Yes, there is.	bread
No, there isn't much . . ., but there's lots of . . .	butter
	meat

Finding and making material

Many textbook exercises can be adapted for *Secret choice I and
II*. Wherever possible, the learners should suggest items for
the list, both to involve them more closely and to make sure
that they understand what they are saying (visual aids are also
useful, where appropriate). They can, of course, suggest
authentic personal information for the lists wherever possible.
All this extends the learners' vocabulary as they ask or look for
language to express their ideas. The language frames and lists
must not only be grammatically and semantically possible,
but also appropriate, and lead to natural exchanges. Often,
inappropriate items only become clear during practice.
Encourage learners to notice and change them. For example,

the *Can you speak . . .?* frame with a list that included *English* led to an answer: *No, I can't speak English, but I can speak Italian* – in English! Further examples of appropriacy, which can be discussed with learners:

– Frames and lists with *tu* or *vous*, *du* or *Sie* should reflect the relative informality or formality suggested by these pronouns. *Es-tu architecte?* is not very probable in adult conversation, but children might well ask each other *Es-tu hollandais/e, italien/ne?* etc.

– The last example shows how attention must be paid to the sex of the answerer if the frame or list includes sex-related words: this provides further useful contextualised practice for the learners.

– The present progressive in English can rarely be used to ask direct questions in the second person. One wouldn't ask: *Are you wearing (blue jeans, blue shoes, a blue shirt)*, etc. – except perhaps on the telephone; but one could use it in the third person, as in enquiring about a missing person: *Is your friend wearing . . .*, etc.

Where possible, learners themselves should suggest a possible context for the mini-dialogue which they have helped to create, i.e. who might say this, and in what situation? This also helps to ensure that they can set the practice in a communicative context, and not simply treat it as an isolated language drill. It is worth taking time to create and adapt frames and lists with the learners in this way, because the activity develops their language awareness and their sense of involvement more than simply providing them with ready-made language items.

In *Teaching material*, contexts are suggested where appropriate, in italics. Full lists are given simply to make the examples clear, but different items can be chosen by the learners. Frames for *Variants 1* and *2* can be adapted from the examples given.

Teaching material

ENGLISH *Secret choice II*

(Comparative, superlatives)

Q: Is your car . . . (1) than a Cadillac?
A: {
  Yes, it's the . . . (2) car you can buy.
  No, but it's . . . (1) than a Cadillac.
	(1) bigger, faster
	more powerful
	more expensive
	(2) biggest, fastest
	most powerful
	most expensive

(*Present perfect / frequency adverbs*)

Q: Have you ever . . .?	visited Buckingham Palace,
A: { Yes, I have. No, I've never . . ., but I've often . . .	met the Queen, stayed at Windsor, danced with the Prince(ss) of Wales

(*Conditional I with* must / needn't)
In a travel agency

Q: If you go to Transylvania, must you . . .?	take a passport,
A: { Yes, you must. No, you needn't . . ., but you must . . .	speak the language, visit Dracula, carry a blood donor card

Variant 3 Parallel questions

(Have got / one)

Q: Have you got a . . . car?	white red
A: { Yes, I have. No, I haven't got a . . . car, I've got a . . . one.	yellow blue, *etc.*

(*Present simple* / ones)

Q: Do you like . . . cars	(*see above*)
A: { Yes, I do. No, I don't like . . . cars, I like . . . ones.	

(*Present progressive*)

Q: Are you thinking about . . .?	money
A: { Yes, I am. No, I'm not thinking about . . ., I'm thinking about . . .	school sport, *etc.*

(*Simple present / frequency adverbs*)

Q: Do you ever think about . . .?	food
A: { Yes, I do. No, I never think about . . ., but I often think about . . .	sex *etc.*

(*Past, simple and progressive*)

Q: Were you . . . when the storm broke?	swimming
A: { Yes, I was. No, I wasn't . . ., I was . . .	shopping sunbathing playing tennis

(Simple past)

Q: Did you . . . when the storm broke?	go (went) home
A: ⎰ Yes, I did.	take (took) shelter
⎱ No, I didn't . . ., I (. . .) . . .	run (ran) away

(Conditional II)

Q: If you won a million pounds, would you . . .?	leave home, buy a boat, buy a Boeing, give it to charity
A: ⎰ Yes, I would	
⎱ No, I wouldn't . . ., I'd . . .	

(Conditional III)

Q: If you had won a million pounds last year, would you have . . .?	left home, bought a Boeing, bought a boat, given it to charity
A: ⎰ Yes, I would.	
No, I wouldn't have . . ., I'd have. . .	

FRANÇAIS *Choix secret II*

(Present / direct object pronouns)

En regardant le plan de la ville

Q: Vous voyez (. . .) . . .?	(le) théâtre
⎰ Oui, je (. . .) vois.	(le) supermarché
R: ⎨ Non, je ne (. . .) vois pas, mais je	(la) poste
⎱ vois (. . .) . . .	(les) magasins, *etc.*

(Reflexive verbs)

Q: Tu t'appelles . . .?	Michel/le
⎰ Oui, je m'appelle . . .	André/e
R: ⎨ Non, je ne m'appelle pas . . .,	Martin/e, *etc.*
⎱ je m'appelle . . .	

Variant 3 Questions parallèles

(Avoir/pas de)

Q: Avez vous (. . .) . . .?	(un) stylo, cahier
⎰ Oui.	(une) règle, gomme
R: ⎨ Non, je n'ai pas de . . ., mais	
⎱ j'ai (. . .). . .	

(avoir / du, en, etc.)

Q: Avez-vous (. . .) . . .?	(du) pain
⎰ Oui, j'en ai.	(de l')eau minérale
R: ⎨ Non, je n'ai pas de . . . (*ou* je n'en ai	(de la) confiture
⎱ pas), mais j'ai (. . .) . . .	(des) croissants, *etc.*

(*Present / possessive pronoun*)

Dans le train

Q: Votre ami cherche . . .?	son billet, portefeuille
R: ⎰ Oui, c'est ça.	sa valise,
Non, il ne cherche pas . . .,	sa carte d'identité
⎱ il cherche . . .	ses cigarettes, clés

(*Plural*)

Q: Vos amis cherchent . . .	leur valise
R: ⎰ Oui, c'est ça.	leur sac de voyage
Non, ils ne cherchent pas . . .,	leurs billets
⎱ ils cherchent . . .	leurs cigarettes

DEUTSCH *Geheime Wahl II*

Variant 3 Parallele Fragen

(Haben / einen)

F: Hast du einen . . .?	Goldfisch
A: ⎰ Ja.	Hund, Hamster
Nein, ich habe keinen . . ., sondern	Kanarienvogel
⎱ einen . . .	

(Haben / eine, ein).

F: Hast du ein(e) . . .?	(e) Katze
A: ⎰ Ja.	(e) weiße Maus
Nein, ich habe kein(e) . . . sondern	Kaninchen, Pony
⎱ ein(e) . . .	

(*Articles* / doch)

F: (. . .) . . . ist nicht alle, hoffe ich?	(der) Tee, Kaffee
A: ⎰ Doch, (. . .) ist leider alle.	(die) Limonade
⎱ Nein, (. . .) nicht, aber (. . .) . . . wohl.	(das) Bier

(*Plurals*)

F: Die . . . sind nicht alle, hoffe ich?	Kekse
A: ⎰ Doch, die sind leider alle.	Bonbons
⎱ Nein, die nicht, aber die . . . wohl.	Brötchen, Äpfel

((Hin)fahren / *dative*)

Im Busbahnhof

F: Entschuldigen Sie, bitte, wohin fährt	zum Flughafen
dieser Bus – bis . . .?	zum Bahnhof
A: ⎰ Ja.	zur Oper
Nein, er fährt nicht . . . sondern	zur Goethestrasse
⎱ bis . . .	zum Kino

(Her)kommen

F:	Entschuldigen Sie bitte, woher kommt dieser Bus – . . .?	vom Kino vom Bahnhof
A:	Ja. Nein, er kommt nicht . . ., sondern . . .	von der Oper, *usw.*

(*Perfect / accusative / adjectives*)

Freunde im Möbelgeschäft

F:	Habt ihr . . . gekauft?	einen grünen/roten Stuhl
A:	Ja, das haben wir. Nein, wir haben . . . gekauft.	eine gelbe/rote Lampe ein blaues/rotes Sofa

(*Future / plural*)

F:	Werdet ihr . . . kaufen?	zwei grüne/rote Stühle
A:	Ja. Nein, wir werden . . . kaufen.	zwei gelbe/rote Lampen zwei blaue/rote Sofas

(Sollen / *accusative*)

Beim Umräumen

F:	Soll ich den Tisch . . . stellen?	auf den Balkon
A:	Ja, bitte. Nein, stellen Sie ihn lieber . . .	auf die Terrasse in das Schlafzimmer, *usw*

(*Dative*)

F:	Steht der Stuhl immer noch . . .?	auf dem Balkon
A:	Ja, sicher. Nein, er steht nicht mehr . . . sondern . . .	auf der Terrasse im Schlafzimmer, *usw.*

(*Word order after* daß)

Konversation zwischen Reiseleitern

F:	Glaubst du, daß die Touristen . . . gehen wollen?	trimmen reiten
A:	Ja, das glaube ich. Nein, ich glaube, daß sie eigentlich . . . gehen wollen.	tanzen schwimmen

(*Word order after* weil)

F:	Warum sind die Touristen unzufrieden – weil sie nicht . . . gehen dürfen?	trimmen reiten
A:	Ja, das glaube ich. Nein, nur weil sie nicht . . . gehen dürfen.	essen trinken

1.5   Hunt the answer
Cherchez la réponse
Die richtige Antwort suchen

Basic gap	Information gap based on personal information
Aim	To find people who can give the required answers to questions; to learn more about one's classmates
Language	Controlled, guided or free
Preparation and material	List of questions on display or handouts (may be prepared with learners)

Stage 1   E,I (5 minutes)

Class   Put a few questions to learners until you get the required answers. Examples:

Lena, can you speak Spanish? – No.
Max, can you? – Yes.
Nico, do you like jazz? – Yes.

Depending on the level, questions may be all of the same pattern or mixed (as in the examples above). Where appropriate, follow up the answers:

How do you say 'Thank you' in Spanish, Max?
Who's your favourite musician, Nico?

This gives extra language practice and, more importantly, shows your interest in what they say and so encourages learners to give authentic information. Learners themselves can suggest questions for stages 1 or 2.

Stage 2   E,I (10 minutes)

Class/team   Learners take turns to choose a question and put it to not more than three classmates to find someone who can give the required answer. Teams may score points for every success. You or the learners can ask follow-up questions where appropriate.

Pairs   Pairs ask each other questions from the list, and keep a record of their successes; the answers they obtain can be reported later.

Changing pairs   Learners each choose a different question or questions (or are given one or more questions on handouts), and circulate in the classroom till they have found, and noted who gave the required answers.

With either form of pair work, learners finally report their results: how many of the required answers did they obtain?

What did they find out about their classmates? Sample replies:
Nico was born in January.
Olga has a hamster, etc.
You or learners can then ask for more details:
What date in January, Nico?
What's your hamster called, Olga? etc.

Stage 3   E,I,A (10 minutes)

Class/team/ pair/changing pairs   As in stage 2, but the questions on display or handouts are phrased indirectly, so that learners must formulate the questions themselves. Examples:
Find someone who:
has never eaten octopus (moussaka, frog's legs, etc.*);*
would like to be an astronaut, etc.

They may also ask follow-up questions, and finally report their results as fully as possible. Note that, although the questions will have the same form, learners may be looking for a *Yes* or *No* answer. The person asking *Have you ever eaten octopus?* hopes to hear *No, never!* Learners are thus encouraged to give honest answers, and not say *Yes* simply to oblige their classmates.

Variant 1   Memory test

In the same or a later lesson, you or the learners check if everyone can remember the reported information, with questions like:
Who's got a pony?
Who didn't watch (TV programme) last week?
Who likes avocado pears?

Variant 2   You too?

Learners can make a statement about themselves and then ask the question:
I always get up late on Sundays – do you?
I can't ride a bike – can you?

Variant 3   Closer and closer

Learners try to guess something about a classmate who answers only with comparatives until the exact answer is found. Examples:
Is your dog (age)?   *No, it's younger/older.*
Have you got (number) cousins?   *No, more/fewer.*

Did you go to bed at (time?)   *No, earlier/later.*

1.3 *Secret choice 1, Variant 1* offers similar practice with given or personal information. 3.6 *Find your partners, Variant 1* and 5.6 *Spot the differences, Variant 3* offer more extensive practice with personal information.

Finding and making material

Questions can be based on structures in the textbook, and vocabulary suited to the learners' level. Encourage learners of English to use short forms in their answers: *Yes, I am/do/have; No, I can't/didn't/wouldn't*, etc.

In *Teaching material*, complete or skeleton question lists are divided between the languages. Some of these lists include mixed language patterns, some are all of one type: which model you follow depends on the level and needs of your learners. Many questions can be used several times, by changing the items given in brackets, or by changing them to the negative/affirmative: *Find someone who likes (doesn't like) horses, cowboy films, pea soup*, etc.

Learners may write their own list of questions, based on the skeleton question forms, and try them out with partners or in changing pairs.

Teaching material

ENGLISH *Hunt the answer*

Skeleton question forms (stages 1 and 2)
(Various tenses)

Are you . . .? / Have you got a/any . . .? / Do you (always, ever) . . .? / Do you like . . .? / Can you . . .? / Have you (ever) . . . (this year, *etc.*)? / Did you . . . (yesterday, *etc.*)? / Were you . . . (last summer, *etc.*)? / Were you (doing) . . . (at six o'clock last night, *etc.*)? / Are you going to . . . (at the weekend, *etc.*)? / Would you like to . . .? / If . . ., would you . . .?

Complete questions (stage 3) (based on the above)

Find someone who:
is afraid of spiders / has a younger brother (sister) / always watches football on TV / doesn't like war films / plays tennis (the piano) / can stand on his/her head / went abroad last summer / was late for school this morning / isn't going to watch TV tonight / is going to have a birthday next month /

wouldn't like to climb Everest / wouldn't lend you (amount in local currency) if you asked, *etc.*

Variant 2 You too?

(*Various auxiliaries in question tags*)

I'm Capricorn – are you? / I don't like Dallas – do you? / I can speak Italian – can you? / I've never visited Spain – have you? / I didn't do my homework last night – did you? / I'd like a cup of coffee – would you? *etc.*

FRANÇAIS *Cherchez la réponse*

Complete questions (stages 1 and 2)
(*Perfect tense, verbs with* être)

Vous êtes sorti(e) de chez vous avant/après (x heures) ce matin?
Vous êtes venu(e) à bicyclette/à pied/en train, voiture, autobus, *etc.*?
Vous êtes arrivé(e) ici avant/après (x heures)?
Vous êtes allé(e) au cinéma, café, théâtre/à la discothèque ces derniers jours?
Vous êtes né(e) en (mois)?
Vous n'êtes jamais tombé(e) d'un mur, arbre, cheval/d'une bicyclette/sur la tête, *etc.*?

Skeleton question forms (stage 3)
(*Various tenses*)

Trouvez quelqu'un qui:
a un(e), des . . . / (fait) . . . / peut . . . / sait . . . / veut (voudrait)
. . . a été . . . / a (fait) . . . / est (allé(e), etc.) . . . / était . . . /
(faisait) . . . / sera . . . (fera) (va faire) . . . / ferait . . . si . . . .

Variant 2 Vous aussi?

Examples:

Je mange beaucoup de bonbons – vous aussi? / Je n'aime pas le football – et vous? / J'aime les films d'Alfred Hitchcock – est-ce que vous les aimez aussi?

DEUTSCH *Die richtige Antwort suchen*

Complete questions for stage 3 (handouts for changing pairs)
(Various patterns)

Finde jemanden: der Schuhgröße (x) hat der ein(e)(n) (*pet, object*) hat der schon mal in (*town, country*) war	Namen:
Finde jemanden: der (*popular entertainer*) nicht mag der (*amount of money*) dabei hat der gestern (*TV programme*) gesehen hat	Namen:
Finde jemanden: der schon mal im Ausland war der eine Platte von (*popular singer or group*) hat der (*language*) sprechen kann	Namen:
Finde jemanden: der (*instrument*) spielt der gestern (*food*) gegessen hat der sich für (*hobby, sport*) interessiert	Namen:
Finde jemanden: dessen Lieblingsfach (*school subject*) ist der ein(e)(n) (*adjective + object*) hat der kein(e)(n) (*food, drink*) mag	Namen:
Finde jemanden: der (*sport*) spielt der in den Sommerferien nach (*country*) fahren wird der mehrere Geschwister hat	Namen:

Variant 2 Sie auch?

Examples:

Ich tanze gern – Sie auch? / Ich mag keine Katzen – Sie auch nicht?

1.6 Questionnaires
Questionnaires
Fragebogen

Basic gap	Information gap based on personal information or opinions
Aim	To complete a graph, report or class profile with information from classmates; to predict the results of the research
Language	Controlled, guided or free
Preparation and material	Minimal – putting simple language frame on display or handouts; or using textbook material

Stage 1   E,I (5 minutes)

Class   Do some 'market research' with a sample of learners: for example, you want to find out when most people get up in the morning – is it before 7 a.m., between 7 and 7.30, between 7.30 and 8 or after 8 a.m.? Ask everyone to write down their predictions. Then ask the sample group: *When do you usually get up?* or *When did you get up this morning?* Fill in the answers on the board, repeating them in the third person: *Helen gets up before 7, Leonora and Patricia get up before 7.30, Gerard, Peter and Luca get up . . .,* etc. Finally, check who made the most accurate predictions.

Stage 2   E,I,A (15 minutes)

Group   Announce the topic for the questionnaire (if the questions are in the textbook or already prepared), or let the class choose a topic and help to devise question(s). If it is a closed questionnaire, as in stage 1, a list of possible answers must also be given. Learners note their personal predictions of the result.

Examples:

1 *Closed questionnaire about pets (Level E)*
   Prediction: most popular pets in correct order
   Question(s): Have you got a/any . . .?
   Answers: cat, dog, goldfish, *etc.*
   Group members may share the questions between them, or one learner (playing the role of a market researcher) can ask for and record all the group's answers: *Who's got a cat/a dog/ any goldfish?* etc.
   Reporting: one group member reports the results, using mainly the third person: *Sylvia and Alan have got hamsters, Karen and I have got cats, Julia hasn't got a pet,* etc. You or a

learner can fill in the results on the board, under each
heading.
2 *Open questionnaire about holidays (Level I or A)*
  Prediction: Most common reply to each question
  Questions: 1 Where did you go on holiday last year?   2 How
  did you travel?   3 Where did you stay?   4 Did you have
  good weather?   5 What did you enjoy most?
  Reporting: go through the questions in turn with the first
  group, and write their answers next to each question
  number.
    Check who predicted the results of the questionnaires most
  accurately, and/or whose answers were most/least typical of
  the class as a whole. Level I and A learners can go on to discuss
  these results and ask each other further questions about their
  holidays.

Example from practice

Adult class, answers to questions 1–3 from first group:
1 *Spain* (2 people), *Sweden, France*
2 *Plane* (2 people), *boat and train, boat and car*
3 *Hotel, with friends, camping* (2 people)
Results from other groups were added to these, which gave
some new headings: 1 *Italy, no holiday;*   2 *Bus, bicycle,* etc.
Finally, there was a complete list of answers given on the
board, plus the number of people who had given each answer.

Stage 3   E,I,A (15 minutes)

Group   As above, without controlled language. There can be more
discussion of their own results within the groups, and any
further details learned in this discussion can be included in the
final reports.

Variant 1 Memory test

As in 1.5 *Hunt the answer, Variant 1.*
  See 2.7 *interviews* and 7.4 *Holiday plans* for further practice
on the topic of tourism. See 3.4 *People and things* for simple
practice, and 7.2 *Order of preference* for more advanced free
practice, based on collecting and comparing opinions.

Finding and making material

Questions can be based on structures and vocabulary in the
textbook for level I and A. Learners' interest is often greater if

they can choose the general topic of the questionnaire, or at least suggest some questions – and the answers for a closed questionnaire. They often acquire new vocabulary via this activity, as they consult you or their dictionaries for the items they wish to ask about. The more advanced the group, the more suggestions they can make.

Many textbooks have exercises designed as, or easily adapted for, questionnaires of this type, as do some magazines for language learners. Questions can also be taken or adapted from opinion polls and surveys published in newspapers and magazines and some textbooks. It can be particularly interesting to compare the class results with those of the original survey; for example, their results in the holidays questionnaire (stage 2), compared with those reported in a foreign newspaper or magazine. Learners can write their own questionnaires to be used in the whole class, or exchanged between groups.

Most of the examples in *Teaching material* can be used as open or closed questionnaires: the former are generally more suitable for learners with a wide vocabulary. The same topics and questions can often be used for either this activity or 1.5 *Hunt the answer*.

Teaching material

ENGLISH *Questionnaires*

1 Open: 'Birthday questionnaire'
  (*Dates*; to be born)

  > Prediction: In which month were most of the class born?
  > Sample questions: When is your birthday? / What month were you born in?
  > Reporting: Who was born in . . . in your group?

2 Open 'Family survey'
  (*Comparatives and superlatives*)

  > Predictions: How many in the class are eldest (*or* youngest, middle, only) children? How large is the average family?
  > Sample questions: have you any brothers or sisters? How many? Are you the eldest/youngest? How many younger/older brothers/sisters have you got?
  > Reporting: How many eldest children are there in your group? *etc.*

3 Closed: 'Experiences'
   (*Present perfect*)
   >Prediction: How many in the class have done these things?
   >Questions: Have you ever . . .?
   >Answers: (*to be suggested by class*) played cricket, visited the
   >Lake District, flown in a helicopter, *etc.*
   >*Reporting: ask follow-up questions as groups report:* Jean has
   >flown in a helicopter, *etc.* – When did you fly in a
   >helicopter, Jean? Where did you play cricket, Rod? (*This
   >also allows you to contrast the tenses.*)

FRANÇAIS *Questionnaires*

1 Questions fermées: 'Étude statistique des peurs et des allergies'
   (Avoir peur de, être allergique à)
   >Pronostic: Combien de personnes ont peur de . . .? Combien
   >sont allergiques à . . .?
   >Questions: Avez-vous peur . . .?   Êtes-vous allergique . . .?
   >Réponses: (*to be suggested by class*) des araignées, serpents,
   >orages; au pollen; à la penicilline, poussière; aux fraises,
   >piqûres de guêpes, *etc.*
   >Compte-rendu: combien de personnes dans ce groupe ont
   >peur . . . sont allergiques . . .?

2 Questions ouvertes ou fermées: 'Sondage touristique'
   (*Conditional II*)
   >Pronostic: Les endroits préférés des touristes
   >Question: Si vous alliez à Paris/en France, est-ce que vous
   >voudriez voir/visiter . . .?
   >Réponses (fermées): (*suggested by class*) La Joconde, le
   >Sacré-Coeur, *etc.*; St Tropez, les châteaux de la Loire, *etc.*
   >Compte-rendu: Combien de personnes dans ce groupe
   >voudraient . . .?

3 Questions fermées: 'Sondage sportif'
   (*Superlatives*)
   >Pronostic: Ce que la classe va dire de chaque sport
   >Question: À votre avis, quel est le sport le plus . . .?
   >Réponses: (*learners suggest adjectives and sports*) dangereux,
   >passionnant, ennuyeux, monstrueux, etc.; le football,
   >hockey, golf, ping-pong; la course automobile (Formule
   >1), corrida, boxe, chasse au renard, *etc.*
   >Compte-rendu: Combien de personnes dans ce groupe
   >trouvent . . .?

DEUTSCH *Fragebogen*

1 Offen: 'Umfrage – Telefonnummer'
   (*Numbers*)

   Frage: Was ist Ihre Telefonnummer?

   Lotterie: *after the questions, draw (or let a learner draw) three or four numbers at random: e.g. 3 – 2 – 5 – 7. The 'winners' are the groups or learners with telephone numbers containing most of these digits, those with the digits in the correct order being preferred.*

   Berichten: Wer in dieser Gruppe hat eine Telefonnummer mit diesen Nummern?

2 Offen: 'Umfrage – Finanzen'
   (*Amounts; comparatives and superlatives*)

   Vorhersage: Was ist der größte (kleinste, durchschnittliche) Betrag?

   Frage: Wieviel Geld hast du im Portemonnaie?

   Berichten: Wer in dieser Gruppe hat mehr/weniger als . . . dabei?

2 Geschlossen: 'Umfrage – Wohlstand'
   (Haben *with accusative, singular and plural*)

   Vorhersage: Wieviele dieser Sachen gibt es in dieser Klasse insgesamt?

   Fragen: Habt ihr/Haben Sie ein(e)(n) . . . zu Hause? Nur einen(e)/eins?

   Antworten: (*learners suggest items*) einen Computer, Fernseher, Mikrowellenherd; eine Waschmaschine, Tiefkühltruhe; ein Auto, ein Schwimmbad, *usw.*

   Berichten: *Ask each group:* Wieviele dieser Sachen besitzt ihr? (*That is, ask for a group answer. I prefer not to ask precisely who has what unless learners wish to reveal this to the whole class.*)

2 Dialogues and role-plays

2.1 Introduction

Role-play may involve assuming a partly or wholly different persona, and/or pretending to be in a different situation. In one sense, therefore, most communication practice in the average FL classroom involves an element of role-play – the speakers pretend that the FL is their only means of communication, even though they may share the same mother tongue. For this reason, role-play activities are found in almost every section of this book. They can take place with wholly scripted or wholly improvised language, and may continue for five minutes or for a whole lesson. Even a simple pattern drill from 1.3 or 1.4 *Secret choice*, set in a given context, is in effect a brief role-play.

2.2 *Smugglers* and 2.3 *Detectives* show how simple drills, based on secret choice, can stress the imagined context in this way; and how these basic situations can then be extended for more advanced levels and more improvised communication practice.

The most common form of role-play in the classroom is perhaps acting out dialogues from the book, particularly situational dialogues such as 'In the shop', 'Asking the way', etc. However, the fact that this language is clearly relevant to future communicative needs is not always sufficient to motivate learners, particularly if the classroom practice is in itself devoid of any communicative elements, so that learners do not feel involved in what they are saying or hearing. If learners are given some choice of what to say, and if there is a clear aim to be achieved by what they say in their role-plays, they may participate more willingly and learn more thoroughly than when they are told simply to repeat a given dialogue in pairs.

2.4 *Shopping* and 2.5 *Finding the way* give the learners tasks to fulfil by communicating with each other, or by listening to communication between others. Their aim is thus not simply to complete the dialogue; they must do something with the information they acquire during the activity, just as they would in an authentic communication situation – though the tasks are adapted to the classroom situation. Learners cannot actually go home with two bottles of claret after acting out a shopping dialogue, but they can, for example, find out which of three classroom shops sells wine at the lowest price; or which has the Mouton Rothschild, which has the *vin de table* and which has sold out. Work with these basic dialogues can also be extended to more varied and improvised communication practice, as is shown in stage 3 or the variants. (See p. 30 for notes on the changing groups and pairs recommended for these two activities.)

2.6 *What are we talking about?* combines role-play with a recognition task for the audience: this format can be adapted for many situations and types or levels of language – either scripted or improvised. Some suggested variants call upon learners to use dramatic expression and intonation in order to convey their message; all of this helps to develop the learners' linguistic and para-lingusitic communication skills in the FL.

The format of 2.7 *Interviews* is more suitable for levels I and A. The content in the main activity is tourist information, but you and the learners can choose any topic of interest.

The different types of role-play in this section offer opportunities for different types of learner. Some will prefer to assume a different persona; many teachers have noticed how a shy or unwilling speaker will suddenly display surprising fluency when playing someone else. Other learners are more comfortable playing themselves in an imagined situation, but one which is realistic and fairly structured, such as shopping. Some people resent having to express feelings or opinions not their own, others enjoy this best; some enjoy acting in front of the class, others are only comfortable in small groups. For all these reasons, learners should choose their roles themselves whenever possible; and this may include choosing to be an actor or a spectator in a given activity (the spectators are not passive observers, but have specific listening tasks in the role-plays described here). The more the learners can decide for themselves, the more successful the role-plays – and indeed most communication activities – are likely to be.

To sum up, role-plays can be introduced from the beginning: from the simple mini-dialogues of *Secret choice*, one can progress in easy steps via practice with more situational dialogues such as 2.2 *Smugglers*, 2.5 *Finding the way*, etc. to the more demanding and imaginative role-plays described in the variants to these activities – and in other activities in this and other sections of the book.

2.2 Smugglers
Contrebandiers
Schmuggler

Basic gap	Information gap based on secret choice
Aim	To catch smugglers; to avoid being caught
Language	Controlled, guided or free

Preparation and material	Minimal – putting simple dialogue frame and list on display or handouts; or using textbook material (optional: visual aids)

Stage 1   E,I (5 minutes)

Class   Take the role of customs officer and invite a few learners (smugglers) each to make a secret choice of one or two objects from a list of five or six, or to draw pictures from an envelope without letting you see them. Go through the dialogue with the smugglers as a demonstration, asking each about three items from the list: the smugglers must give up any which they have. Any other items are successfully smuggled, but must be shown or declared when the dialogue is completed. This ensures that the smugglers answer truthfully! (The number of items chosen and asked about can of course be adjusted to suit the time available or amount of practice required.)

Pronunciation and intonation can be practised at this stage, and a learner or learners can also practise the role of customs officer.

Stage 2   E,I (5 minutes)

Team/group/ pair   The roles of customs officers and smugglers are divided among the learners; the latter select items from the list, or the envelope. The officers question them as demonstrated in stage 1, and points are scored for every object successfully smuggled, or confiscated (pictures can be handed over): the winners are the learners or team with the most points or pictures at the end.

Stage 3   E,I,A (5 minutes)

Team/group/ pair   As in stage 2, without using the dialogue frame. This gives scope for more improvisation and level A learners often act out quite dramatic scenes, explaining away any items they are caught smuggling, etc. They may regard this as extremely useful practice!

See 4.4 *The speechless tourist* for further practice in the same situation.

Finding and making material

Many textbooks have a dialogue which can be used for this activity. Picture cards make the role-play more realistic. Advertisements for wines, perfume, cigarettes, etc. provide a plentiful supply of suitable pictures, which can be used for

many other communication activities, for example, 2.4
Shopping, 3.3 *Duets*, 3.4 *People and things*, etc. (See 5.2 *General notes on visual material.*)

Teaching material

ENGLISH *Smugglers*

(Some, any, *etc.*)

Customs officer: Have you got anything to declare?
Smuggler: No, nothing.
Customs officer: Have you got any . . .? (*3 times*)

| Smuggler: No, I haven't. *or* No, I haven't got any . . .
 Customs officer: Thank you, you can go through. | Yes, I have. *or* Yes, I have got some . . .
 Open your case please! |

List: wine, whisky, sherry, perfume, cigars, cigarettes

FRANÇAIS *Contrebandiers*

(Du, de la; pas de; en)

Douanier: Avez-vous quelque chose à déclarer?
Contrebandier: Non, (je n'ai) rien.
Douanier: Avez-vous d- . . .? (x 3)

| Contrebandier: Non, je n'en ai pas. *ou* Non, je n'ai pas de . . .
 Douanier: Merci, vous pouvez passer. | Ah oui, j'en ai.
 ou Ah oui, j'ai d- . . .
 Ouvrez la valise, s.v.p.! |

Liste: du vin, parfum; de la vodka; de l'eau de toilette; des cigares, cigarettes

DEUTSCH *Schmuggler*

(Kein-)

Zollbeamter: Haben Sie etwas zu verzollen?
Schmuggler: Nein, nichts.
Zollbeamter: Haben Sie . . .? (× 3)

| Schmuggler: Nein, ich habe kein – . . .
 Zollbeamter: Danke schön, Sie können weiter. | Nun ja, ich habe . . . dabei.
 Machen Sie bitte Ihren Koffer auf! |

Liste: -en Wein, Schnaps; -e Schokolade; -Parfüm; -e Zigarren, Zigaretten

2.3 Detectives
Policiers
Detektive

Basic gap	Information gap based on secret choice
Aim	To discover who was present at the time and place of a crime
Language	Controlled, guided or free
Preparation and material	Minimal – putting simple dialogue frame and list on display or handouts; or using textbook material (optional: visual aids)

Stage 1   E,I,A (10 minutes)

Class   Take the role of chief detective and explain that some learners were guests in the house last night when a crime took place (invent details) between 10 p.m. and midnight. The guests write down a place from the list or plan (level I and A learners can choose two or more places and the times they moved from one to the other). Interrogate the guests, using the frame or asking for details from more advanced learners. The other learners are assistant detectives who make notes of the places (and times). One or two can also take turns to ask questions. Finally, announce the exact place and time of the crime (you can write this down in advance or make it up on the basis of what the learners have said). Check with your assistants which guests were in the given place: they are arrested as suspects!

Stage 2   E,I (10 minutes)

Group   Write down, or ask a learner to write down, the time and place of the crime. One member of each group is the detective: the rest write down where/when they were in the house. Detectives question their groups as in stage 1. At a given time limit, the place and time of the crime are announced and the detectives report any suspected criminals in their groups. This may be done in reported speech at levels I or A. Example:

(*Sir Jasper was murdered at 10.30 p.m. in the library.*)
Detective 1: *Sybil says she was in the library from ten o'clock until quarter to eleven.*
Detective 2: *Christopher says he was in the library from ten thirty till midnight.*

Stage 3 E,I,A (15 minutes)

Group   As above, without using a dialogue frame. More
improvisation can be encouraged at all levels (depending on
the examples given in stage 1). When the detectives report,
you can ask for more details from them or from the suspects
themselves. Level I and A learners may be able to make up
stories to prove their innocence. Example:

(Continued from stage 2)
Sybil: *I saw Christopher come into the library with a gun in his hand.
I hid under the table and I saw him shoot Sir Jasper*, etc.
The detectives ask further questions to test such stories.
The learners can use communication strategies to express
themselves (see 4.1 *Introduction* to *Communication strategies*).
The discussions continue to the time limit, or until the class or
a jury panel agrees that one or more suspects must be guilty.

See 1.2 *Catch* for simpler practice.

Variant 1 Town or country

With town instead of house plan: *One of the shops*, etc. *was
robbed last Saturday when you were all shopping in town. You must
say when you visited various shops (and what you bought)*. Finally
announce e.g.: *The butcher was robbed at 3.30 (by someone buying
sausages)*, and see which learners are suspects.

With a map of the country: *Last July there was a bank robbery
in one of these towns* (name e.g. ten towns). *You were all touring
in the area and must say where you were and on which dates*. Finally
announce e.g.: *The Crédit Lyonnais in Dijon was robbed on July
15th*, and see who are suspects.

Variant 2 Alibi

Two learners prepare an alibi together, to cover several hours.
While one learner waits outside, the other is questioned by
classmates. The second learner then enters and is also
questioned: the classmates try to discover contradictions and
inconsistencies in the two stories. If they can find any, the pair
are guilty of the crime. (This is described in many books of
language games: e.g. Wright *et al*. 1979, 1984, p. 165 in
Booklist 2a.)

Finding and making material

Many textbooks have suitable house or town plans. Some books have lessons on the topic 'crime' for which this activity is appropriate. In general, it can be used in association with the past tense of *to be* and *to go*.

Teaching material

House plan   (alternative to list)

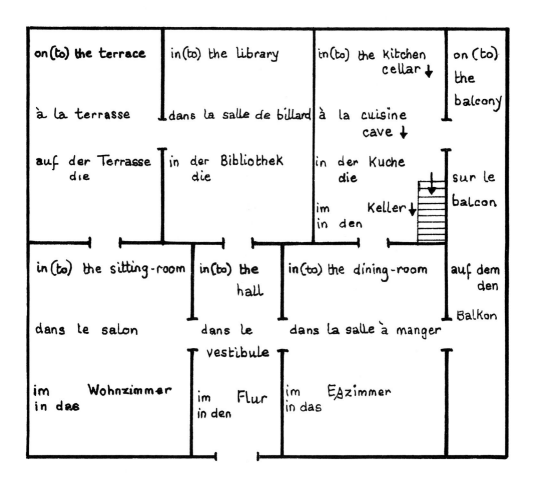

From *Developing Communication Skills* by Pat Pattison
© Cambridge University Press 1987

ENGLISH *Detectives*

(*Simple past of* to be, to go, to stay; *optional: reported speech*)

Q: Where were you between 10 o'clock and midnight last night? – And you? *etc.*

A: I was . . . from 10 o'clock until . . . Then I went . . . and I stayed there until midnight.

(Detective: X says s/he was . . . from . . . till . . .: Y and Z say they were . . ., *etc.*)

FRANÇAIS *Policiers*

(*Past tense of* être, aller, rester; y; *optional: reported speech*)

Q: Où étiez-vous entre dix heures et minuit? – Et vous? *etc.*

R: J'étais . . . jusqu'à . . . et puis je suis allé(e) . . . et j'y suis resté(e) jusqu'à minuit.

(Policier: X dit qu'il/elle était . . . de . . . jusqu'à . . .: Y et Z disent qu'ils/elles étaient . . ., *etc.*)

DEUTSCH *Detektive*

(*Past tense of* sein, gehen, bleiben; *optional: reported speech*)

F: Wo waren Sie zwischen zehn Uhr und zwölf Uhr gestern Nacht? – Und Sie? *usw.*

A: Ich war von zehn bis . . . . . . und dann ging ich . . . und blieb da bis Mitternacht.

(Detektiv: X sagt, daß er/sie . . . war, von . . . bis . . .: Y und Z sagen, daß sie . . . waren, von . . . bis . . ., *usw.*)

2.4 Shopping
Faire des courses
Einkaufen

Basic gap	Information gap based on secret choice or split information
Aim	To find the lowest prices in the shops
Language	Controlled, guided or free
Preparation and material	Minimal if there is shopping dialogue in textbook; otherwise, put dialogue frame and shopping list on display or handouts (optional: visual aids)

Stage 1   E,I (5 minutes)

Class   Ensure learners know the exchange rate between their own and the foreign currency. Take the role of shopkeeper: learners come in turn to ask for one item from the list, until the class has heard all the prices. Make some prices much higher and some much lower than in the native country so that learners can work out which items are 'best buys' in their own country and which in the foreign country. The dialogue can be repeated with a learner playing the shopkeeper, and new prices.

Stage 2   E (10 minutes)

Class   Three or four learners take the roles of shopkeepers and may sit at the front of the class. They decide the prices of the items in their shops (secret choice), ensuring that each one has a fair ratio of high and low prices; or you can give each shopkeeper a price list in advance. Other learners take it in turns to play the customers. Each customer goes to just one shop and buys one or two items, while the others note the prices they hear. Encourage consecutive customers to ask for different things in different shops; systematically working through the list makes it too easy for the listeners!

When all the items have been bought from each shop, the learners report where each can be bought most cheaply. The shopkeepers will confirm the prices. Alternatively, learners can practise their mathematics by working out at which shop you need spend the least money to buy all the articles.

Team   Team members can take it in turns to visit the shops and ask for items, making sure the team buys at least one of each article on the list. The winning team is the one which has made the most 'best buys' – i.e. paid the lowest prices for the most articles.

Stage 3   E,I,A (15 minutes)

Class/team   As in stage 2, without using the dialogue frame.
Changing   The shopkeepers sit in different corners of the room. Group
groups   members divide the shopping list between themselves: e.g. A buys pens and pencils, B buys exercise books and biros, C buys rulers and erasers, etc. Each group member then goes to find the price of the chosen items in each shop. To keep everyone moving, each customer asks for only one item before going to another shop. The first group to declare the list of 'best buys' has won.

See 2.6 *What are we talking about?, Variant 1* for more practice in listening and completing lists or graphs.

Variant 1 Sold out!

With amounts: the customers are told that no shop has more than, for example, five litres or kilos of each item. They take it in turns to buy a litre or kilo of something from the list (but they may not ask for the same item, in the same shop, as the customer immediately before them). All the customers must keep a check of what has already been bought because the winning team or group is the one which can buy the most before hearing the words: *Sold out!*

Variant 2 Find what you want

A list of four or five items is put on display: next to each item is a further choice of three or four sizes, colours, materials, etc. Each shopkeeper makes a secret choice of just two sizes or colours, etc. for each article. Example:
Shop A: blue and white shoes, in sizes 5 and 6
Shop B: grey and black shoes, in sizes 4 and 5, etc.
(or you can give each shopkeeper a list prepared in advance). The customers choose what they want, and take it in turns to go to a shop. The winners are (as in real life!) those who manage to get what they want in the first shop they try. This can be done in changing groups (see stage 3 above), or in pairs: each learner takes turns to be the shopkeeper. Finally, they compare which of them came closest to getting exactly what was wanted. Prices can be included – each shopkeeper decides the price, the customers decide the maximum they will pay. This makes the activity more complicated but even more realistic.

   This variant can be used in other situations, such as finding hotel rooms (see example under DEUTSCH in *Teaching material*); or clients may visit various dating agencies, looking for their ideal partners (there are no examples for this in *Teaching material* – the lists may be left to the imagination of level A learners!).

Variant 3 Value for money

Each shopkeeper sells the same articles for the same price, but each offers different quality or amounts. The customers try to discover or decide which shops offer best value for their money. This provides useful free communication practice when organised in changing groups (see stage 3 above). If there are two sales people in each shop, they can deal with more customers at once. Level I and A learners often display unexpected talents as sales people, trying to persuade shoppers that, for example, a plastic suitcase is much better than leather, or a nylon shirt better than a silk one because . . . There is also more discussion within the groups of customers, as they try to decide which shop offers best value for each item. Finally all the groups report their list of 'best buys' and there may be further discussion between groups which have made different decisions – discussion which the shopkeepers can join in with.

This variant can also be used with hotels instead of shops: hoteliers may think up extra attractions for their rooms – a telephone, television, balcony, view of the sea, etc. – to make decisions more difficult. To complicate matters, one can also vary the prices in each hotel.

Finding and making material

Nearly all textbooks have one or more dialogues which can be used for this activity, with little or no adaptation.

There are examples of dialogues in each language for the basic activity and for *Variant 3* in *Teaching material*; dialogues for the other variants are divided between the languages.

Visual aids are recommended to ensure that level E learners know what they are buying and selling, and to add realism for learners of any level. See 5.2 *General notes on visual material*, particularly sources (d), (e) and (g).

For *Variant 3*, English teachers can use Birt and Fletcher 1981, 'Bargain hunting' *Booklist* 2a.

Teaching material

ENGLISH *Shopping*

(Dialogue)	Shopkeeper: Good morning/afternoon. Can I help you? Customer: Good morning/afternoon. I'd like . . . please. Shopkeeper: Here you are. Anything else? Customer: No, thank you. How much is it? Shopkeeper: (*price*) Customer: Here you are. Thank you. Goodbye. Shopkeeper: Thank you. Goodbye.

List (suggested prices in £)				
	a pot of jam	£1.50	60p	£1.00
	a loaf of bread	30p	50p	80p
	a packet of washing powder	95p	£1.70	£1.20
	a tin of cat food	65p	45p	30p
	a dozen eggs	£1.00	60p	85p
	eighty teabags	£1.00	£1.20	95p

Variant 1 Sold out!   See FRANÇAIS or DEUTSCH.

Variant 2 Find what you want

List: a shirt, sweater/some boots, sandals
Sizes: 8–10–12–14 / 3–4–5–6
Colours: red, white, blue, black

Shopkeeper: Good morning/afternoon. Can I help you?
Customer: I'd like . . . please.
Shopkeeper: Yes, and what size?
Customer: Size . . . please.

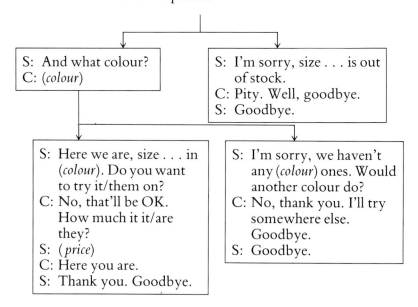

S: And what colour?
C: (*colour*)

S: I'm sorry, size . . . is out of stock.
C: Pity. Well, goodbye.
S: Goodbye.

S: Here we are, size . . . in (*colour*). Do you want to try it/them on?
C: No, that'll be OK. How much it it/are they?
S: (*price*)
C: Here you are.
S: Thank you. Goodbye.

S: I'm sorry, we haven't any (*colour*) ones. Would another colour do?
C: No, thank you. I'll try somewhere else. Goodbye.
S: Goodbye.

Variant 3 Value for money

> *List:* pens, watches, dictionaries, jeans

✂--

> *Dialogue frame*
> Shopkeeper: Good morning/afternoon. Can I help you?
> Customer: Good morning/afternoon, have you got any . . .?

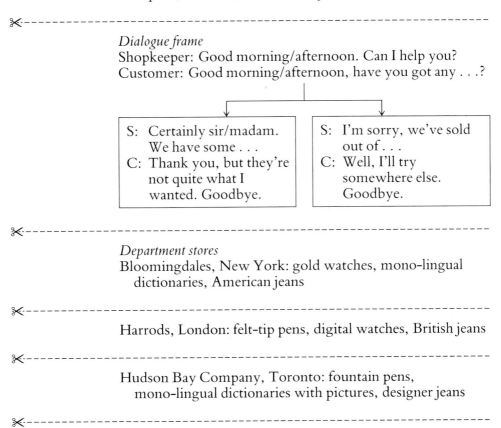

| S: Certainly sir/madam. We have some . . .
 C: Thank you, but they're not quite what I wanted. Goodbye. | S: I'm sorry, we've sold out of . . .
 C: Well, I'll try somewhere else. Goodbye. |

✂--

> *Department stores*
> Bloomingdales, New York: gold watches, mono-lingual dictionaries, American jeans

✂--

> Harrods, London: felt-tip pens, digital watches, British jeans

✂--

> Hudson Bay Company, Toronto: fountain pens, mono-lingual dictionaries with pictures, designer jeans

✂--

> Myers, Sydney: ball-point pens, waterproof watches, bi-lingual dictionaries.

FRANÇAIS *Faire des courses*

(*Dialogue*)

> Patron(ne): Bonjour, monsieur/madame/mademoiselle.
>   Vous désirez?
> Client(e): . . . s'il vous plaît.
> Patron(ne): Voilà. C'est tout?
> Client(e): Oui merci. Ça fait combien?
> Patron(ne): Ça fait (*prix*).
> Client(e): Voilà. Au revoir, monsieur/madame/
> mademoiselle.
> Patron(ne): Merci, monsieur/madame/mademoiselle. Au
> revoir.

> *Liste:* (*prices suggested in French francs*)

une bouteille de vin rouge	18,–	20,–	17,–
une boîte de sardines	2,50	3,50	3,–
une tablette de chocolat	4,–	3,–	3,50
une baguette (pain)	3,–	4,50	5,–
un paquet de sucre	7,50	5,–	6,–
un tube de moutarde	4,–	5,–	4,50

Variant 1 *Je n'en ai plus*

> Patron(ne): Bonjour, monsieur/madame/mademoiselle.
>   Vous désirez?
> Client(e): Vous avez d – . . .?
> Patron(ne): Oui, j'en ai. Combien en | Je regrette, je n'en ai
>   voulez-vous? | plus.
> Client(e): J'en veux un kilo/litre, s'il vous plaît.
> Patron(ne): Ça fait dix francs.
> Client(e): Voilà dix francs. Merci monsieur/madame/
> mademoiselle. Au revoir.
> Patron(ne): Au revoir, monsieur/madame/mademoiselle.

> *Liste:* du vin, de l'eau minérale (un litre); de la confiture, des
> pommes (un kilo)

Variant 2 *Trouvez ce qu'il vous faut*

See ENGLISH or DEUTSCH.

From *Developing Communication Skills* by Pat Pattison
© Cambridge University Press 1987

Variant 3 En avoir pour son argent

Liste: des chemises, des cartes postales, des disques de Charles Aznavour, des valises

✂---

Dialogue

Patron(ne): Bonjour, monsieur/madame/mademoiselle.
Vous désirez?

Client(e): Vous avez des . . .?

P: Oui, nous avons des . . . C: Merci, ce n'est pas tout à fait ce que je voulais. Merci quand même. Au revoir. P: Au revoir, M/Mme/ Mlle.	P: Je regrette, nous n'avons plus de . . . C: Eh bien, tant pis. Au revoir P: Au revoir, M/Mme/ Mlle.

✂---

Magasins

Uniprix, Genève: chemises en soie, cartes postales géantes en noir et blanc, petites valises en cuir

✂---

Monoprix, Bruxelles: chemises en nylon, disques trente-trois tours, grandes valises en cuir

✂---

Prisunic, Paris: chemises en coton, cartes postales géantes en couleur, disques trente-trois tours en stéréo

✂---

Prixbas, Quebec: cartes postales en noir et blanc, disques compacts, grandes valises en plastique

From *Developing Communication Skills* by Pat Pattison

DEUTSCH *Einkaufen*

(Dialog)   Verkäuferin: Guten Tag. Was wünschen Sie, bitte?
Kund(e)(in): Ich hätte gerne . . .
Verkäuferin: Gerne. Sonst noch etwas?
Kund(e)(in): Das ist alles, danke schön. Wieviel macht das?
Verkäuferin: *(Preis)*
Kund(e)(in): Bitte.
Verkäuferin: Danke schön. Auf Wiedersehen.
Kund(e)(in): Auf Wiedersehen.

Liste: (suggested prices in Deutschmarks)

einen Kasten Bier	11,–	9,50	7,80
einen Sack Kartoffeln	4,80	5,10	6,40
eine Tafel Schokolade	1,50	1,10	1,25
eine Büchse Sardinen	1,50	1,30	1,10
ein Glas Marmelade	2,–	1,90	2,50
ein Eis	–,60	–,70	1,–

Variant 1 Ausverkauft

See FRANÇAIS.

Variant 2 Aussuchen

Dialog   Tourist: Guten Tag. Ich hätte gerne ein Einzel/Doppelzimmer
im Hotel   für das Wochenende, bitte.
Rezeption: Mit Bad oder Dusche?
Tourist: Mit . . . bitte.

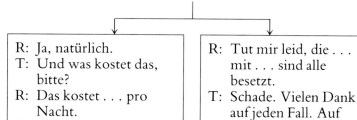

R: Ja, natürlich.
T: Und was kostet das, bitte?
R: Das kostet . . . pro Nacht.
T: Das nehme ich dann.

R: Tut mir leid, die . . . mit . . . sind alle besetzt.
T: Schade. Vielen Dank auf jeden Fall. Auf Wiedersehen, *usw.*

Hotels
Hotel Vier Jahreszeiten, Wien: Einzel/Doppelzimmer mit
  Dusche, 1500/2000 Schilling
Dolder Grand Hotel, Zürich: Einzelzimmer mit Dusche, 230
  Franken; mit Bad, 280 Franken
Hotel zur Post, Köln: Einzel/Doppelzimmer mit Bad, 80/100
  Mark
Berlin Hilton: Doppelzimmer mit Dusche, 250 Mark; mit
  Bad, 300 Mark

From *Developing Communication Skills* by Pat Pattison
© Cambridge University Press 1987

Variant 3 Der beste Kauf

Liste: Mäntel, Kuckucksuhren, alkoholische Getränke, Pralinen

✂--

Dialog
Verkäufer(in): Guten Tag. Sie wünschen?
Kund(e)(in): Guten Tag. Haben Sie . . .?

V: Ja, wir haben . . .
K: Danke, ich muß mir
    das erst noch überlegen.
V: Ja, gut, auf
    Wiedersehen.
K: Auf Wiedersehen.
	V: Tut mir leid, damit
	    kann ich Ihnen nicht
	    helfen.
	K: Schade. Auf
	    Wiedersehen, *usw.*

✂--

Warenhäuser
KaDeWe, West Berlin: Regenmäntel, Russischer Wodka, große Schachteln Pralinen

✂--

AHerzmansky, Wien: Lodenmäntel, kleine Kuckucksuhren, Slivovitz

✂--

Globus, Basel: große Kuckucksuhren, Weißwein, mittelgroße Schachteln Pralinen

✂--

Kaufhof, Düsseldorf: Pelzmäntel, Kuckucksuhren aus Plastik, kleine Schachteln Pralinen

2.5 Finding the way
Trouver le chemin
Den Weg suchen

Basic gap   Information gap based on split information
Aim   To find places by exhanging information
Language   Controlled, guided or free
Preparation and material   Blank map on display; sets of (incomplete) maps on handouts; dialogue frame on display or handouts; or use textbook material

Stage 1   E,I,A (5 minutes)

Class   Put a blank map on display and let learners ask the way from the bus stop to places of their choice – *café, cinema, station*, etc. – while you improvise directions to any blank location on the map (at level E), pointing out the way as you speak. You can also claim not to know the way to certain places (using phrases from the dialogue frame). Learners can make up directions in answer to each other's questions, or claim not to know the way. Continue until the map is complete or until the learners have had enough practice with the language.

Stage 2   E,I (10 minutes)

Group   Learners work in groups of four, in which each learner has one map from the sets A–D or E–H. They all play the roles of tourists at the bus stop and know two or three places in the town (shown on the maps they have), but not the two places they want to visit (given in the notes with each map). Without showing each other their maps, they ask for and give directions, following the dialogue frame and the examples in stage 1. At the time limit, learners repeat the directions to the places they have found, so that you or a learner can fill in a blank map on display.

   The sets of maps can be used in larger groups by letting some learners share; the maps can also be adapted for pair work.

Stage 3   E,I,A (15 minutes)

Group   As above, without using the dialogue frame.
Changing pairs   All the maps are dealt out to the learners (one for you too). Everyone then moves round the class trying to find people

who can give them the directions they need (always starting from the bus stop). They ask and answer one question at a time, before changing partners again and speaking to someone else. Maps A–H are so designed that, as an alternative to the whole class, the changing pairs can take place within groups of eight: extra learners can take any map and join any group.

Level I and A learners can improvise more details – offering extra suggestions and help:

I don't know where the post office is, but perhaps you can buy stamps at the hotel?

or explaining why they need to go to the places they are looking for. Map G offers scope for telling dramatic stories to the police!

At the time limit, learners report back as in stage 2. Some may also volunteer to repeat their conversations in front of the class.

Variant 1 Map dictation

Learners have or make a copy of a blank map: for listening practice, describe the location of various places, so that learners can fill in these places on their blank maps:

The café is in the second street on the left, and it's the first building on the right, etc.

For speech practice, learners can also take it in turns to describe the location of buildings to the class, the group or their partner. Finally the completed maps are checked to see how well they followed the directions.

See 6.3 *Destination words* for simpler practice with directions. See also 4.6 *Picture dictation* for practice in following or giving descriptions of any kind.

Finding and making material

Very simple maps are given in *Teaching material*. These are easy to copy; many learners quickly 'get lost' when using complicated maps, and so fail because of poor orientation, rather than poor communication skills. Locations are not numbered; otherwise, learners can simply say 'The café? It's number 3' instead of giving directions.

To make sets of four maps as in *Teaching material*:

1 Make a list of eight locations and set them out twice as in the table below: this gives two locations to be shown on each map and two locations which the holder of the map must look for. It ensures that no one can get the required directions from one person only.

Table

	Map shows . . .	Map-holder looks for. . .
Map A	1 Theatre	3 Museum
	2 Town hall	5 Tennis courts
Map B	3 Museum	1 Theatre
	4 Bookshop	7 Car park
Map C	5 Tennis courts	4 Bookshop
	6 Pub	8 Bank
Map D	7 Car park	2 Town hall
	8 Bank	6 Pub

2 Draw a simple street map with eight blank locations: copy it four times on to one sheet; label the maps A, B, C and D.

3 Write in the eight locations on your original map (this then becomes the key map from which you can make the others, and also check that learners' reports are correct).

4 Fill in the 'Map shows . . .' and 'Map-holder looks for . . .' information on the sheet of A, B, C and D maps, according to the table and the key map. The 'Map holder looks for . . .' instructions can be very simple for level E and more indirect for levels I and A, as in *Teaching material*.

5 Make several copies of this sheet, cut them up and put each set of four maps in envelopes ready for use. See further notes in 5.2.2(d).

Note: You can add a few more blank locations to the map in order to make learners give more detailed directions:
Is it the first or second building on the left? etc.

You can also add a few street names and traffic signs to various maps to provide richer practice:
The pub is in Coronation Street – do you know where that is? Turn left at the traffic lights, cross the bridge, etc.

Without these additions, maps A and B from the set described above will look like this (level E):

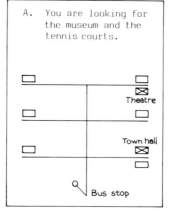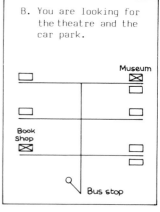

Learners (in pairs or groups) can make lists of locations, fill in the table and prepare sets of maps. If each group chooses a set of different locations (which can mean, for example, using hotels, cafés, cinemas, etc. with different names), you will obtain many different sets of maps which can be exchanged between groups for repeated practice, or used for changing pairs in the whole class.

The numbers given above can be adjusted to allow practice in pairs, or to let learners exchange information about only one location, or several.

The dialogue frames in *Teaching material* omit complete directions: for completely controlled practice, add the dialogue frames from 6.3 *Destination words*.

Teaching material

ENGLISH *Finding the way*

Q: Excuse me, do you know the way to . . .?
   Excuse me, is there a . . . near here?
A: Yes, certainly, . . .
   I'm sorry, I'm afraid I can't help you.
   I'm sorry, I'm a stranger here myself.

FRANÇAIS *Trouver le chemin*

Q: Excusez–moi M/Mme/Mlle; le/la . . . s'il vous plaît?
   Excusez–moi, il y a un(e) . . . près d'ici, s'il vous plaît?
R: (Oui) . . .
   Désolé(e), M/Mme/Mlle; je ne sais pas du tout.
   Désolé(e), M/Mme/Mlle; je ne suis pas d'ici.

DEUTSCH *Den Weg suchen*

F: Entschuldigung, wie komme ich zum/zur . . .?
   Entschuldigung, gibt es hier ein(e)(n) . . .?
A: (Ja) . . .
   Tut mir leid, das weiß ich nicht.
   Tut mir leid, ich bin selber fremd hier.

ENGLISH FRANÇAIS DEUTSCH

Finding the way
Blank map
Key map

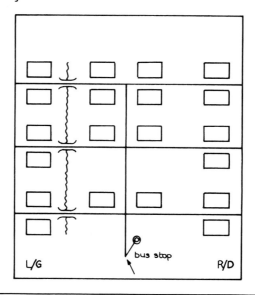

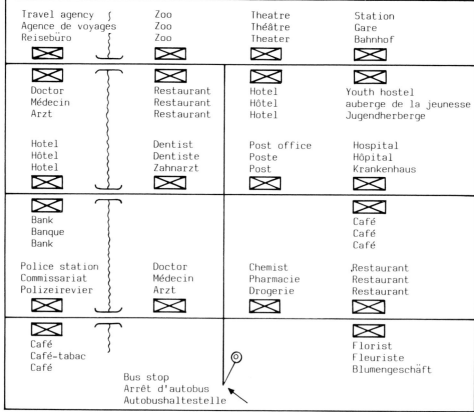

Travel agency Agence de voyages Reisebüro	Zoo Zoo Zoo	Theatre Théâtre Theater	Station Gare Bahnhof
Doctor Médecin Arzt	Restaurant Restaurant Restaurant	Hotel Hôtel Hotel	Youth hostel auberge de la jeunesse Jugendherberge
Hotel Hôtel Hotel	Dentist Dentiste Zahnarzt	Post office Poste Post	Hospital Hôpital Krankenhaus
Bank Banque Bank			Café Café Café
Police station Commissariat Polizeirevier	Doctor Médecin Arzt	Chemist Pharmacie Drogerie	Restaurant Restaurant Restaurant
Café Café-tabac Café	Bus stop Arrêt d'autobus Autobushaltestelle		Florist Fleuriste Blumengeschäft

From *Developing Communication Skills* by Pat Pattison

ENGLISH *Finding the way*

A. You want to change some money and then buy an airline ticket.

zoo

hospital

bus stop

L   R

B. You want to find a youth hostel and then visit a zoo.

travel agency

chemist

bus stop

L   R

C. You want to buy some flowers, and then you must visit the hospital.

dentist

youth hostel

bus stop

L   R

D. You want to buy some aspirin, and then visit a dentist.

bank

florist

bus stop

L   R

From *Developing Communication Skills* by Pat Pattison
© Cambridge University Press 1987

85

E. You are looking for the station and a hotel not too far away from the station.

post office

doctor   restaurant

bus stop

L   R

F. You want to buy some stamps and then have a cup of coffee. You don't want to walk too far.

theatre   station

doctor

bus stop

L   R

G. You must find a doctor immediately. Then you want to talk to the police.

restaurant

hotel

café

bus stop

L   R

H. You are looking for the theatre and somewhere to have dinner, not too far from the theatre.

hotel

police station

café

bus stop

L   R

From *Developing Communication Skills* by Pat Pattison

FRANÇAIS *Trouver le chemin*

A. Vous voulez changer de l'argent et ensuite acheter un billet d'avion.

le zoo

l'hôpital

ARRÊT D'AUTOBUS

G D

B. Vous cherchez l'auberge de la jeunesse. Vous voulez visiter le zoo.

une agence de voyages

une pharmacie

ARRÊT D'AUTOBUS

G D

C. Vous voulez acheter des fleurs et puis vous devez visiter l'hôpital.

le dentiste

l'auberge de la jeunesse

ARRÊT D'AUTOBUS

G D

D. Vous voulez acheter des aspirines et ensuite vous voulez trouver un dentiste.

la banque

un fleuriste

ARRÊT D'AUTOBUS

G D

From *Developing Communication Skills* by Pat Pattison
© Cambridge University Press 1987

E. Vous voulez trouver la gare
   et un hôtel pas trop loin de
   la gare.

la poste

un
médecin

un
restaurant

ARRÊT
D'AUTOBUS

G   D

F. Vous devez acheter des
   timbres et vous voulez boire
   un café. Vous ne voulez pas
   aller très loin.

le théâtre   la gare

un
médecin

ARRÊT
D'AUTOBUS

G   D

G. Vous devez trouver un médecin,
   très vite! Ensuite vous
   voulez parler avec un agent
   de police.

un hôtel   un
           restaurant

un café

ARRÊT
D'AUTOBUS

G   D

H. Vous voulez aller au théâtre
   et ensuite manger dans un
   restaurant pas trop loin du
   théâtre.

un hôtel

le
commissariat
de police

un café tabac

ARRÊT
D'AUTOBUS

G   D

From *Developing Communication Skills* by Pat Pattison
© Cambridge University Press 1987

DEUTSCH *Den Weg suchen*

A. Sie müssen Geld wechseln;
   danach wollen Sie eine
   Flugfahrkarte kaufen.

der Zoo

das
Krankenhaus

AUTOBUS
HALTESTELLE
L   R

B. Sie suchen die Jugend-
   herberge; dann wollen Sie
   einen Tiergarten besuchen.

ein
Reisebüro

eine
Drogerie

AUTOBUS
HALTESTELLE
L   R

C. Sie wollen Blumen kaufen
   und müssen dann das
   Krankenhaus suchen.

der
Zahnarzt

die
Jugendherberge

AUTOBUS
HALTESTELLE
L   R

D. Sie wollen Aspirin kaufen
   und dann müssen Sie einen
   Zahnarzt finden.

die Bank

ein
Blumen-
geschäft
R

AUTOBUS
HALTESTELLE
L

E. Sie wollen zum Bahnhof und suchen ein Hotel das nicht allzuweit vom Bahnhof entfernt ist.

die Post

ein Arzt

ein Restaurant

AUTOBUS HALTESTELLE

L   R

F. Sie müssen Briefmarken kaufen und dann wollen Sie eine Tasse Kaffee trinken. Sie wollen nicht allzuweit laufen.

das Theater   der Bahnhof

ein Arzt

AUTOBUS HALTESTELLE

L   R

G. Sie müssen so schnell wie möglich zu einem Arzt! Gleich danach wollen Sie einen Polizisten sprechen.

ein Restaurant

ein Hotel

ein Café

AUTOBUS HALTESTELLE

L   R

H. Sie wollen ins Theater gehen und suchen ein Restaurant nicht allzuweit vom Theater.

ein Hotel

das Polizei- revier

ein Café

AUTOBUS HALTESTELLE

L   R

From *Developing Communication Skills* by Pat Pattison
© Cambridge University Press 1987

2.6 What are we talking about?
De quoi est-il question?
Worüber sprechen wir?

Basic gap	Information gap based on secret choice
Aim	To recognise what the speakers are talking about
Language	Controlled, guided or free
Preparation and material	Dialogue frame and sets of similar material (words or pictures) on display or handouts; or use textbook material

Stage 1 E,I,A (5 minutes)

Class/team Act out (alone or with a learner) a dialogue referring to one picture or text from the set, e.g. a restaurant dialogue, with several lists of orders on display (see *Teaching material DEUTSCH*). Listeners try to recognise which of the lists is being referred to. When the scene is complete, check which learners, or how many from each team, have identified the list correctly.

Stage 2 E,I (10 minutes)

Group/pair Learners prepare role-plays based on their choice from the sets of words or pictures on display, with the help of the dialogue frame, and act these out in class. The listeners can win points for correct identification, as in stage 1.

Stage 3 E,I,A (10 minutes)

Group/pair As above, without dialogue frame. Learners can also take one frame from a series of pictures or picture story (in textbooks or on display or handout) and act out an appropriate dialogue, while classmates try to recognise which picture they are referring to.

Variant 1 Follow the conversation

Instead of recognising what is being talked about, listeners must fill in a form or graph, or complete a picture, a route on a map, etc., according to the dialogue they hear.

See 2.4 *Shopping* for similar practice in listening to dialogues and filling in a list and 4.6 *Picture dictation* for listening and drawing practice.

Variant 2 Recognition

For receptive practice, play short extracts from textbook tapes and ask learners to identify the situation. These may be from an earlier unit (as revision) or a forthcoming one (as introduction).

For speech practice, volunteers act a short dialogue and listeners try to identify the situation, the roles of the speakers, and what they are doing. At levels E and I this also gives opportunities for revision; learners choose or adapt extracts from earlier situational dialogues – *In the restaurant, hotel, train,* etc. Level I and A learners can adapt or create dialogues with more subtle clues, or which are open to several interpretations. Questions can include, besides the above:
What is the relationship between the speakers? What are they feeling? Why? What has happened/is happening/is going to happen? etc.
This can lead to further discussion, as actors and audience suggest different interpretations of the scene.

Variant 3 Interpretations

A group or groups of volunteers act out the same brief dialogue, but interpret it differently each time by changing the non-linguistic elements – stress and intonation, pauses, emotional expression, gestures, etc. Actors and audience then discuss the different versions, to see how well the actors' interpretations were understood, and to expand on or explain the scene further. Learners may acquire or practise a lot of vocabulary concerning emotions while discussing the scenes (both here and in *Variant 2*):
I think s/he was annoyed, shy, delighted, embarrassed, evasive, etc.
At level E, this discussion may take place in the mother tongue.

Examples from practice

1 Level A English learners acted out a dialogue consisting of repetitions of the words: *Yes, Marsha – No, Johnny!* and ending with Marsha saying *Oh!* Interpretations:
   a) Eager man trying to persuade coy woman to marry him. He finally produces an engagement ring.
   b) Confident boy trying to persuade nervous girl to dive from the highest board at the swimming pool – he finally pushes her.
   c) Brother trying to persuade sulky sister to let him share her bag of sweets – he finally snatches the bag.
2 Level I German learners using textbook dialogue (translated):

A: Hallo, Bernard. Come in.

B: Hallo, Mrs Schmidt. Is Christine in?

A: Yes, she's in her room. I'll call her. Christine! Bernard's here.

C: Coming!

Interpretations:

a) Boy calling for girlfriend, speaks to mother. He is shy.

b) Idem – boy is uncomfortable as the mother makes it clear that she disapproves of him. Girl is pleased to see him.

c) Boy sounds threatening. Woman and girl are both afraid of him, etc.

If necessary, you can suggest such interpretations in advance to the volunteers, but sessions usually go better if this is left to their own imagination.

See 5.4 *Find the picture* for simpler practice, and 5.8 *Strange pictures* for role-plays based on pictures. 3.5 *Split dialogues* offers further practice in making up or discussing mini-dialogues. 4.5 *Silent film* has mime followed by interpretation and discussion.

Finding and making material

Dialogue frames can be adapted, and lists compiled, from textbook material. Many books also have suitable sets of pictures or picture stories. See 5.2.2 *General notes on visual material*, source (d) for information about making sets of similar pictures; 5.3 *Visual material* has suitable sets of pictures, which are referred to in *Teaching material* below.

Conversations for *Variants 2* or *3* can be taken from the textbook or adapted from such books as Maley and Duff 1978, and Mortimer 1985, in *Booklist* 2a.

Teaching material

ENGLISH *What are we talking about?*

(*Demonstration dialogue for stage 1, referring to* 5.3 Visual material, No. 3 Faces)

A: Why is Jack looking so happy today?
B: He's got a new girlfriend.
A: Did she persuade him to shave off his moustache?
B: Yes, and next week he's going to get some more modern glasses.
A: I hope he'll get his hair cut too.
B: Don't talk so loud! He's looking at us.

Question: Which man are we talking about?

Variant 1 *Follow the conversation*

(*'Dress' the outline figure in accordance with the dialogue*)

A: Look at that girl over there, the one with (curly/straight, blonde/black) hair.
B: The one who's wearing (jeans *or* a long/short skirt)?
A: Yes, and she's wearing a (T shirt/blouse/sweater).
B: With (long/short) sleeves?
A: No, (short/long *or* sleeveless). And she's wearing (black/white shoes/boots/sandals).
A: Yes, I see the girl you mean. What about her?
B: Well, she's carrying (*use your imagination!*) just like mine.

Variant 2 *Recognition*

A: What colour would you like? B: Black.
A: What size? B: Four. Can I try them on?

From *Developing Communication Skills* by Pat Pattison
© Cambridge University Press 1987

FRANÇAIS   *De quoi est-il question?*

(*Dialogue frame for stage 2, referring to* 5.3 Visual material, No. 4 Rooms)

> A: C'est une photo de la salle à manger?
> B: Oui, me voilà devant (derrière) la table. (Tu vois, j'ai une lettre à la main.) Et ça, c'est mon chat, assis sur la chaise (par terre).
> A: Mais, qu'est-ce qu'il y a au-dessus de la porte (entre la porte et la fenêtre)? Un ballon?
> B: Mais non, c'est une pendule. D'ailleurs, la pièce n'est plus comme sur cette photo: maintenant, la table est devant la porte (fenêtre).

> *Question:* De quelle photo est-il question?

Variant 1   *Suivre la conversation*

> À l'hôtel: remplir le formulaire
>
> NOM _____   NATIONALITÉ _____
> PASSEPORT_____   DATE DE DÉPART_____
> CHAMBRE_____
>
> Touriste: Bonjour. J'ai reservé une chambre.
> Employé(e): Bonjour. Vous êtes M/Mme/Mlle Dupont?
> A: Non, je m'appelle . . .
> B: Comment? Voulez-vous l'épeler, s'il vous plaît?
> A: . . .
> B: Merci. Et quelle est votre nationalité, s'il vous plaît?
> A: Je suis (*nationalité*).
> B: Et le numéro de votre passeport?
> A: . . .
> B: Et vous restez jusqu'à quand?
> A: Je pars (*jour*) le (*date et mois*).
> B: Merci. Vous avez la chambre numéro . . . Voici la clé.
> (*Noms:* JACOBOVITZ, LEJEUNE, HARPER, GARY, etc.)

Variant 2   *Reconnaître*

> A: Je vous fais le plein?
> B: Non, vous m'en donnez pour soixante-dix sept francs.
> A: De l'ordinaire?
> A: Oui, de l'ordinaire.

DEUTSCH *Worüber sprechen wir?*

(Dialogue frame for stages 1 or 2, referring to lists of orders in a restaurant)

Kellner: Bitte schön, was möchten Sie?
Gast 1: Ich hätte gerne . . ., und . . .
Kellner: Und was möchten Sie?
Gast 2: Ich möchte . . . und . . .
Kellner: Sonst noch etwas?
Gast 1: Nein danke, das wär es.

Liste:

1 2 Apfelsaft, 1 Kartoffelsalat, 1 Hamburger
2 2 Apfelsaft, 1 Kartoffelsalat, 1 Bockwurst
3 1 Apfelsaft, 1 Bier, 1 Kartoffelsalat, 1 Bockwurst
4 2 Bier, 2 Bockwurst
5 1 Bier, 1 Limonade, 2 Bockwurst
6 2 Limonade, 1 Bockwurst, 1 Hamburger

Variant 1 Aktiv zuhören

Use the dialogue above: listeners write out the orders according to what they hear.

Variant 2 Erkennen Sie den Dialog?

A: Sie müssen umsteigen.
B: Gibt es keine direkte Verbindung?
A: Doch, um zehn Uhr.
B: Den nehme ich! Vielen Dank!

From *Developing Communication Skills* by Pat Pattison

2.7 Interviews
Interviews
Interviews

Basic gap	Information gap based on personal ideas
Aim	To find who has had or plans to have the most interesting holiday
Language	Guided or free
Preparation and material	Model sentences on display; tourist information (brochures, etc.) in the FL; or textbook material

Stage 1   I,A (10 minutes)

Class   Let learners choose the basic context and roles, either:
a) foreigners being interviewed at the start or end of a visit to the learners' own town or country, or:
b) themselves being interviewed at the start or end of a visit to any foreign country or city where the FL is spoken. The choice may depend on what brochures, etc. are available. Prepare for stages 2 and 3 by discussing possible reasons for visiting the chosen destination(s), what visitors might do or plan to do and see, and what kind of questions they would ask visiting foreigners, or expect to be asked on a visit to a foreign country. A list of suggestions and model questions and answers can be put on the board. If necessary, act the part of interviewer or interviewee with a learner or learners to demonstrate the language that might be used.

Stage 2   I,A (Time decided with class)

Group and class   All groups agree on the basic context and roles, (a) or (b), but each may choose a different destination, influenced by the discussion in stage 1, the brochures and other information available, and on places which learners have visited themselves. Add extra interest by telling them that the group with the most interesting plans for or account of their visit can win a prize offered by a travel company – a free holiday in the country of their choice. Visitors may need time to prepare their stories, at home or in class. Interview groups briefly and invite other learners to ask them questions, before inviting the class or a jury panel to decide which group should win the prize. (Unfortunately, the travel company has meanwhile gone bankrupt: the group may be given brochures or foreign stamps, etc. as a consolation prize!)

Stage 3 I,A (Time decided with class)

Group   Learners choose roles of reporter(s) and visitor(s) within their groups. Proceed as in stage 2, giving both reporters and visitors time to prepare if necessary. A time limit of three to five minutes can be set for the interviews themselves, after which reporters tell the class briefly what they have discovered: this may take the form of a short (radio or TV) report in which the tourists are asked to repeat some of their replies. Finally, the class, or a jury panel, may decide who has won the prize.

See 1.6 *Questionnaires* for controlled practice on the topic of holidays, and 7.4 *Holiday plans* for more extensive practice.

Variant 1 Find the reason

Some learners (preferably in pairs) can invent or be given roles, involving specific reasons for visiting the chosen destination. Other learners, the reporters, are told the age and sex of the visitors (assuming this is not clear from their appearance) and have the task of discovering why the people are in the country. The visitors may not always want to volunteer the information, and will try to answer non-committally (*Yes, sometimes, No, not exactly*, etc.); however, they must answer direct questions honestly. In the final reporting stage the visitors can reveal anything which the reporters failed to find out.

Example from practice

Level A group questioning the teacher playing a visitor to the Caribbean.

Q: Is this your first visit to this region?   A: No, it isn't.
Q: Have you any relations here?   A: No.
Q: Are you here on business?   A: No, not really.
Q: What else can you do? You go fishing?   A: Not exactly, but you're close.
Q: You're going on the sea?   A: Yes, I am.
Q: Diving?   A: Yes.
Q: For pearls?   A: Perhaps for pearls.
Q: Something in the sea. You're interesting – interested in archaeology?   A: You mean like the Greeks and Romans? No, not so long ago.
Q: You're looking for a ship; a famous ship?   A: No, it's not famous but it is a ship.

From this point, the group quickly discovered that the tourist was looking for treasure on a sunken pirate ship; but they did not discover that she had found the pirate's map in her home town.

See 6.4 *Quizzes* for similar practice.

Variant 2 Space ship souvenirs

Learners imagine they are going to Mars in a space ship, alone or in pairs. What five (or more) objects will they take on the journey, to keep them occupied or entertained, or just to remind them of their life on earth – and why? The ship has all they need for basic survival, plus cassette and video players, so they may choose favourite books, tapes, video tapes of films or TV programmes and any other items; but no living creatures or items too large for the ship – a guitar but not a grand piano!

Learners may be interviewed by the class, group or partners (using future or conditional: *What will/would you take . . .?* etc.), and the different lists should finally be displayed or reported for further comparison and discussion in the class.

See 7.3 *Choices* for discussion practice on a similar basis.

Variant 3 Natural disaster

Some learners play the inhabitants of islands where there have been earthquakes or floods; others play reporters who ask them about which (how many) people or animals have been hurt, wounded, drowned, killed; which (how many) roads, buildings, etc. have been damaged, flooded, burned down, destroyed, etc. A preliminary brainstorming session with the class can provide ideas and model questions. The various islanders are interviewed and all the information is reported. This can be done in the passive: *Three goldfish were drowned, the school was flooded . . .* and combined with indirect speech: *They told me all the roads had been destroyed.*

The class or a jury panel (see p. 30) can now act as a United Nations relief agency and decide which island needs help most urgently.

See 6.4 *Quizzes* for simpler practice with the passive.

Finding and making material

Textbooks or other school books usually have information on which interviews can be based. See 5.2 *General notes on visual material*, sources (f) and (g) for brochures and other material; not forgetting tourist brochures of the native country in FL versions. You and any learners who have visited foreign countries can use personal experience in the interviews, as well as any authentic material collected here, such as postcards, guidebooks, etc.

Material for *Variant 1* can be improvised, or written by you or the learners in advance. The examples in *Teaching material* ENGLISH are based on roles written by a level A learner of English.

Teaching material

ENGLISH *Interviews*

(*Model questions*)

Is (was) this your first visit to . . .?
Why have you decided (did you decide) to come here (again)?
What do (did) you like/dislike about our country?
How long are you going to stay (have you been here)?
Where are you going to (did you) stay?
How did you learn to speak our language so well?
What is (was) the first thing you want (wanted) to see?
Is there anything you'd like to ask (say to) me about our country?

Variant 1 Find the reason

In Amsterdam: American hippies who have come to Amsterdam for drugs
A Canadian couple who have come to see the places the husband had helped to liberate in 1945
In Rotterdam: A British football manager and coach who have come to Rotterdam to 'steal' one of the Rotterdam football players.
A film star and director looking for locations for their next film about a hijacked oil tanker.

FRANÇAIS *Interviews*

(*Model questions*)

Est-ce que c'est (c'était) votre premier séjour à . . . / en . . .?
Qu'est-ce qui vous a poussé à choisir cet endroit?
(*Au debut du séjour*) Qu'est-ce qui risque de vous gêner? (temps, langue, nourriture, *etc.*)
(*A la fin du séjour*) Qu'est-ce qui vous a plu/déplu?
Combien de temps allez-vous rester (êtes-vous resté(e)(s))?
Où allez-vous loger (avez-vous logé)?
Qu'est-ce que vous visiterez d'abord (qu'avez-vous vu d'abord)?

Comment avez-vous appris à si bien parler notre langue?
Avez-vous des remarques à faire sur votre séjour?

Variant 1 Trouver la raison

À Paris: Nous sommes couturiers/ières, et nous voulons confectionner des modèles de grands couturiers, mais sans permis. Nous assisterons à un défilé de mode chez Dior (Chanel, St Laurent, Cardin, etc.)

Sur la Côte d'Ivoire: Nous y sommes pour acheter de l'ivoire, bien que la vente de l'ivoire soit interdite par l'Organisation Mondiale pour la Protection de la Nature

À la Guadeloupe: Nous voulons louer un bâteau pour découvrir le trésor d'un corsaire; on a trouvé une carte

Variant 2 Le vaisseau de l'espace

(*Conditional*)

Q: Qu'est-ce que vous prendriez – et pourquoi?
Que prendriez-vous d'autre?
R: Je prendrais . . ., parce que . . .

Variant 3 Catastrophe naturelle

(*Passive*)

Tremblement de terre, inondation, etc.
X personnes, animaux ont été blessé(e)(s), noyé(e)(s), tué(e)(s), etc.
X batiments, routes, etc. ont été endommagé(e)(s), brûlé(e)(s), détruit(e)(s), etc.

DEUTSCH *Interviews*

(*Model questions*)

Ist (war) dies Ihr erster Besuch in . . .?
Warum haben (hatten) Sie sich (noch einmal) für diese Reise entschlossen?
Wie lange bleiben Sie (sind Sie geblieben)?
Wo werden Sie wohnen (haben Sie gewohnt)?
Was ist (war) das erste, was Sie gerne sehen möchten (wollten)?
Was werden Sie sonst noch tun (haben Sie sonst noch getan)?
Wo haben Sie unsere Sprache so gut gelernt?
Gibt es etwas in unserem Land, wonach Sie mich gerne fragen würden?

Variant 1 Entdecke den Grund

In West-Berlin: Verwandte leben in Ost-Berlin, wollen aber in den Westen fliehen; wir wollen ihnen (von West-Berlin aus) helfen

In Wien: Wir haben ein Restaurant in (*native country*); wir treffen uns im Hotel Sacher mit fünf Meisterköchen, um Rezepte auszutauschen; wir interessieren uns besonders für Mozartkugeln und Sachertorte

In Sankt Moritz: Wir sind Trainer der (*native country*) Skiläufer(innen) und interessieren uns für die neuen Skier, die in der Schweiz entwickelt werden; wir möchten uns gerne in den entsprechenden Fabriken umsehen

Variant 2 *Raumschiff Souvenirs*

(*Conditional*)

F: Was würden Sie mitnehmen – und warum?
  Was würden Sie sonst noch mitnehmen?
A: Ich würde . . . mitnehmen, weil . . .

Variant 3 *Naturkatastrophe*

(*Passive*)

Das Erdbeben, die Überschwemmung, *usw.*
X Menschen, Tiere, *usw.* wurden verwundet, verletzt, getötet; sind ertrunken, *usw.*
X Straßen, Gebäude, *usw.* wurden beschädigt, vernichtet; sind abgebrannt, *usw.*

3 Matching activities

3.1 Introduction

In the communication activities of this section, the learners' aim is to recognise matching items, or to complete pairs or sets. The section includes versions of familiar activities such as 'Bingo', 'Happy Families' and scrambled sentences, adapted in ways which increase their communicative elements. They can all be practised with controlled, guided or free language, and are adaptable for all levels.

In 3.2 *Clock bingo*, learners match times instead of numbers; the activity can be adapted for question and answer practice. Other items for matching are suggested in the variants.

3.3 *Duets* is a more communicative version of 'Happy Families' (sometimes called 'Quartets'): learners match items of vocabulary, or information about the foreign culture or literature, while practising request forms. It differs from the original game in that the learners themselves decide what to ask for, instead of repeating what their cards tell them. Thus they actively recall their knowledge, and review meanings and associations in order to match paired items.

3.4 *People and things* is based on an opinion gap. Learners are asked to match objects with people, and may give reasons: variants suggest matching other items, such as weather with places.

In 3.5 *Split dialogues*, learners match given phrases. This may cover grammar, vocabulary and idioms (as in a scrambled sentence exercise), but it can also be used to extend the learners' sensitivity to language in use, making them aware that the same phrases can be used to communicate different meanings, depending on intonation, context, the attitude and relationship of the speakers, etc. The split dialogues can be further developed into role-plays to demonstrate these possibilities more clearly.

3.6 *Find your partners* is an extremely versatile communication activity, with controlled, guided or free language, in which learners seek someone who can complete or match the information they hold. It can be based on given or personal information.

Many of these matching activities are most effectively practised in changing pairs: this is fully described on p. 30.

3.2   Clock bingo
Loto à l'horloge
Uhr-Lotto

Basic gap	Information gap based on split information
Aim	To complete a bingo card
Language	Controlled, guided or free
Preparation and material	Bingo cards, with clocks, as handouts; language frame on display; or textbook material

Stage 1   E,I (5 minutes)

Class   Learners or pairs are given (or make) bingo cards showing clocks or times. Call out various times from the master card (see *Teaching material*). Learners cross out the times they find on their papers, calling out *Full House!* ([F] *Là,* [D] *Voll!*) when they complete a line (working with lines instead of complete papers speeds up the activity and allows more learners to win within the time limit). For purely receptive practice, learners calling *Full House!* can repeat their times for checking in the mother tongue.

Stage 2   E,I (5 minutes)

Class   Ask individual learners the time: they answer with one of the times on their cards, and they and any other learners with this time on their cards can cross it out. Continue until *Full House!* is called and let the winner(s) prove their score by repeating the times in the FL.
At level I ask the class more precise questions:
What time did you have breakfast?
What time will school finish?
(choose questions to match the times on the master card). Any learners who indicate that they have an appropriate time may answer. If their answer is appropriate, all learners with that time on their cards can cross it out. See *Example from practice* in stage 3.

Stage 3   E,I,A (5 minutes)

Class/group   Learners take it in turns to ask others in the class or group what time it is; the answers and scoring continue as in stage 2. Level I or A learners can ask more precise questions in order to elicit, if possible, one of the times on their own papers:

Example from practice

Q: What time do many people go to bed? (*Various learners raised their hands.*) Yes, Angela?
A: Ten thirty.

This was an appropriate answer, so Angela and others with *ten thirty* on their papers could cross it out. The questioner was unlucky: she was hoping to hear *eleven forty-five* but chose the wrong person to answer her question!

There may be some argument as to what is an appropriate answer (*Nobody goes to bed at ten thirty!*); encourage this, so long as it takes place in the FL.

In groups, learners may call *Full House!* when half their times are crossed out, whether or not these are in a line.

Variant 1 Varied bingo papers

Bingo cards can be made with words or pictures to practise any vocabulary. Questions can be adapted according to level. For example, questions about picture bingo cards could be direct: *Have you got a cat/a pen?*; or indirect: *Who's got an animal that drinks milk/something you can write with?*

See 3.3 *Duets, Variant 2* for further practice in eliciting a required answer.

Finding and making material

Learners or pairs can make their own bingo cards: they divide a card into, for example, six boxes and choose what to put in them from, for example, twenty items on display or in their textbooks, so that everyone may create a different combination. This may result in too many nearly identical cards; or you may wish to save classroom time by advance preparation, as described below.

Fill an A4 sheet with twenty-four items (clocks, words, pictures) and make eight copies. Each of these sheets (but not the master sheet!) can be cut up in a different way to give twenty bingo cards with six items each. The sets of numbers below refer to the master sheet in *Teaching material*, and show the ways in which the copies can be cut up (read the numbers from top left to bottom right, e.g. the first card contains clocks numbered 1, 2, 5, 6, 9, 10).

Copy 1: (four cards)	(1) 1 to 10,	(2) 3 to 12,
	(3) 13 to 22,	(4) 15 to 24
Copy 2: (two cards)	(5) 2 to 11,	(6) 14 to 23
Copy 3: (two cards)	(7) 5 to 14,	(8) 7 to 16
Copy 4: (two cards)	(9) 9 to 18,	(10) 11 to 20
Copy 5: (three cards))	(11) 1 to 7,	(12) 9 to 15,
	(13) 17 to 23	
Copy 6: (three cards)	(14) 2 to 8,	(15) 10 to 16,
	(16) 18 to 24	
Copy 7: (two cards)	(17) 5 to 11,	(18) 13 to 19
Copy 8: (two cards)	(19) 6 to 12,	(20) 14 to 20

Notes

– If you write the numbers shown in brackets on the back of each card, you can easily check if any are missing after use in class.

– Cards made from *copy 1* have no overlapping items, so they must not all be given to the same group in stage 3 group work.

– When *copy 2* is cut two side strips are left: these can be used as vertical bingo cards (21) and (22), reading downwards 1–21 and 4–24.

– In classes with more than twenty (or twenty-two) learners, some cards can be shared.

– As these papers are not scientifically designed, two or more learners may call *Full House!* at the same time. This is not a disadvantage (since you are not handing out valuable prizes!), but rather increases learner interest: but you can make the one who calls first the winner, or the one who can read back the items on the bingo card most correctly (at level E).

– As with all *Teaching material*, the bingo master sheet is presented in the form which teachers found to be simplest and most efficient. For example, six items per card made the scoring faster and more interesting in class than nine or more. Only the most necessary numbers are added to the clock faces (and you can of course simply write *10.15 3.20*, etc.). You can (perhaps with learners' help) make master sheets to include more than twenty-four items; but this takes more time and gives fewer overlapping items, which are needed for stages 2 and 3.

– The master sheet in *Teaching material*, and No. 1 *Miscellany* in 5.3 *Visual material* (for work with pictures) are designed for level E, and can be adapted for other levels.

Teaching material

ENGLISH   FRANÇAIS   DEUTSCH   *Clock bingo*

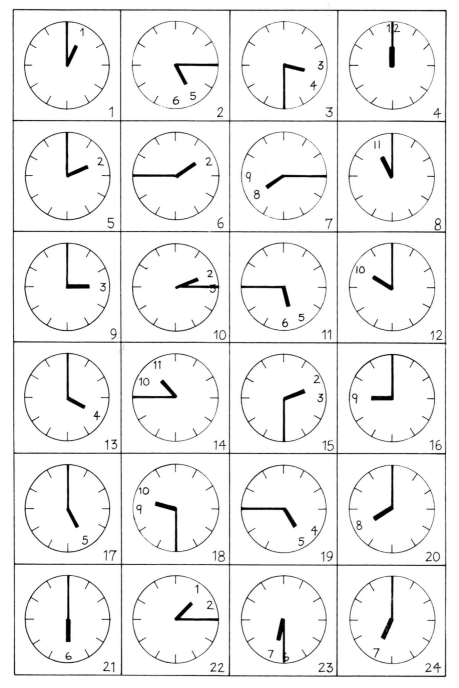

From *Developing Communication Skills* by Pat Pattison
© Cambridge University Press 1987

3.3 Duets
Duo
Duette

Basic gap Information gap based on split information
Aim To collect pairs of associated items
Language Controlled, guided or free
Preparation and Language frame on display or handout; or textbook material;
material sets of cards or papers with words or pictures

Stage 1 E,I,A (5 minutes)

Class Remind learners of 'Happy Families', in which the cards show one item and list three others which the players must ask for in order to form a set. In *Duets*, they only have to form pairs, but their cards do not tell them what to ask for: they must think of an associated item for themselves. You will tell them if the pairs are based on a particular principle, such as a thing plus a person or place associated with it. They must name one of the items they hold (e.g. *CAT*) and then ask the group as a whole for any item that they think could form a pair. If the pairs are all living things, they might ask for a *MOUSE* or a *DOG*. If it is animals plus things, they might ask for some *MILK*, etc. Cards which form a pair always have the same symbol written on them so players can check to see if they match. Demonstrate the activity with a group of four or five learners and a set of eight or ten cards.

Procedure:
1 Learners do not get an extra turn if they complete a pair, nor if they ask for an item which nobody has.
2 Learners do not have to give up cards if they are not asked for correctly, and if the speaker cannot correct the mistake.
3 If learners cannot think of anything to ask for, they must still name an item they hold, to give others the chance to recognize an association: see the exchange between George and Mai in Example 2.

Examples from practice

(Numbers refer to the notes above. Asterisks indicate a mistake.)
1 Level E group working with cards from *Set 1* in *Teaching material* ENGLISH:
    Marie: I've got a tourist and I'd like – a suitcase, please.
    Lisa: Here you are.

Marie: Thank you. (*Puts the papers together. The symbols don't match.*) Sorry, that's wrong. (*Returns the paper to Lisa.*)

Philippe: I've got a taxi and I★ like – a taxi driver.

Marie: What? (*phrase to indicate mistake*) (2)

Philippe: (*Looks at language frame again*) – er – I'd like a taxi driver please.

Marie: Here you are.

Philippe: Thank you. (*The symbols match so he keeps the pair.*) (1)

Lisa: I've got a suitcase and I'd like – a customs officer please (*knowing from Marie's first request that 'tourist' is wrong*) . . . etc.

2 Level A group, working without a language frame and with cards about British cultural background.

Mai: I've got Shakespeare. Would someone be so kind as to give me – Stratford-on-Avon please. (*No response from the group so the next learner carried on.*) (1)

George: I've got the Globe Theatre and I'd like – er, I don't know what I'd like. (3) (*Gasp from others who saw the connection which George had missed. Mai had not missed it, however, and waited until her turn came round again.*)

Rod: I've got 10 Downing Street so who's got Maggie Thatcher?

Jean: Would you mind repeating that? (2)

Rod: I mean Mrs Thatcher. (*Jean still would not accept this. It was then her turn.*)

Jean: I've got the Prime Minister. Rod, would you kindly give me 10 Downing Street? (*Loud protests from Rod but the group supported Jean's strict interpretation of the rules!*) (2)

Mai: I've got Shakespeare. Would you mind giving me the Globe Theatre?

George: Here you are. (*George thus learns or is reminded that there is a connection between the two!*) (3)

Stage 2   E,I (10 minutes)

Group   Each group has an envelope of cards to share out – not the same as those used in the demonstration! Learners try to form pairs while you circulate and deal with any problems that arise. Tell the groups about any language points they should look out for, such as articles:

[E] *I've got Nelson and I'd like – Trafalgar Square or ★The Trafalgar Square*
[F] *J'ai un boucher et je voudrais – de la or ★du viande*
or adjective agreement:
[D] *Ich habe ein kleines Haus; und ich möchte einen kleinen Garten haben*

The cards or papers themselves show the correct form so learners can correct each other where necessary. This usually takes the form of not handing over a paper if the speaker cannot correct a mistake, and then requesting the paired item correctly when the holder's turn comes round. Learners are very motivated to check mistakes and to avoid any mistakes themselves, so that they can collect the maximum number of pairs!

All groups can work with identical sets of papers but you may prefer to let groups work with a set suited to their needs, interests or abilities. To take the German example above, some may have a set with adjectives, some without, and others a set consisting entirely of words with *einen*, etc.; or some groups may work with sets based on language, while others work on cultural background or literature. Groups who finish early can choose another set.

At the time limit, ask who has made the most pairs (and ask all groups to put their papers back in the envelopes!).

Stage 3   E,I,A (10 minutes)

Group   As above, without using language frames.

Variant 1 Connecting pairs

Learners who make a pair in *Duets* must also name the connection between them (not suitable for controlled language practice). Examples:
[E] *Shakespeare's plays were performed in the Globe Theatre.*
[F] *Un boucher vend de la viande.*
[D] *Die meisten kleinen Häuser haben einen kleinen Garten.*
Alternatively, cards are placed face down and drawn one by one. Learners who can explain a connection between two consecutively drawn cards can claim the pair. Example (from the level E group in stage 1; cards were drawn in the following order):
Tourist – suitcase: a tourist carries a suitcase.
Taxi driver – customs officer: when a taxi driver goes on holiday, he must pass the customs officer: or the customs officer takes a taxi to go to work, etc.

See 5.8 *Strange pictures, Variant 1* for practice in making up stories or role-plays to connect random items.

Variant 2 Matching quiz

Hand out all the papers from one or two identical sets, so that all learners have at least one paper. Ask questions based on the items on the cards. Anyone holding the paper with the answer reads it out. The following questions are based on the examples from stages 1 and 2 above:

E *Where were Shakespeare's plays first performed? (the Globe Theatre)*
Who wrote Hamlet? (Shakespeare)
F *Qui est-ce qui vend de la viande? (un boucher)*
Qu'est-ce qu'on mange avec des légumes? (de la viande)
D *Wie heißt das Gebäude, in dem man wohnt? (ein Haus)*
Was sieht man vor vielen Häusern? (einen Garten)

You can suit the question to the form of the item on the paper for totally receptive practice, as here, or let learners alter the item appropriately in their answers:

D *Wo findet man Blumen? (in einem Garten)*

It is useful to ask a second question for the same answer now and then so that those learners whose papers have already been asked about know they may have another chance:

E *Name a famous London theatre in the time of Elizabeth I (the Globe – again!)*

This form of quiz ensures that all learners can participate, as they only have to recognise the relation between the questions and the papers they hold. The quicker or better informed learners thus do not dominate the answering so much as in other types of quiz. The quiz can also be organised as a competition between groups or teams, by distributing two (or more) identical sets of cards between two (or more) teams.

For more speech practice, a group of learners can be given the list of items, and try to collect the papers from the others by asking questions designed to elicit the appropriate words.

See 3.2 *Clock bingo*, stage 3, for similar practice in eliciting particular replies; and see 6.4 *Quizzes* for more traditional types of quiz.

Finding and making material

You and the learners can look through a few units in the textbook, or any material the learners have for cultural background or literature, and list possible pairs, if necessary based on a single principle – *person + thing*, etc. Eight to twelve pairs are enough for groups of four or five learners (and are considerably easier to find than four-item sets for 'Happy Families'!). If this is done by the learners it gives them useful practice in considering and categorising vocabulary and other items. Keep the original lists for reference. Then you or the learners themselves set out the sixteen or more items on an A4 sheet, in the grammatical form that will fit into the request frame, and add the symbols to each pair. For beginners, sheets can include simple pictures drawn or traced from the textbook with the words added below: No. 1 *Miscellany* in 5.3 *Visual material* can be adapted in this way. See *Teaching material* under ENGLISH for examples of completed level E cards with words, pictures and symbols. See further notes on making handouts in 5.2.2 source (d). Lists and papers made by learners can be exchanged between groups so that none work with their own material.

Language frames can be adapted from language in the textbook. *Teaching material* below gives a list of phrases from which you can select according to learner's needs.

Teaching material

ENGLISH *Duets*

(*Model phrases*)

1 *Requesting items*
   I've got . . . Please can/may I have . . .?
   I've got . . . and I'd like . . . please.
   I've got . . . and I'd like somebody to give me . . . please.
   I've got . . . Has anybody got . . . please?
   I've got . . . Would you mind giving me . . .?
   I've got . . . but I don't know what I want/but I don't know what to ask for/and I've no idea what to ask for.
2 *Offering and accepting papers*
   Here you are – Thank you.
3 *Non-pair*
   No, sorry. Sorry, that's wrong. They don't match. They're not a pair.
4 *Reactions to a mistake*
   What? What did you say? Try again. Say that again please? Would you mind repeating that?
5 *General*
   Nobody's got that. Bad luck!
   It's your turn. Whose turn is it? Is it my turn? etc.

SET 1   (24 papers)   person or animal + thing

| a teacher | a red pen | a tree | a dog |

a student	–	a book
an air hostess	–	an aeroplane
a milkman	–	a bottle of milk
a taxi driver	–	a taxi
a man	–	an umbrella
a lady	–	a handbag
a boy	–	a shirt
a girl	–	a skirt
a customs officer	–	a suitcase
a tourist	–	a passport

SET 2   (24 papers)   General knowledge of Great Britain: place(s) + person, place or thing

The F.A. Cup Final	–	Wembley Stadium
The Boat Race	–	Oxford and Cambridge
Windermere	–	the Lake District
Queen Elizabeth	–	Buckingham Palace
The Prime Minister (or name)	–	10 Downing Street
London	–	England
Edinburgh	–	Scotland
Cardiff	–	Wales
Belfast	–	Northern Ireland
The Houses of Parliament	–	Westminster
Nelson's Column	–	Trafalgar Square
William Shakespeare	–	Stratford-on-Avon

FRANÇAIS *Duo*

(Model phrases (see under ENGLISH above))

1 J'ai . . . et je voudrais . . . s'il vous plaît.
J'ai . . . et j'aimerais bien avoir . . .
J'ai . . .: qui a . . .?
J'ai . . .: il y a quelqu'un avec . . .?
J'ai . . .: est-ce que je pourrais avoir . . .?
J'ai . . .: est-ce que vous pourriez me donner . . .?
J'ai . . .: est-ce que quelqu'un pourrait me donner . . .?
J'ai . . ., mais je ne sais pas ce que je veux!/mais je ne sais pas que demander/et je n'ai aucune idée (que demander)!

113

2 Voilà/voici . . . – Merci – Je vous en prie. De rien.
3 Dommage. Dommage, ça ne va pas. Ça ne va pas ensemble.
Ce n'est pas une paire.
4 Quoi? Vous dites? (Essayez) encore une fois. Voulez-vous
répéter, s'il vous plaît?
Ça n'existe pas. Pas de chance.
C'est votre tour. À qui le tour? C'est mon tour? *etc.*

SET 1   (24 papiers)   Des choses; un(e) + du, de la, des

une allumette	–	des cigarettes
une bibliothèque	–	des livres
une boulangerie	–	du pain
une brasserie	–	de la bière
une chocolaterie	–	du chocolat
une canne à pêche	–	des poissons
un restaurant alsacien	–	de la choucroute
une banque	–	de l'argent
un boucher	–	de la viande
une bouteille	–	du vin
un café crème	–	du sucre
un chat	–	du lait

DEUTSCH *Duette*

(Model phrases (see under ENGLISH above))

1 Ich habe . . . und ich möchte . . . (haben).
Ich habe . . . und ich würde gerne . . . haben.
Ich habe . . .: darf ich bitte . . . haben?
Ich habe . . .: wer kann mir . . . geben?
Ich habe . . .: können Sie mir bitte . . . geben?
Ich möchte gern . . ., weil ich schon . . . habe.
Ich habe . . . aber ich weiß nicht, was ich will!/und ich habe
keine Ahnung, was ich fragen soll.
2 Bitte schön – Danke schön – Bitte schön.
3 Schade. Schade, das geht nicht. Sie passen nicht zusammen.
Das ist kein Paar. Nein, das paßt nicht dazu.
4 Wie bitte? Was sagen Sie? Ich glaube, ich habe Sie nicht
richtig verstanden. Würden Sie das bitte wiederholen?
5 Das gibt's nicht. Pech (gehabt).
Sie sind dran (an der Reihe). Wer ist dran? Bin ich dran? *usw.*

SET 1   (16 Papiere)   Gegenstände, Einzahl oder Mehrzahl;
jedes Paar hat dasselbe Adjektiv
*(To make it more difficult, you can have two or more pairs with the
same adjective.)*

ein ledernes Sofa   –   zwei lederne Sessel

ein altes Bücherregal	–	alte Bücher
einen großen Tisch	–	vier große Stühle
ein kleines Bett	–	einen kleinen Nachttisch
rote Schuhe	–	rote Socken
eine weiße Hose	–	ein weißes Hemd
einen blauen Mantel	–	einen blauen Hut
einen grünen Kugelschreiber	–	einen grünen Ordner

SET 2   (22 Papiere)   Landeskunde, BRD: Stadt + Assoziation

Hamburg	–	die größte Hafenstadt Deutschlands
Kiel	–	(den) Nord-Ostseekanal
München	–	das Oktoberfest
Bonn	–	das Parlament
Ost-Berlin	–	das Brandenburger Tor
West-Berlin	–	(den) Kurfürstendamm
Essen	–	die Firma Krupp
Wolfsburg	–	das Volkswagen-Werk
Hannover	–	die Industriemesse
Garmisch-Partenkirchen	–	(den) Wintersport
Heidelberg	–	die älteste Universität Deutschlands

3.4 People and things
Des gens et des choses
Menschen und Dinge

Basic gap	Opinion gap based on shared information
Aim	To assign appropriate objects to people
Language	Controlled, guided or free
Preparation and material	Minimal – putting simple frame and list on display; or using textbook material (optional: visual aids or realia)

Stage 1   E,I (5 minutes)

Class   Point to items from the list (or show flashcards or realia), and assign them to an appropriate person, according to the frame:
It's the man's lighter.
Let's give her the flowers.
If the language frame is set out widely enough across the board, you can place or stick flashcards under the people they are assigned to (using Blu-tack, for example). You can also

suggest why you assign the objects:
It's the man's lighter; he smokes a lot, etc.

Stage 2   E,I (5 minutes)

Class   You or volunteer learners continue naming or showing items and let other learners decide how best to match them to the people in the language frame (with or without reasons). Other learners can disagree:
No, it's the woman's lighter.
No, let's give her the wine, etc.

Group/pair   The groups have lists of items or sets of cards to assign. Finally, groups compare their decisions.

You can arrange the items so that they can be divided equally between the people in the frame. If the objects are not equally divided at the end, or, for example, *the man* has not got enough and the only things left are *a dress* and *a lipstick*, learners must re-match the objects they had already assigned.

Stage 3   E,I (5 minutes)

Class/group/ pair   As above, without using the language frame

Variant 1   Find the owners

Collect a selection of belongings from the class, including yourself (pens, books, bags, etc.). You or a learner can hold them up one by one with the question:
Whose is this ruler? or *Who shall I give this book to?*
Learners answer:
It's Charlotte's; It's yours; Give it to Carol, etc.
and can win (team) points if they choose the correct owner. If not, the owner can claim it:
It's mine; Give it to me!

Variant 2   Free choice

Without lists or flashcards; learners can suggest objects to be assigned to each person in the frame, from their own vocabulary; or make up a list of famous people, with the learners' help. Learners enjoy assigning appropriate or wildly unsuitable items to them:
Let's give Princess Diana a big shopping bag, because she buys so many things, etc.

Variant 3 Choosing presents

Without language frames: the learners decide on a list of four or five celebrities or anyone well-known to the whole class (such as the head of the school, yourself, or someone in the class who has a birthday). Each group then takes a set of five or more advertisements, and discusses what presents they would give to which people and why. They report and explain their decisions. The class or a jury panel can discuss these choices further and/or vote on the best presents for each person.

Example from practice

Level A English groups. Presents suggested for the Princess of Wales:
1 An exercise bicycle because it's a better way to lose weight than anorexia nervosa.
2 A wool suit because she's so fond of clothes.
3 A slide for her children to play on.
4 A cookery book in case her chef leaves.
The class decided the exercise bicycle was the best present: the suit wasn't fashionable enough, the slide was dangerous, and she could always get a new chef. Learners pick up a lot of new vocabulary from advertisements, which they can use in their discussions and reports.

Variant 4 Who is what

Learners match adjectives to people (famous people, nationalities, animals, sports, etc.) in the frame. For example – which of the following adjectives will learners assign to *men* and *women*, *boys* and *girls*?:
sympathetic, likeable, friendly, sensible, sensitive, intelligent, tall, strong, ambitious, kind, silly, etc.
(These words were chosen because they are often confused in various FLs, or often applied in stereotyped ways.) The results can lead to some lively discussion in level I and A co-educational classes! Note that French adjectives must be changed to suit the gender of the person or thing described.

See also 1.6 *Questionnaires* for other practice in collecting opinions. The kind of discussion in *Variants 3* and *4* is dealt with more fully in Section 7 *Discussions and decisions*.

Variant 5 Weather and places

You and the learners can choose a list of widely different countries such as *Iceland, India, Kenya, Britain, Australia.* Some learners make a secret choice of country and talk to the others (or answer their questions) about the weather there, as if on the telephone, until the country is guessed. The choices may reflect popular prejudice rather than meteorological fact! Examples:

Q: *What's the weather like (where you are)?*
A: *It's raining and it's foggy. It's not very hot and not very cold.*
(Britain)
It's snowing and it's very cold. (Iceland)
It's hot and it's raining very hard. (India)

Alternatively, some learners can choose a month or season in their own country and the others try to guess which it is from their answers about the weather or what they are wearing; or they can mime their reactions to the weather for the others to guess.

See *Section 4* for more uses of mime.

Finding and making material

Language frames can be based on textbook material. Simple drawings of the people in the frames are useful at level E. Flashcards can be based on the textbook or taken from the sources given in 5.2 *General notes on visual material* (particularly sources (d) and (e)). A set can include any of the following: *clothes, food, drinks,* and items such as *cameras, watches, jewellery, flowers, books, records, cars, toys,* etc. You can also use some of the pictures from No. 1 *Miscellany* in 5.3 *Visual material*.

The frames in *Teaching material* can be presented bit by bit for level E or for remedial work, and together for more advanced learners. Specialised examples are divided between the languages: ENGLISH has frames for the past tense and for complex sentences. FRANÇAIS has a complete frame for possessive pronouns, and FRANÇAIS and DEUTSCH have frames including adjectives. The later frames for each language are given in compressed form.

Variant 3: a single edition of a magazine like *Reader's Digest* (in the FL edition) provides enough advertisements for a whole class – everything from dandruff cures (this was always a popular choice for Kojak) to dieting aids. I do not mount these on cards – partly because there are often useful advertisements on both sides of the page, and partly because learners often become fascinated by reading parts of the articles on the same pages: and this may induce them to read the magazines themselves.

Teaching material

ENGLISH *People and things*

Language frames

(Singular or plural possessive forms)

    Q: Whose (hat/s) is this/are these? *or*
    Who does this/do these (dog/s) belong to?

A: It's They're	the man's (his) woman's (her) family's (their)	(hat/s) (dog/s)
It's They're	the men's (their) women's girls' boys'	(book/s)

(Direct and indirect object pronouns)
With names or pictures on display: e.g. a man, woman, two children

    Q: Who shall we give the . . . to?
    A: Let's give it/them to him/her/them.
    Let's give him/her/them the . . ., (because . . .)

(Past tense)

    Q: Who did you give the . . . to (last Christmas)?
    A: I (We) gave it/them to . . . *etc.*

(Complex sentences)

    Q: Who do you think we should give the . . . to?
    A: I think we should give it/them to . . ., (because . . .)

FRANÇAIS *Des gens et des choses*

Language frames

(A qui, etc. (adjectives optional))

    Q: C'est à qui, ce/cette/cet/ces . . .?

R: C'est le/la/l' . . . Ce sont les . . .	au vieil homme au vieux professeur à la vieille dame aux vieilles dames, *etc.*

(Possessive pronouns, singular and plural)

Q: C'est le/la . . . Ce sont les . . .	de l'homme? du professeur? de la femme?

R1: Oui, | c'est son/sa . . .
         | ce sont ses . . .
R2: Non, | ce n'est pas son/sa . . ., c'est le/la . . .
         | de l'homme
         | ce ne sont pas ses . . ., ce sont les . . .
         | du professeur, *etc.*
Q: C'est le/la (ce sont les) . . . des petits garçons?
                                   des petites filles?
R1: Oui, | c'est leur . . .
         | ce sont leurs . . .
R2: Non, | ce n'est pas leur . . ., c'est le/la . . .
         | des petits garçons
         | ce ne sont pas leurs . . ., ce sont les . . .
         | des petites filles

(*Direct and indirect objects, pronouns*)

List, flashcards or objects all on display)

Q: Voulez-vous donner le/la/les . . . | au père?
                                        | à la mère
                                        | aux enfants?
R1: Non, je préfère lui/leur donner le/la/les . . .
R2: Non, je préfère le/la/les donner au père, à la mère, *etc.*
    (parce que . . .)

DEUTSCH *Menschen und Dinge*

Language frames for selection: various cases
(*adjectives optional*)
(*Nominative*)

F1: Wer hat so ein(e)(n)/solche . . .?
A1: Der (nett-e) Mann/Die (-e) Frau/Das (-e) Kind

(*Genitive*)

F2: Wessen . . . ist (sind) das?
A2: Es ist (sind) der/die/das . . .
    des (nett-en) Mannes/der (-en) Frau/des (-en) Kindes

(*Dative*)

F3: Wem gehört (gehören) der/die/das . . .?
A3: Er/sie/es gehört (gehören)
    dem (nett-en) Mann/der (-en) Frau/dem (-en) Kind

(*Accusative*)

F4: Für wen ist (sind) der/die/das . . .?
A4: Er/sie/es ist (sind) für
    den (nett-en) Mann/die (-e) Frau/das (-e) Kind

(*Direct and indirect objects; dative*)
List, flashcards or objects all on display

F1:	Was möchten Sie	dem	Mann, Kind	geben?
	möchtest du	der	Frau	
		mir		
		uns		

A1:	Ich möchte	ihm	den . . .	geben
		ihr	die . . .	
		dir, Ihnen	das . . .	
		euch, Ihnen		

F2: Wem geben Sie den/die/das . . .?

A2:	Ich gebe ihn/sie/es	dem Mann, Kind
		der Frau
		den Männern, Frauen, Kindern
		(weil . . .)

3.5 Split dialogues
Dialogues éclatés
Getrennte Dialoge

Basic gap	Information gap based on split information
Aim	To match phrases making a mini-dialogue
Language	Controlled (may include free practice)
Preparation and material	Scrambled list of phrases on display or handouts, or in textbook, for stage 1; on separate papers for stages 2 and 3

Stage 1   E,I,A (5 minutes)

Class/team   Learners study lists of phrases and suggest those which can be combined to form mini-dialogues. You or other learners can accept or reject these on the basis of grammar, lexis or appropriateness, while the others defend or further explain their suggestions if possible. Example:

Level E or I.

1 *How old is your little sister?*	A *Two hours*
2 *How long have you been waiting?*	B *Two*
3 *What time does the train leave?*	C *Two years*
4 *How long did you live in France?*	D *I don't know*
5 *How many people live in that house?*	E *Two o'clock*

1B, 2A, 3D or E, 4C, 5B or D form natural combinations: 1D,

2C or D, 3B, 4D are possible, but learners should explain how and why. Other combinations are totally improbable or impossible: invite learners to explain why.

With some examples, you can demonstrate how changing the intonation can suggest a different context or different relationships for the speakers. Invite learners (or pairs) to read out mini-dialogues in different ways, if necessary adding extra phrases to make the differences clearer. Examples:

What time does the train leave?   I'm sorry, I don't know. (politely) / **I** *don't know!* (rudely)

What *time does the train leave?* (incredulously) – *Two o'clock –* (*In the* **morning**??)

What *time does the train leave?* (angrily) – *Two o'clock – (That's* **much** *too late.)*

At level E, any discussion about the suggested dialogues can take place in the mother tongue. At all levels, the aim is to develop the learners' sensitivity to meaning and appropriateness, as well as to grammatical and other clues, and to develop their awareness of what can and cannot be done with particular language.

Stage 2   E,I,A (10 minutes)

Class   You and the learners (or pairs) each have a paper with one phrase from a mini-dialogue. Those who think they have a beginning sentence read this out, and those who think they have a response to it reply. Sometimes they may find that what seemed to be a beginning sentence (or question) functions better as a reply. Example:

It's very cold in here.
Do you want me to shut the window?

Sometimes several combinations seem possible and the learners can discuss these. For example, *Would you like some hot chocolate?* and *Yes, please* can combine with each other but also with the phrases above.

Encourage learners to read their mini-dialogues in different ways and in different combinations, as in stage 1.

Stage 3   E,I,A (10 minutes)

Changing pairs   You and the learners each take a paper, and memorise the phrase written on it. Everyone then puts down the papers and circulates, repeating the memorised phrases to everyone they meet – even if they think their own phrase cannot possibly combine with the one they hear, as the partner may notice a possibility they have missed. Everyone notes the people who have phrases which might form a mini-dialogue with their own. After two to five minutes (depending on the size of the class) everyone sits down. Those who have not found any phrases to match their own now read these out, to see if someone in the class can suggest matching phrases. Then those who found combinations report them. The discussion of the suggested mini-dialogues, and different ways of combining or interpreting the phrases, takes place as in stages 1 and 2.

Examples from practice

German level I group (translated):
A: *You may not lean out of the window here.*
B: *Why not?*
C: *Are you enjoying the journey?*
D: *No, absolutely not.* (überhaupt nicht)
D, spoken in tones of strong agreement, could combine with A; A could be spoken with a questioning intonation, taking D as a negative reply. B, accompanied by a careless shrug, is a possible response to C.

   An unexpectedly motivating characteristic of this exercise emerged in practice: learners often noticed and exploited the possibility of making jokes by deliberately putting incongruous phrases together (often by stretching linguistic possibilities to breaking point!).
French level I group:
Est-ce que tu connais Sylvie Vartan?
(Regretfully) *Non, je suis né à Salzburg.*

English level A group (using sentences from first edition of Maley and Duff 1978 and 1982, in *Booklist* 2a):
Who said you could borrow that lighter? and
Why don't you stop picking your nose?
both received the same reply:
Oh sorry, I didn't know it was yours!

   See 2.6 *What are we talking about? Variant 3* for more practice in using intonation, etc. to affect the meaning of speech.

Variant 1 Complete the dialogue

Pairs or groups prepare a full dialogue incorporating two or more of the phrases in any combination: some dialogues can be acted out in front of the class. This is particularly interesting when some groups have chosen the same phrases but combined or developed them in quite different ways.

Finding and making material

Many textbooks contain exercises with scrambled dialogues or questions and answers to be matched. If required, you can often add to or adapt these in order to ensure that some of the sentences can be combined with several others: this encourages learners to think about the alternative meanings and contexts for the language they are using (and not only to match grammar and lexis). Learners, preferably in pairs, can make up four or five mini-dialogues, following the same guidelines. You can help learners to correct these and use the best for further practice with the whole class.

Examples from practice

Level I French and English teenage classes. The following combinations were accepted, after the necessary corrections, and used in class to the great enjoyment of the learners:

F *Veux-tu coucher avec moi?*
   Non, tu as de trop grands pieds. (It must be said that not many people recognised the connection!)

E *Do you think our teacher is sexy?*
   Well, that's a matter of opinion. (Originally: *Well there can be different opinions about that.* The new idiom *a matter of opinion* proved to be applicable in many mini-dialogues and was therefore widely used and very well learned by the class!)

The quickest way to make material is for pairs to write the two phrases of a mini-dialogue on two pieces of paper, put these in a box and let all the learners draw out a paper, exchanging it if it is one they wrote themselves. When making sets for repeated use, it is advisable to number the papers discreetly so that you can check if any are missing. Keep a master list (as in *Teaching material*) so that, if you need only part of the set, you know which numbers you can discard without leaving any unmatched phrases.

The examples in *Teaching material* are mostly based on second year material or beyond, but the activity can be used as soon as the learners know a few phrases in the FL.

For more suggestions, see Maley and Duff, 1978 and 1982, in *Booklist* 2a.

Teaching material

ENGLISH *Split dialogues*

(Based on mini-dialogues written by level I learners)

1 Do you speak English?
2 How are you?
3 How do you do?
4 How do you do it?
5 Why do we always come to school?
6 Don't you think our teacher is sexy?
7 I hate teachers.
8 Are you married?
9 Have you done your homework?
10 Are you going to the party on Saturday?
11 I think it's going to rain.
12 Did you make that yourself?
13 Can you lend me £/$100?
14 Do you like English food?
15 Can I borrow this bicycle?

16 Yes, very well.
17 Very well, thanks.
18 How do you do?
19 Do what?
20 I guess we'll never know.
21 Well, that's a matter of opinion.
22 Why do you say that?
23 What a stupid question!
24 Not yet.
25 I hope so.
26 I hope not.
27 Yes – do you like it?
28 Why do you ask?
29 You must be joking!
30 Don't ask me – it's not mine.

FRANÇAIS *Dialogues éclatés*

1 Que penses-tu de cette robe?
2 Encore du café?
3 C'est vachement cher, ça!
4 Tu connais Sylvie Vartan?
5 Il faut te reposer un peu
6 Quelle heure est-il, s.v.p.?
7 Vous allez bien?
8 Salut (*nom*), ça va?
9 Vous avez un journal?
10 Qu'est-ce que tu prends?
11 Tu as fait bon voyage?
12 Vous êtes d'ici?
13 Tu les connais, ces gens-là?

16 Elle est un peu courte.
17 Non, ça va, merci.
18 Tu n'as pas assez d'argent?
19 Bien sûr que je la connais!
20 Je n'ai pas le temps.
21 Onze heures et demie.
22 Très bien, merci.
23 Ça va, et toi?
24 Voici *le Figaro*.
25 Un jus d'orange.
26 Très bon, merci.
27 Non, je suis né(e) à Salzburg.
28 Non, je ne les connais pas.

14 As-tu envie d'aller à la discothèque ce soir?
15 Ce manteau est très chic.

29 Mais qui va payer?

30 Mais non, il est beaucoup trop court.

DEUTSCH *Getrennte Dialoge*

1 Gefällt Ihnen die Reise?
2 Das hier ist ein Nichtraucher-Abteil.
3 Sie sitzen auf meinem Platz!
4 Soll ich Ihren Koffer tragen?
5 Was fehlt Ihnen denn?
6 Was suchen Sie?

7 Es gibt noch einen Zug um zehn Uhr.
8 Meine Tasche ist so schwer.
9 Hier darf man sich nicht hinauslehnen.
10 Ich möchte nach Wiesbaden.
11 Gibt es keinen Speisewagen?
12 Können Sie mir sagen, wo ich umsteigen muß?
13 Ist hier noch ein Platz frei?
14 Willst du einen Fensterplatz?
15 Steig ein!

16 Nein, überhaupt nicht.
17 Na, und?
18 Tut mir leid.
19 Danke, nicht nötig.
20 Mir ist schlecht.
21 Ich kann meine Fahrkarte nicht finden.
22 Soll ich den nehmen?
23 Soll ich sie nehmen?
24 Warum nicht?
25 Wann wollen Sie fahren?
26 Doch, zwei Wagen weiter vorne.
27 Nein, das weiß ich auch nicht.
28 Ja, gewiß.
29 Das ist mir egal.
30 Ich kann nicht einsteigen.

3.6 Find your partners
Trouvez les partenaires
Partner finden

Basic gap Information gap based on split information
Aim To find someone with the same items as yourself
Language Controlled, guided or free
Preparation and material Language frame on display, or handouts; duplicated sets of similar pictures on handouts

Stage 1   E,I,A (5 minutes)

Class   Make two copies of a set of, for example, six similar pictures. Hand out eleven pictures to learners or pairs and keep the twelfth. Describe your picture and ask any learners who think they have the same one to indicate this.

You may either describe your picture completely and ask who has the same one; or begin the description and then ask learners a few questions. Example, based on No. 2 *Families* in 5.3 *Visual material:*

Teacher: *The man in my picture is carrying an umbrella, and the girl is wearing a black dress.* Corrie, Nel, Frances, Dick and Marcel all raise their hands.)
You think you have the same one, Corrie? Is the boy in your picture carrying an umbrella? No? Sorry, it's not the same.
Yes, Nel? (but Nel, hearing the previous answer, shakes her head. Corrie and Nel both have picture B.)
Is the woman in your picture wearing a white dress, Marcel? Yes? perhaps it's the same.
Frances, is the girl in your picture taller than the boy? No? Sorry, it's not the same. (Hearing this, Dick also drops out. He and Frances have picture F.)
I think we have the same picture, Marcel. What's the letter?
(Teacher and Marcel both have picture E.)

Encourage the learners holding pictures to ask some questions themselves, as preparation for stages 2 and 3.

Stage 2   E,I (10 minutes)

Class   Each learner or pair is given one picture from the duplicated sets. Learners take turns to describe their pictures. Others ask questions (soon after the description begins) until they find out if they have the same picture. Learners can copy the phrases you used in stage 1 when they find the pictures cannot be identical:
   F *Non, je regrette, ce n'est pas le même.*
   D *Nein, tut mir leid, es ist nicht dasselbe.*

Stage 3   E,I,A (10 minutes)

Class/
changing pairs   As above, without using the substitution table or language frame. For more intensive practice in a shorter time, changing pairs is recommended. Tell the learners how many partners they have to find: for example, if the picture set was duplicated three times, each learner or pair has to find two others with the

127

same picture. You and the learners take pictures and move round the class, taking it in turns to ask and answer a question with those you speak to, until there is an answer showing that the two pictures cannot be identical. Then break off the conversation with a phrase such as *No, sorry . . .* (as in stages 1 or 2), and move on. No one may show the pictures they hold at any time. The pairs go on questioning each other until everyone has found all possible partners and can sit down; or until the time limit. Everyone then reports which partners they found. Those who did not find partners can ask and answer questions in the whole class, as in stage 2.

Number the pictures on the back so you can check that at least two of each picture have been handed out: warn learners not to use the numbers to find their partners! However, they can be used at the end of any stage as a quick way of checking if learners have indeed got identical pictures.

As there is no controlled language for stage 3, you can hand out different sets of pictures in the class – a set of similar faces, similar families, similar houses, etc. – so long as there are at least two copies of each. This works most efficiently in changing pairs: if one learner begins, *The man in my picture has got a moustache*, learners who have not got a picture of a man can say immediately, *No sorry, it's not the same*, and move on to question someone else.

The activity is a useful follow-up to 5.4 *Find the picture*. 5.6 *Spot the differences* provides more extensive practice in discovering differences and similarities between pictures.

Variant 1 Partners

Instead of pictures, you can work with purely verbal information. Write two or more questions on the board and several possible answers to each, with the help of the learners. The chosen items will depend on the learners' level, and on the information learners wish to ask about or give (it is thus an opportunity for them to extend their vocabulary in areas of personal interest). Learners then choose their own answers to each question from those on display, and try to find out who has made exactly the same choices. Example:

When are you going on holiday? – *in May, June, September, December*
Where are you going? – *to Tahiti, Hawaii, Bondi Beach, Israel*
How long are you going to stay? – *for a weekend, two weeks, a month, six weeks*
Responses: *So am I/Oh, I'm not*
The answers can be based on authentic personal information.

Establish questions and possible answers with the class first.
Examples:

What's your favourite spectator sport?   – tennis, baseball, cricket, none, etc.
What kind of music do you like best?   – classical, pop, jazz, none, etc.
What are your hobbies?   – reading, listening to music, jogging, stamp-collecting, etc.
What's your favourite TV programme?   – any current programmes, etc.
(Various responses are possible; only one example is given)
I like . . . too / Oh really?

Learners ask each other the questions and give personal answers (not necessarily the same as those on display) to see if anyone has identical or near-identical choices. (This is one way to find learners with similar interests if you wish to form groups on this basis for any activity.) See 1.3 *Secret choice I, Variant 1* for practice with simpler frames, and 1.5 *Hunt the answer* for simpler guided practice with authentic personal information; see also 1.6 *Questionnaires*, and 5.6 *Spot the differences, Variant 3.*

Finding and making material

For the basic activity at level E, Nos. 2, 3 or 4 from 5.3 *Visual material*, and the corresponding substitution tables from 5.4 *Find the picture* can be used. *Finding and making material* in 5.4 describes how to make sets of similar pictures. Any picture stories with similar pictures can be duplicated, including those in 5.3, and used for levels I and A. See 5.2 *General notes on visual material* for other notes on finding and making material. The number of pictures in the set and learners in the class determines how many duplicates must be made. Learners should not see the complete sets or picture stories in advance, in case they note that there are just one or two essential differences between some of the pictures, and limit their descriptions or questions accordingly.

   Variant 1: questions and answers can be based on textbook material (particularly for level E). Examples from *Teaching material* for 1.3 and 1.4 *Secret choice*, 1.5 *Hunt the answer* and 1.6 *Questionnaires* also provide ideas.

Teaching material

ENGLISH *Find your partners*

Variant 1 **Partners**

(Present perfect and simple past)

Which of Shakespeare's plays have you seen?
– Hamlet, Macbeth, Othello, King Lear
So have I (Oh, I haven't)
Where did you see it?
– in Adelaide, Los Angeles, Stratford-on-Avon, Stratford Ontario
So did I (Oh, I didn't)
What did you think of it?
– I though it was fantastic, terrible, quite good, so-so
So did I (Oh? I thought it was . . .)

FRANÇAIS *Trouvez les partenaires*

Variant 1 *Partners*

(Conditional)

Si vous pouviez aller où vous vouliez, où iriez-vous?
– *(Learners make suggestions)*
Si vous pouviez avoir ce qui vous plairait le plus, que choisiriez-vous?
– *(Learners make suggestions)*
Si vous pouviez être quelqu'un d'autre, qui aimeriez-vous être?
– *(Learners make suggestions)*
Moi aussi (Ah bon!)

DEUTSCH *Partner finden*

Variant 1 *Partners*

Wer ist Ihr Lieblingsschriftsteller/Filmstar?
– *(Learners suggest names)*
Ja, ich finde ihn/sie auch sehr gut (Ja? Ich mag lieber . . .)
Haben Sie schon . . . gelesen/gesehen?
– *(Learners suggest titles of books or films)*
Ich auch (Ich aber nicht)
Wie fanden Sie es?
– Sehr spannend/interessant/ein bißchen langweilig/schrecklich
Ich auch (Oh ja? Ich fand es . . .)

4 Communication strategies

4.1 Introduction

We can reasonably assume that, during their language course, learners will not master every item they may need for communication. They will need communication strategies in order to compensate for the gaps in their knowledge. The strategies for speech can be very broadly categorised as:

1 *Paraphrase or approximation*   Using the words you do know to replace or describe those you do not.
2 *Borrowing or inventing words*   For example, using words from any language (usually the mother tongue) in place of unknown FL words, often adjusting the form or pronunciation in the hope they will be understood.
3 *Gesture*   Anything from pointing to elaborate mime.
4 *Asking for feedback*   Either directly: *How do you say . . .? Do you know what I mean?* (see list of phrases at the end of this introduction); or indirectly, by constantly watching the other person's reactions, or speaking with questioning intonation to check if you have understood, or been understood, correctly.
5 *Reduction*   Simplifying, changing or even abandoning those parts of the message which are too difficult to express.

(See Littlewood 1984 pp. 83–87, in *Booklist* 3, for a fuller description of these strategies.)

Example from practice

Between Italian and English speakers, outside the classroom (the numbers refer to the strategies listed above).

I: Have you got an – /aːg/? *(2) Adapting the Italian word* ago *to make it sound more English; (4) questioning intonation, and watching English speaker's face.*

E: What? *(4) Feedback – message not understood.*

I: I must . . . My dress is . . . *(5) This part of message abandoned as the words* mend *and* torn *were unknown.* I must *(miming sewing)* – how do you say? I need a thing to do this. *(3) and (4) Gesture and request for feedback.*

E: Oh, you want a needle! *Communication successfully achieved – and a new word acquired.*

The strategies scarcely need to be taught; everyone uses them naturally, even in the mother tongue. Sometimes, however, they are suppressed or even forbidden in FL lessons, even though learners will find them essential in FL communication outside the classroom, and even though insistence on using correct forms at all times runs the risk of creating learners who are unwilling to open their mouths or try to express anything for which they do not know the exact FL words. In communication practice, you can encourage learners to use these strategies with maximum effectiveness, so that they do not make excessive use of (5) by falling silent, or saying only what they know is correct, instead of what they intend (asking for *scissors*, a word they know, instead of a *needle*, which is what they want); or inappropriate use of (4) by relapsing into the mother tongue and asking for direct translation (*Come si dice 'ago' in inglese?*) whenever they have difficulties. These reactions will be of little use in contact with native speakers who do not know the learners' mother tongue, or whenever the aim is to communicate meaning, and not simply to produce correct sentences.

Teachers, of course, also need to be proficient in these strategies, particularly paraphrase and mime, if they are to convey meaning to their learners during communication practice, without relapsing into direct translation.

The emphasis in the preceding three sections of this book was on helping learners to master basic language items for communication; this section puts more emphasis on providing motivation to communicate even though they do not know all the language they need. The strategies specifically practised here can and should be used wherever appropriate with any communication activity, since they are an important component of oral communication skills. They can thus be used with activities from all sections of the book to encourage learners to express themselves and to acquire any new language items they need (see also p. 14 and p. 17 on giving feedback on errors, and using the FL in the classroom). Most teachers and learners find a mixture of the two types of oral practice is most valuable. Controlled communication practice with given language can alternate with more spontaneous practice in communicating with any words and in any way. In the latter type of practice, learners should always feel that they are being encouraged and helped to express themselves, not that their knowledge of the language is being tested in any way.

The activities in this section allow learners to practise the most useful communication strategies: various forms of paraphrase and mime, combined with asking for feedback. There is a minimum of guided practice with frames or word lists, though you can influence the language used by the choice of topic. The learners' aim in all these activities is to convey (and understand) meaning. You should offer help with language after, rather than before their attempts to communicate, so that they learn to cope without constant reliance on the teacher or book, and find out how much they can do independently. Feedback from you and classmates will show how far they are succeeding. Having discovered in this way what language items they need in order to communicate more easily, learners are often more receptive to the linguistic help you can give them: they now know from personal experience how much they need it! (See *Examples from practice* in this section and in 5.6 *Spot the differences*.) The most important of the new language items can be written on the board after the exercise, for the learners to copy into their notebooks. You can often organise the practice so that the new items will be met in subsequent textbook units, reading or listening material; or they can be used again in other, more guided communication activities such as 1.3 and 1.4 *Secret choice*, 3.3 *Duets*, etc.

In 4.2 *Guess the word*, learners have to convey the meaning of words which they all (should) know, for their classmates to guess, without actually naming the item. The activity is particularly useful for practising various forms of paraphrase. In 4.3 *What's it called?* this exercise becomes more realistic: the learners use communication strategies to deal with words they really do not know in the FL.

The next two activities concentrate on gesture and mime. These are both useful communication strategies and a valuable stimulus to communication – creating an information or opinion gap concerning the interpretation of the wordless message. In 4.4 *The speechless tourist*, learners mime and guess words and phrases within a defined context – what does somebody want to buy in a shop? – etc. In 4.5 *Silent film*, they mime complete scenes for their classmates to interpret.

4.6 *Picture dictation* requires learners to describe, or to draw the pictures described. It is both motivating and useful for them to see classmates translate their words and gestures into pictures, showing immediately whether or not they have made themselves understood, and stimulating repeated attempts at communication, until the picture is faithfully reproduced.

Phrases for feedback

ENGLISH

What's that (called) in English? How do you say that in English?
Sorry, I don't understand what you mean/what X means. I'm afraid I can't follow: do you mean . . .? What does X mean?
Could you repeat that please?
Do you understand? Do you know what I mean?

FRANÇAIS

Qu'est-ce que c'est en français? Comment dit-on cela en français?
Je ne comprends pas: qu'est-ce que cela veut dire/vous voulez dire?
Je n'ai pas tout à fait compris: vous voulez dire . . .?
Que veut dire X? Qu'est-ce que cela veut dire – X?
Vous pouvez répéter, s'il vous plaît?
Vous comprenez? Vous comprenez ce que je veux dire?

DEUTSCH

Was ist/Wie heißt das auf Deutsch? Wie sagt man das auf Deutsch?
Verzeihung, ich verstehe nicht ganz: was bedeutet das/meinen Sie? Sie meinen . . .?
Entschuldigung, können/würden Sie das bitte wiederholen?
Verstehen Sie? Verstehen Sie, was ich meine?

4.2 Guess the word
Devinez le mot
Das Wort raten

Basic gap	Information gap based on split information
Aim	To convey the meaning of words without naming them: to understand the word conveyed
Language	Free, with any communication strategies
Preparation and material	Minimal – words on papers (optional)

Stage 1   E,I,A (5 minutes)

Class/team   Ask the learners to guess the word(s) you will describe with the help of communication strategies. Teams can win points for the number of words they recognise in a given time, such as one minute per team; or score 3 points for guessing a word at the first definition, 2 points if a second definition is needed, and one point after a third definition – after which you give the answer. Learners can act as time-keepers and scorers. If necessary, tell them that your definitions concern particular types of word – nouns, verbs, adjectives, etc. – or a particular topic, such as 'Houses and gardens'.

Moving from receptive practice, learners give definitions for you to recognise, either choosing words themselves or being given words on papers; the latter is useful for reviewing recently-learned or particular types of vocabulary. Learners may fail to communicate because they adapt mother-tongue words inappropriately, misinterpret the original word, or have very faulty pronunciation, etc. Respond as native speakers would in such situations, negotiating meaning by querying unclear descriptions, asking for clarification and giving help.

Examples from practice

English learner of French took a paper with the word *cloche* and pointed to her watch and then drew a large circle in the air (misinterpretation).
Teacher: *Un horloge? Ah, plus grand – une pendule?*
(Learner had second thoughts – and was prompted by a fellow team member!)
L: *Non – er – ding-dong* (accompanied by drawing the shape of a bell in the air)
T: *Ah, une cloche!*

French learner of English described *boat* as: *Like a sheep* (mispronunciation of /ɪ/).
T: *Like a sheep – you mean an animal? a goat – a cow?*
L: *No, no, a sheep – on the sea!*
T: *A sheep on the sea – a swimming sheep? Do you mean a sheep or a ship?*
(Teachers can occasionally pretend to be rather slow or literal-minded native speakers! – in this case to demonstrate the importance of differentiating /ɪ/ and /iː/.)

There are more examples on p. 17 in *Dealing with errors*.

Stage 2   E,I,A (5 minutes)

Class/team   Hand out papers with selected words written on them, or let learners choose their own words. They define these by using the strategies you demonstrated in stage 1, and may direct their definitions to a selected person or group in their own team. Encourage these selected learners to give feedback as you did in stage 1, *Sorry, I don't understand – do you mean . . .?* etc. Learners can act as time-keepers and scorers while you act as referee, intervening only when it seems that they would not communicate their meaning to a native speaker, even though their classmates may understand them (as they might understand *cloche* as *clock* in the example above).

Stage 3 E,I,A (5 minutes)

Group/pair Learners take papers or choose words and take turns to define them for their partners. Groups declare their scores at the time limit, and some learners can demonstrate their definitions for the whole class to guess.

Variant 1 Limited definitions

You or the learners may decide on strict rules for the ways in which the words may be defined: e.g. by sentences in which the word might occur (it is replaced by a nonsense word or sound), by synonyms, antonyms or other one-word definitions, by mime and gesture, etc. You may be able to refer to well-known television games in selecting one of these rules.

Examples from practice

Sentences: *You go to a restaurant when you want to eat a BLANK.* (*Meal*)
One-word definitions: *Garden* – (*Fence*); *Happy* (singing) – (*Birthday*)
   For examples of extensive mime, see 4.4 *The speechless tourist* and 4.5 *Silent film.*

Variant 2 I'm thinking of . . .

Learners can give descriptions of people or things using a fixed pattern. Examples:
I'm thinking of something that – is small and white and you write on the board with it. (*Chalk*)
I'm thinking of someone who – was married to Elizabeth Taylor. (*Various possibilities!*)
   See 4.4 *The speechless tourist, Variant 2* for other practice with fixed patterns.

Variant 3 Split crosswords

Teams or pairs have handouts with half-completed crosswords: a different half for each team or partner. Learners take turns to ask each other for definitions of the words they have not got in order to complete their crosswords.

Alternatively, give half the learners blank crossword frame A, and the completed frame or answers for crossword B. The other half get the completed crossword frame or answers for A and the blank frame for B. Working in pairs, they can exchange information by defining the words they have, to enable all the learners to complete their blank crosswords.

Finding and making material

No preparation is necessary, but you may find particular sets of words from the textbook (or other sources) lead to useful practice of communication strategies. Such words can be put on papers and kept in envelopes labelled with the level and/or topic area, for repeated use.

Variant 3: Crosswords can be taken from the textbook or other sources, or made up by you or the learners. For the examples shown in *Teaching material*, make two blank copies and half fill in each. As numbering crosswords can be complicated, I suggest keeping a consecutively numbered list of all the words in the crossword, across and then down, and adding these numbers to the frame, with arrows showing in which direction the words are to be read. Blank squares need not be blacked out: learners must ask each other, *What's 2 across? How many letters?*

Note: the crosswords for *Variant 3* are placed together at the end of *Teaching material*, for easier photocopying.

Teaching material

FRANÇAIS *Devinez le mot*

Variant 2 *Je pense à...*

Je pense à quelque chose qui – roule sur un chemin de fer
et que – vous trouvez dans une gare
(Train)
Je pense à quelqu'un qui – a perdu une bataille à Waterloo
et que – les Anglais ont envoyé à Sainte
Hélène (Napoléon)

DEUTSCH *Das Wort raten*

Variant 2 *ich denke an...*

Ich denke an etwas, das – fliegt
und worin –Menschen sitzen (Flugzeug)
Ich denke an jemanden, der – gesagt hat: Ich bin ein
Berliner (Kennedy)
(*He should have said* Ich bin
Berliner.)
der – die Eroica komponiert hat
(Beethoven)

ENGLISH   *Guess the word*

Variant 3 Split crosswords

✂---

A

	8↓		9↓			10↓				11↓
1→ S	U	P	E	R	M	A	R	12↓ K	E	T
	2→ S	A	T							
					3→ S	A	W			
								4→		
	5→ P	A	R	T	Y					
					6→ O↓	N	E	13↓ S		
7→ P	O	S	T	O	F	F	I	C	E	

Across →

1 supermarket
2 sat
3 saw
5 party
6 ones
7 post office

Down ↓

✂---

B

	8↓ B		9↓ R			10↓ B				11↓ S
1→	U		E			A		12↓ K		T
	S		S			N		N		A
2→ S			T			K		E		T
	T		A			3→ S		W		I
	O		U						4→ T	O
5→ P			R							N
			A			6→ O↓		13↓ S		
			N			F		E		
7→			T			F		E		

Across →

4 to

Down ↓

6 off
8 bus stop
9 restaurant
10 banks
11 station
12 knew
13 see

✂---

From *Developing Communication Skills* by Pat Pattison
© Cambridge University Press 1987

FRANÇAIS   *Devinez le mot*

Variant 3 Mots croisés

✂---

A

1→ ↓S	E	10 ↓P	T	11 ↓E	12 ↓M	B	13 ↓R	E
P		A		2→				
O		R					3→	
4→ R	A	T			5→			
T		6→ I	L				7→	
8→ S	U	R		9→				

Horizontal →

1 septembre
4 rat
6 il
8 sur

Vertical ↓

1 sports
10 partir

✂---

B

1→ ↓		10 ↓		11 ↓E	12 ↓M		13 ↓R	
				2→ S	A		E	
				T			3→ S	I
4→					5→ O	N	T	
		6→					7→ E	N
8→				9→ P	O	U	R	

Horizontal →

2 sa
3 si
5 ont
7 en
9 pour

Vertical ↓

11 est
12 ma
13 rester

✂---

From *Developing Communication Skills* by Pat Pattison
© Cambridge University Press 1987

DEUTSCH *Das Wort raten*

Variant 3 Kreuzworträtsel

✂--

A

1→ ↓A	R	9 ↓B	E	I	10 ↓T	E	N
C		A					
2→ H	E	U		3→		11 ↓	
T		E		4→	12 ↓		
5→ Z	U	R		6→			
E							
7→ H	E	13 ↓U	T	14 ↓E		8→	
N		M		R			

Waagerecht →

1 arbeiten

2 Heu

5 zur

7 heute

Senkrecht ↓

1 achtzehn

9 Bauer

13 um

14 er

✂--

B

1→ ↓		9 ↓		10 ↓T			
				A			
2→			3→ I	N		11 ↓A	
			4→ Z	12 ↓E	H	N	
5→			6→ E	I	N		
			N		U		
7→	13 ↓	14 ↓	8→ U	N	S		
				G			

Waagerecht →

3 in

4 zehn

6 ein

8 uns

Senkrecht ↓

10 tanzen

11 Ahnung

12 Ei

✂--

From *Developing Communication Skills* by Pat Pattison
© Cambridge University Press 1987

4.3   What's it called?
Comment ça s'appelle?
Wie heißt das?

Basic gap	Information gap based on split information
Aim	To find out unknown words in the FL
Language	Guided and free, with any communication strategies
Preparation and material	Minimal – putting model phrases on display, or on handouts; (optional: pictures or mother tongue words on display or on handouts; same pictures or words with mother tongue equivalents on handouts required for stage 3)

Stage 1   E,I,A (5 minutes)

Class   Play the role of an FL native speaker who wants to find out certain words in the learners' mother tongue, but cannot speak their language. Use any communication strategies to ask about a few words (preferably some which learners do not yet know in the FL). Example:
(Mime sewing) *What do you call the little thing you use to do this – it's very small and you put cotton through it* (mime threading a needle), etc.
Learners give you the word in their mother tongue.
Encourage them to use any model phrases on display to ask you for the FL equivalent: *What's that called in English?* etc.

Stage 2   E,I,A (5 minutes)

Class   You are still the mono-lingual native speaker, but now it is the learners (individually or in pairs) who try to find out from you words they do not know in the FL, using the model phrases and the kind of communication strategies you have already demonstrated.

Example from practice

Level A (Dutch) learner:
L1: *I come to school on a – bus bike. How do you say that in English?* (translation and adaptation of mother tongue equivalent, 'buzz-bike' mispronouncing /z/)
T: *You mean a bike you can take on a bus?*
L2: (helping L1) *No, it makes a noise – brmm brmm.*
T: *Oh, a motorbike? You have a motorbike?* (surprised intonation)

L1: *Not a big bike. It has a little motor, and you use your feet like this.* (moves hands in pedalling motion) *What do you call that?*

T: *I think you mean a moped.* (Writes word on board)

Instead of choosing words freely, learners can choose from pictures (or mother tongue words) on display. Some items may be very similar (*a bench, a stool,* etc.) so that attempts to identify them must be very precise (*Something you sit on* is not enough). As soon as you recognise (or judge that a native speaker would recognise) what they mean, you can provide the words both orally and in writing, for learners to make a note of. Learners may be given points for themselves or their teams for describing words so clearly that you can recognise them immediately.

Stage 3   I,A (5 minutes)

Class/group/ pair   One or two learners in the class, group or pair have a set of pictures or mother tongue words with their FL equivalents. The rest see only the pictures or mother tongue words (on display), which they describe until the others recognise what they mean and give them the FL equivalents. Both sides can use the model phrases and techniques demonstrated in stages 1 and 2 when asking for and giving feedback.

Team   One or two learners from each team sit in front of the class, with the complete set of mother tongue – FL words. Each team describes a picture or word from those on display, for their own team member(s) on the panel to recognise. Once recognised, the words are written beside the items on display. Points are scored as in stage 2.

Act as referee offering help where required, as with the pronunciation of new words, or pointing out when the questioners would not be understood by native speakers.

Variant 1 New words

Learners can use their dictionaries to look up two or three FL words which they would like to know, or which interest them as they look through the dictionary (checking the pronunciation with you if necessary). Some or all of these FL words can then be written on the board, or on papers which are then re-distributed in the class. Learners ask about the meanings of words they do not know, and those who chose them must convey their meaning, using any communication strategies.

Finding and making material

See *Feedback phrases* in 4.1 for model phrases. Learners will find bi- and mono-lingual dictionaries useful in preparing material.

Teaching material

ENGLISH *What's it called?*

stool   bench   deck chair
screw   nail   drawing pin (thumb tack)
tray   shelf
tap   garden hose   drainpipe
dress/coat hanger   coat hook
double bed   cot   bunk beds
ball of string   ball of wool   rubber band

FRANÇAIS *Comment ça s'appelle?*

un tabouret   un banc   une chaise longue (de bord)
une vis   un clou   une punaise
un plateau   une étagère
un robinet   un tuyau   un tuyau d'écoulement
un cintre   une patère
un grand lit   un lit d'enfant   des lits superposés
une pelote de ficelle   une pelote de laine   un élastique

DEUTSCH *Wie heißt das?*

r Hocker   e Bank   r Liegestuhl
e Schraube   r Nagel   e Reißzwecke
s Tablett   s Regal
r Wasserhahn   r Gartenschlauch   s Regenrohr
r Kleiderbügel   r Garderobenhaken
s Doppelbett   s Gitterbett   s Etagenbett
s Knäuel Bindfaden   s Wollknäuel   s Gummiband

4.4 The speechless tourist
Le touriste muet
Der stumme Tourist

Basic gap	Information gap based on split information
Aim	To convey meaning by mime: to interpret the mime in words
Language	Free, with any communication strategies; mime and gesture
Preparation and material	Minimal – papers with words or messages to be mimed

Stage 1 E,I,A (5 minutes)

Class   Play the role of a mono-lingual foreign tourist in, for example, a department store in the learners' own country. You have lost the power of speech so you have to communicate what you want in gestures and mime. The learners are staff or onlookers who try to interpret what you mean. They make all their suggestions in the FL, since you understand nothing else. Indicate whether or not they are close to the right answer by gestures – including repetition or adaptation of the mime to help them.

In interpreting the mime, learners may find that they do not know all the correct words in the FL: they themselves must use communication strategies such as paraphrase, etc. These are acceptable so long as a foreigner would understand them, e.g. *You've lost your *marriage ring?* However, learners must come as close as possible to the full message: if you want to buy, or have lost, *a Japanese camera with telephoto lens*, then you would not accept just *a camera*.

When the mime is guessed, or when the time limit is reached, you can give the class the original message and/or write it on the board (and so they learn the term *wedding ring*).

Stage 2 E,I,A (10 minutes)

Class   Volunteers for the tourist role are given or make up a message, and the miming and guessing proceed as in stage 1. If you do not know the message, you can join in the guessing. Otherwise, you need only intervene if the tourist accepts interpretations which are insufficient, or which would be incomprehensible to a real foreigner; or if the class needs help in making suggestions. (Too much teacher intervention can make the learners self-conscious.)

It is perhaps better to ask for volunteers for this activity as not all learners enjoy miming in front of the class (but see stage 3).

Team   Team members take it in turns to act out a mime for their teams alone to guess. In a large class, this means fewer people are calling out suggestions at once. If the 'home team' doesn't guess within the time limit, other teams can make suggestions.

Stage 3 E,I,A (10 minutes)

Team   If possible, divide the class into teams so that each can use a corner of the classroom or other suitable space. Teams now work simultaneously instead of in turns. Some team members take a paper or make up a message to mime. When they think their team has interpreted this satisfactorily, they call you to hear the result. If the message is not complete, the tourists and interpreters try again. Otherwise, show them the original message, and let another member choose the next message. Teams can see how many messages they can guess within the time limit. Many learners are more willing to mime in front of a small group than in front of the whole class, so that you need not work only with volunteers. Some of the mimes from each team can be repeated for the whole class to guess.

Variant 1 The game

Many learners will be familiar with the game in which words and sayings, or the titles of films, plays, books or songs are mimed for others to guess, often with accepted signs for 'First/second word, First/second syllable, It's a short word, It sounds like, it's a book, song, film title,' etc. In the FL class, this provides an opportunity to revise vocabulary and idioms, and cultural background.

Variant 2 The sentence game

Learners mime situations which can be expressed in a single sentence. This can provide useful practice with particular structures: given an example of the chosen structure in advance. Examples:

You want us to (give you a drink, open a window, etc.)
You're going to (wash the windows, play tennis, etc.)
You were . . .ing X when Y. . .ed (playing tennis when it started to rain, etc.)
She's been (shot, stung by a bee, etc.)

    Two or more people can mime together; with passive constructions, for example, the learners must say what is

happening or has happened to the second 'actor'.
See 4.5 *Silent film* for more extensive miming.

Finding and making material

The messages to be mimed can be based on textbook vocabulary, structures or situations, particularly for levels E and I. When learners are used to the activity, they can make up messages themselves: keep the best of these for future use!

Contexts for the activity are given under ENGLISH in *Teaching material*, and suggested messages for each context are divided between the languages.

For further ideas, see Maley and Duff 1978 in *Booklist* 2a.

Teaching material

ENGLISH *The speechless tourist*

(*The restaurant*)
The learners are waiters or other clients in the restaurant, who try to interpret the tourist's wishes (or complaints).
Messages: ordering any food or drinks. Complaints about particular items being too cold or not fresh, etc., dirty crockery, cutlery, foreign objects or insects in the food:
>There's lipstick on this glass.
>There's cigarette ash on my ice cream.
>Waiter, there's a fly in my soup! *etc.*

(*Customs*)
In response to the question Have you anything to declare? *the tourist mimes putting a container on the counter and describing its contents. Other learners are customs officers and other travellers.*
Messages:
>X bottles of red/white wine (champagne, perfume)
>X boxes or packets of cigars (cigarettes)
>Gold watch (diamond ring, pearl necklace)
>Bottles of medicines for headache (toothache, stomach ache, sore throat, sleeping tablets)
>Box containing a cat (dog, parrot, poisonous snake, baby crocodile, tarantula)

(*The department store*)
The tourist is trying to find a particular department and/or buy one or more objects (descriptions may be detailed for levels I or A), including items typical of the learners' own country (a Scottish kilt, a cowboy hat, a toy kangaroo etc.); or has a complaint about something bought previously. Other learners are sales assistants and shoppers. See
DEUTSCH.

(*The hotel*)
The tourist comes to the reception desk of the hotel with a request or complaint. Other learners are hotel staff or guests. See FRANÇAIS.

(*The hospital*)
The tourist walks (or staggers!) into the hospital and tells the nurse what has happened to him/what's wrong with him: anything from toothache *to* a broken leg. *See* FRANÇAIS.

FRANÇAIS   *Le touriste muet*

(L'hôtel)

L'ascenseur ne fonctionne pas.
Je voudrais qu'on me serve le petit déjeuner au lit demain matin s.v.p.
J'ai perdu ma valise – je l'avais laissée là, près de l'entrée.
Je voulais une chambre avec bain et vous m'en avez donné une avec douche.
Je ne peux pas ouvrir la porte de la garde-robe.
J'ai laissé tomber mon alliance dans le trou du lavabo. Est-ce que quelqu'un peut m'aider à l'attraper?

(A l'hôpital)

J'ai mal à la tête (au genou, aux dents).
J'ai été(e) renversé(e) par une voiture: j'ai mal partout.
Je suis tombé(e) de cheval: je crois que je me suis cassé(e) le bras gauche.
J'ai mangé des champignons – ils étaient vénéneux.
J'ai été aggressé(e) dans la rue par un voyou; il m'a blessé(e) au visage – j'ai perdu quelques dents.
J'ai été mordu(e) par un chien enragé.

Variant 2   Jeu des phrases

– Vous avez (soif)
– Vous vous (lavez/êtes lavé(e) la tête)
– Vous allez/êtes en train de/venez de (manger)

DEUTSCH   *Der stumme Tourist*

(*Das Warenhaus*)

Ich suche die Spielwarenabteilung (Fotoabteilung).
Ich möchte ein Spielzeug-Känguruh (einen Cowboyhut, einen Schottenrock, chinesischen Tee, eine Flasche Champagner, eine Platte von (*any easily mimed artist*) kaufen
Beschwerden:
Dieses Hemd (diese Hose, diese Schuhe) ist (sind) zu klein (groß).

An diesem Hemd (Mantel) fehlt ein Knopf.
Dieses Transistorradio (dieser Kassettenrecorder) ist kaputt.
Ich kann diesen Koffer nicht schließen; das Schloß ist kaputt
(der Schlüssel paßt nicht).

Variant 2 Das Satzspiel

– Sie setzen eine Brille auf (machen ein Fenster zu)
– Sie haben mir (ihm, ihr, uns) eine Blume (ein Buch) gegeben
– Er wird gewaschen

4.5 Silent film
Film muet
Stummfilm

Basic gap Information gap based on split information
Aim To interpret a mimed scene
Language Free, with any communication strategies; mime and gesture
Preparation and material Minimal if textbook material is used; or prepare papers with scenes to be mimed

Stage 1 E,I,A (5 minutes)

Class At level E, perform a simple series of actions and give a commentary at the same time: *I'm opening the door, I'm coming in, I'm sitting down.* At other levels, give volunteers a few scenes to choose from, or let them make up their own. They prepare to mime the scene, as in a silent film (if necessary as homework). A volunteer (*the master of ceremonies, l'animateur, der Moderator*) can set the scene and identify the characters, so far as necessary:
Val is Mrs Smith, she's at home, and Justin is the postman,
or:
Oliver is an old man, Aimée is a child, etc.
You then give a running commentary, or a summary of their performance, guided or corrected by the MC if necessary.

Example 1 (running commentary by teachers):

The man is walking somewhere – he's cold – (MC: Where is he?) – he's outside – in the street – he's looking at something – perhaps at the windows? (MC: No.) – the doors of the houses? (MC nods) – he's found the door he wants – he's knocking at the door – a woman opens the door – I don't think she knows him – he's smiling, he's saying 'It's me!' – she's looking puzzled – she's looking at him very closely – he's smiling and nodding – now she's saying 'Oh!' – she's recognised him – she's slammed the door in his face. (MC: *The end!*)

Ask the actors to repeat part of the scene if it is not clear. (See *Variant 1* for discussion of open-ended scenes like the above.)

Stage 2   E,I,A (10 minutes)

Class   Volunteers prepare a scene as in stage 1, while you or the MC encourage a group of learners to give a commentary or summary of the action. In discussing the scene afterwards, you can ask other learners about details the first group did not mention, and help all the learners to express their ideas more clearly. All language items that are new or difficult can be put on the board. Example, summary (based on the telegram story in *Teaching material*, DEUTSCH):

The man heard somebody at the door, he went to the door, the postman gave him a letter – (MC: *Not a letter.*) – *a telegram?* (MC nods) – *he opened it, it *were bad news.*

In the subsequent discussion, you might ask for further details (and give further practice with tenses!) by asking:

What was he doing when he heard the postman at the door? (watching TV)

What did he do then? (switched it off)

and deal with problem items similarly:

You said it was bad news; how do you know it was bad news? (and write *It was bad news* on the board.) The actors can repeat the scene, for a different group of learners to give a more polished commentary or summary; and they may suggest suitable dialogue for the scene (see *Variant 2*).

Stage 3   I,A (10 minutes)

Class   As in stage 2, without your intervention during the commentary or summary.

Team   If there is space, two or three acting groups may perform simultaneously in different parts of the room, while their 'audiences' give commentaries or summaries. You can subsequently answer questions about language items they found difficult. One or more groups and team members may repeat their performance and commentary for the whole class to discuss.

Variant 1 Explanations

Some of the mimed stories may be incomplete, so that learners, in groups or in the whole class, can discuss their ideas about the whole story, the characters and their situation, what past events led to this scene, what may happen next, etc. Example (based on the mime in stage 2):
Was the man expecting a telegram? What was in the telegram? Who sent it? What will the man do next?
Group discussions on these lines may lead to comparison of the class or groups' interpretations with those of the actors; to written stories – or to the presentation of further mimes.

Variant 2 Soundtracks

One group mimes while a second group not only describes the action but also suggests a suitable dialogue for the actors. The rest of the class comment and suggest alternatives or improvements.

   If you have suitable film strips, or scenes in films or video, these can be shown without sound for the class or groups to interpret the action and make up the dialogue.

Variant 3 Directors

In the days of the silent film, directors called out instructions to the actors while a scene was being filmed. Learners or pairs can prepare such instructions and try them out in class with a group of volunteer actors. Other learners can comment on how well the actors followed the instructions, and, at levels I and A, discuss the scene further, as in *Variant 1*.

   See 3.4 *People and things, Variant 5*, 4.2 *Guess the word*, and 4.4 *The speechless tourist* for simpler or more contextualised mimes. 5.5 *Memory tests, Variant 3* describes other uses of mime.

Finding and making material

You or learners may write scripts for the mimes. These can be in the mother tongue: it is the non-actors who must translate the mime into the FL as best they can. Mimes can be based on personal experience (see *Teaching material* ENGLISH and FRANÇAIS). Picture stories, such as Nos. 8, 11 and 15 in 5.3 *Visual material*, can also form the basis for mimes, or the situations in 4.4 *The speechless tourist* can be extended. Encourage learners to add extra details to these scripts in performance.

Variants 1 and *4:* Writers prepare an incomplete scene, leaving opportunity for discussion.

Variant 2: Groups can prepare mimes based on material which all the learners have read, to provide revision of the language used. Select and adapt situations from the textbook or other sources. Examples:

Access to English 2, 15: At the police station
Tricolore 2, 6: Fifi Folle va voir le médecin
Deutsch Konkret 1, 14B: Ein spannendes Buch

For further ideas, see Maley and Duff 1978 and 1982, in *Booklist 2a.*

Teaching material

ENGLISH *Silent film*

(*The hotel room* – two people)

Enter hotel room – show the porter where to put your suitcase – give him a tip – porter leaves – open your case and take out piece of clothing (dress, jacket, etc.) – take it to wardrobe, open wardrobe door – find wardrobe is full – react with surprise or puzzlement – put your clothes back on top of your suitcase – go to dressing table or chest of drawers and open drawer – take out article of clothing (socks, a tie, a bra, a pair of tights) – replace clothing and shut drawer angrily – go to telephone and telephone reception to complain.

FRANÇAIS *Film muet*

(*Dans le train* – two or more people)

Vous lisez un livre dans le train – le contrôleur vient pour contrôler les billets – vous ne trouvez pas votre billet – vous donnez de l'argent au contrôleur pour acheter un autre billet – mais ça coûte très cher – vous payez à contre coeur – le contrôleur sort – vous prenez votre livre et l'ouvrez – le billet est dedans – vous vous levez pour appeler le contrôleur – haussez les épaules – rasseyez-vous et continuez à lire.

(*Pendant la nuit* – two people)

Vous lisez au lit – entendez un bruit – vous vous levez et allez sur la pointe des pieds vers la porte – l'ouvrez avec soin – écoutez, avec l'air inquiet – allez vers le téléphone, tournez le dos à la porte, composez un numéro – entendez entrer quelqu'un – laissez tomber le combiné – regardez derrière vous – réagissez comme vous voulez.

2e acteur: entrez – regardez l'autre acteur – réagissez comme vous voulez.

DEUTSCH *Stummfilm*

(*Das Telegramm* – two people)
Du siehst fern zu Hause – jemanden an der Tür hören –
Fernseher ausmachen – Tür aufmachen – Postbeamter
überreicht ein Telegramm – Tür nicht zumachen –
Postbeamter wartet, beobachtet dich – Telegramm ansehen,
besorgt aussehen – mit zitternden Händen Telegramm öffnen,
lesen – laß es fallen und schlage die Hände vors Gesicht –
Postbeamter hilft dir, dich hinzusetzen.

4.6   Picture dictation
Dictée par le dessin
Bild Diktat

Basic gap	Information gap based on split information
Aim	To give and follow descriptions to reproduce a picture
Language	Guided and free, with any communication strategies
Preparation and material	Minimal – if textbook picture is used; picture on display or handouts; model phrases on display or handouts

Stage 1   E,I (5 minutes)

Class   Give the learners a general description of a scene to be drawn,
and then give the detailed description slowly enough for them
to draw the picture. Encourage them to ask questions (in the
mother tongue for purely receptive practice). Note: left and
right in the descriptions refer to the spectators' point of view.
Finally the learners see the original picture, and compare it
with their own. Discuss any differences and why they
occurred (in the mother tongue or FL): for instance, if the
initial, global description was not clear or was misunderstood,
learners may have drawn things in the wrong size or position,
making it impossible to fit later elements into the picture. This
discussion is a useful preparation for stage 2.

Stage 2   E,I,A (15 minutes)

Class   Ask a volunteer to leave the room while the others see, or
select from their books, the picture to be drawn. The
volunteer need not be a good artist but should understand the
language well. The learners who remain behind may ask you
about language items they will need and may copy the picture

153

if necessary. Warn them that you will not give them any more help with language once the volunteer has returned: it is up to them to convey their meaning by any communication strategies they can. The drawing itself and feedback from the volunteer will show them how successful they are.

After two or three minutes, remove or cover the picture and call back the volunteer, who may be asked to play a role: he or she is an artist of any nationality who speaks the FL but not the mother tongue of the class. Thus the FL is their only means of communication, even though none of them is a native speaker.

In a large class, arrange for pairs to describe the picture in turn. Example:
– The first pair gives a global description of the picture. The artist does not start drawing yet, but may ask this pair questions.
– In all following pairs, the first speaker describes a part of the picture and answers any questions from the artist, who only now starts drawing; the second speaker corrects the drawing and answers further questions.
– When each pair is satisfied, the next pair takes over, describing another part of the picture.

Stress that no one should speak out of turn, or correct already completed parts of the picture. You may set a time limit, such as ten or fifteen minutes (for a large class): if the drawing is finished before this, or before all pairs have spoken, learners may correct or add details. You or (preferably) a learner can act as referee, preventing interruptions and if necessary setting a time limit of a minute or less for each pair. You and the learners can make a note of their problems for later discussion: you may also note words or expressions which the artist can follow but which a native speaker probably would not (e.g. the *cloche – clock/bell* confusion mentioned in 4.2 stage 1).

Example from practice

An Italian-speaking level E French learner was told *Dessinez un* /gɑtoː/ *sous la chaise*, and drew a cat under the chair (*gatto* = cat.). The next speaker corrected *sous* to *sur* immediately, and the *gatto/chat* confusion was queried a few turns later. The teacher asked afterwards what a real French artist would have drawn in response to /gɑtoː/ (a cake!).

If there is an OHP or a board which can be turned round, the artist's drawing can remain hidden from the class until finished: in general, however, I let the class see the drawing in progress, as the immediate feedback from the artist is so valuable in demonstrating how well they have communicated. Finally, the artist also sees the original drawing and the two pictures are compared as in stage 1: what is different – what parts of the communication went wrong – why?

Now learners can ask you for the language items they needed and did not know; and you can give or write on the board any other items you noted during their descriptions. You or the learners can also remind particular speakers of more effective communication strategies they might have used.

Example from practice

A learner in an adult level E French class spent some time explaining the word *fenêtre* in words and gestures, but didn't think of pointing to the classroom window!

Stage 3 E,I,A (5 minutes)

Group/pair   One learner in each group is the artist. The others can choose or draw a picture which they must then describe for the artist to draw. The artists may ask questions and they can choose whether or not they let the describer see what they are drawing. No. 5 *Monsters* in 5.3 *Visual material* is the result of pair work in which the describer could not see what the artist was drawing.

Variant 1 Teacher as artist

A learner or learners choose or draw a picture for the rest of the class to see while you look away (or leave the room); the learners then describe the picture so that you can draw it. You can thus give immediate feedback in the role of an FL native speaker:
Did you say 'pan' or 'pen'?
She's pushing an *aspirator? Sorry, I don't know what you mean.
(Learners then described a vacuum cleaner with gesture and the brand name Hoover.)

Variant 2 Complete the picture

Learners follow descriptions to complete or add details to a picture (which may be in their textbook). Examples:
– They trace the route of a fly round a room; a burglar in a house; a tourist on a street map: an escaping prisoner in an outdoor scene, etc.

– They draw features on a face, or clothes on a figure; furniture in a room or house; people, vehicles or buildings in a street scene, etc.

See *Variant 1* of 2.5 *Finding the way* and 2.6 *What are we talking about?* for similar practice (the latter in dialogue form).

Variant 3 Moving things

Learners follow descriptions to arrange objects or picture cards. Example:
Put the book in the middle of the table. Put the eraser inside the book. Put the ruler on top of the book, with one end on the bottom left corner and one end on the top right corner, etc.
The original arrangement can then be uncovered and compared.

If there are enough sets of material, this can be done in groups or small teams. One learner from each group goes repeatedly to look at a complicated arrangement of objects or shapes (e.g. on the teacher's desk) which the others cannot see. These learners describe the arrangement to their groups so that they can reproduce it. If they begin to communicate almost entirely by gesture at this point, ask them to work with their hands behind their backs – frustrating but effective! At the time limit, the groups can see who has made the best copy.

See 5.5 *Memory tests, Variant 1* for practice with similar material.

Finding and making material

Draw simple pictures or choose them from the textbook, to practise particular language items. For freer practice, eliciting more communication strategies, draw or choose pictures or photographs from any source, including future textbook units. You and learners may describe places, things, or people known to you. 5.2 *General notes* and 5.3 *Visual material* supply further ideas.

Drawings for display in stage 2 must be on a part of the board which can be covered, or on the OHP or a poster. The larger the class, the more details the picture must contain. The picture in *Teaching material* was used with classes of twenty to thirty learners (ten or fifteen pairs). Both the original and the copies were on OHP transparencies (and the artist in the copy shown here was only told by the last speaker that the woman was holding the right-hand curtain!). Pictures drawn and reproduced on OHP transparencies in stage 2, or produced by pairs in stage 3, can often be used for 5.6 *Spot the differences.*

Learners can make up pictures and descriptions: these may also be used for writing and reading practice, as can the examples in *Teaching material*.

Variant 2: you can draw a basic outline on the board for learners to copy and complete, or make copies, for example of a textbook or other picture, from which details can be blanked out, so that learners can simply compare their completed drawings with those in the book. For example, No. 4 *Rooms* in 5.3 *Visual material* can be used in this way for level E.

Variant 3: classroom objects can be used, as in the given example. If available, use plastic or wooden building blocks, Lego pieces or cuisinaire rods. Sets of pictures can be cut up and re-arranged in a given order: see No. 1 *Miscellany* in 5.3 *Visual material*.

Teaching material

Picture dictation

(*Example of original and learner's copy*)

From *Developing Communication Skills* by Pat Pattison
© Cambridge University Press 1987

ENGLISH   *Picture dictation*

(*Model phrases*)

> Draw . . . in the middle of the picture; in the top/bottom
> left/right-hand corner.
> There's a . . . (standing, *etc.*) . . .
> (It) is more to the left/right, higher/lower, bigger/smaller
> (than) . . . *etc.*

(*Model dictation for stage 1*)

General description

> There's a house in the middle of the picture. There's a woman
> standing on the right of the house, and on the left there's a
> garage. There's a car in the garage, and a dog under the car.

Detailed description

> Draw the house in the middle of the picture, with a closed door
> in the centre and a window on each side. On the first floor there
> are three windows, and there's also a window in the middle of
> the roof. The chimney's on the left. Draw the woman on the
> right of the house. She's holding a bunch of flowers in front of
> her with both hands. Draw the garage on the left, with the
> door open. There's a car in the garage, and a little dog is lying
> underneath it. There's a black cat standing on the roof, facing
> left. There's a tree behind the garage. It's as high as the house.

FRANÇAIS   *Dictée par le dessin*

(*Model phrases*)

> Dessinez . . . / Il y a . . . au milieu, en haut, en bas, à gauche, à
> droite de l'image
> En haut à gauche, en bas à droite; dans le coin gauche en haut,
> le coin droit en bas, *etc.*
> Plus à gauche, plus haut, plus grand(e), plus petit(e), *etc.* que ça.

Variant 2 *Complétez l'image*

*Based on a tourist map of Paris. As an alternative to tracing the route, learners wrote down
the places visited (see list at end of text). This can be done even without a map, if learners
are sufficiently knowledgeable!*

> *Un Américain à Paris*
>
> Suivons le trajet d'un touriste américain qui veut découvrir
> certains des endroits les plus connus du centre de Paris. Son
> itinéraire débute dans le vieux Paris, là où la ville a été fondée,
> sur l'Ile de la Cité. Là, il va visiter la Cathédrale de Paris. (1) Il
> quitte l'Ile de la Cité, traverse le pont le plus ancien de Paris (2)

et il suit le Quai du Louvre pour aller voir le grand musée. (3)
Après avoir admiré la Joconde et la Vénus de Milo, il traverse
le parc devant le musée (4) jusqu'à la grande place où se dresse
l'Obélisque et où le roi Louis XVI a été décapité. (5) Il monte
ensuite les Champs Elysées, pour aller voir le monument qui
est le symbole des victoires de Napoléon. (6) Là se trouve aussi
la tombe du Soldat Inconnu, au centre de la place qui s'appellait
autrefois la Place de l'Étoile. (7) De là, il prend l'avenue
Kléber, pour se rendre au Palais de Chaillot. Il traverse la Seine
par le pont juste avant le Palais pour aller visiter le monument
qui est peut-être le plus connu de la ville, d'où il a une superbe
vue sur tout Paris. (8) Malheureusement, en se penchant pour
faire une photo, il se penche un peu trop, et voilà comment
finit sa visite à Paris!

1 NOTRE DAME   2 LE PONT NEUF
3 LE LOUVRE   4 LE JARDIN DES TUILERIES
5 LA PLACE DE LA CONCORDE   6 L'ARC DE
TRIOMPHE   7 LA PLACE CHARLES DE GAULLE
8 LA TOUR EIFFEL

DEUTSCH *Bilddiktat*

(Model phrases)

Zeichnet/Zeichnen Sie . . . in der Mitte des Bildes, links/rechts
oben/unten im Bild, *usw.*
Oben/unten/rechts/links im Bild ist ein(e)/gibt es ein(e)(n) . . .
Ein(e) . . . steht/liegt/sitzt, *usw.* . . .
Links/rechts neben, unter, vor, auf, *usw.* dem/der . . ., steht
ein(e) . . ., *usw.*
Weiter links, rechts; höher, tiefer; größer, kleiner, *usw.* als . . .

(Model dictation)
General description

Wir stehen in einem Zimmer und zeichnen, was wir sehen.

Detailed description

Zeichne ein liegendes Rechteck. Dies ist jetzt die Wand des
Zimmers. In der Mitte der Wand ist ein Fenster mit Gardinen.
Draußen scheint die Sonne. Rechts ist eine Tür. Vor dem
Fenster steht ein Tisch. Unter dem Tisch liegt ein Buch. Auf
dem Tisch steht ein Glas. Links neben dem Tisch steht ein
Stuhl. Über dem Stuhl hängt eine Uhr an der Wand. Es ist jetzt
sechs Uhr. Zwischen Tisch und Tür sitzt eine Katze. Sie
schaut zur Tür hin, weil sie nach draußen will.

5 Pictures and picture stories

5.1 Introduction

Pictures and picture stories are widely used for oral practice, and particularly for 'free' speech practice: often, however, learners are asked to describe a picture or re-tell a story which everyone can see, so that there is no information gap which could give their practice real communicative force. This section shows how practice with pictures can be given a clear communicative purpose and result by the introduction of any of the following:

– An information gap, by use of secret choice between several similar pictures, or by dividing pictures between learners (5.4 *Find the picture*, 5.6 *Spot the differences*, 5.7 *Split picture stories*).
– An observation gap: learners see the same pictures and must try to recall details, or to recognize differences between them (5.5 *Memory tests*, 5.6 *Spot the differences*).
– An opinion or ideas gap, by the use of incomplete, confusing or ambiguous material (5.7 *Split picture stories*, 5.8 *Strange pictures*).

Most of the activities can be used with controlled, guided or free language. Pictures without texts are useful for practice with communication strategies: see 4.1 *Introduction* to *Communication strategies* for more details, and 4.6 *Picture dictation* for examples.

The activities in this section make demands on learners' powers of observation and recall, or on their imagination and creativity: work with pictures can thus be varied to suit different kinds of learner. The greater confidence and fluency which result from this practice seem to have positive effects on learner performance in any kind of oral test based on pictures.

The *Teaching material* in this section contains language frames and other texts, with references to the appropriate pictures in 5.3 *Visual material*. All these pictures are cross-referenced to activities throughout the book, and may be photocopied.

5.2 General notes on visual material

5.2.1 Finding material

Many textbooks and supplementary school books have suitable visual material. Work with textbook pictures often provides useful introductory, supplementary or revision practice with the language of the associated lessons. The same pictures can also be used quite separately from these lessons, for communicative practice at different levels and with different language items.

Other sources:

a) children's picture books, picture puzzle books and picture games in the FL or mother tongue.

b) Children's pages of newspapers and family magazines, including radio and television guides.

Much of this material is designed to develop young children's language skills, and is thus suitable for non-native beginners of any age, since they are more or less at the level of young children in their use of the FL. If the material is introduced frankly in these terms, beginners of most ages (except adolescents) will use it with both pleasure and profit.

c) Cartoons and picture strips, from comics, (teenage) magazines, newspapers or books, with or without words (which can easily be eliminated or changed with type-out paint such as Tippex).

d) Newspapers, colour supplements and magazines, particularly the advertisements. Specialist magazines on TV or the cinema, etc. are useful for pictures of famous people or dramatic scenes; magazines on hobbies or topics such as cars, geography, photography, sports, etc. are useful for special items.

e) Mail order catalogues, advertising brochures, etc. for pictures of objects.

Many of these sources have pictures or photographs which are not culture-specific, so that mother tongue material can be used. However, FL sources are preferable, for their authentic details – food, drinks, clothes, house interiors, etc.

f) Posters, brochures, maps, slides, films, etc. from travel companies, hotel chains, railways, shipping and air lines, and offices of tourism at home and abroad; national and commercial companies such as post offices, banks, various manufacturers, and from foreign consulates and institutions like *The British Council, L'Institut Français, L'Alliance Français, Intercodes, Inter Nationes, das Goethe Institut* (in most capital cities).

g) Realia: models, toys, toy money, (empty) containers of foreign goods; items such as postcards, travel and other tickets, timetables, theatre programmes, immigration or hotel forms, menus, etc.

All the above can be collected on holidays abroad. Education authorities, schools – and the taxman – may contribute to the cost. You can show friends, colleagues, learners and their parents examples of what is needed and ask them to collect such material when they can. Contacts in the foreign country can also be asked to send tickets, menus, etc. or suitable pages from sources (a) to (e): this is less expensive than sending whole magazines or catalogues.

5.2.2 Making material

a) *Drawings for display*   You or gifted colleagues (from the art department?) and learners can draw or copy pictures for transparencies, posters and flashcards.

Posters are easier to store and to use if they are folded rather than rolled up. The drawing or writing can be designed round the fold marks, to avoid putting important details or letters on a crease.

b) *Copying for display*   If you have an overhead projector, you can trace any pictures directly on to transparencies, making what alterations you wish. An OHP can also be used to make posters or flashcards: the pictures are traced or drawn on a transparency, then projected on to sheets or cards stuck on the wall. Trace the projected outlines on these cards with thick felt-tip pens, and you have your large size copies. The same technique can be used with slides, though photographs are not so easy to trace.

The easiest way to display posters is with plastic adhesives such as Blu-tack, or with crepe sticky tape, if felt- or magnet-boards are not available.

c) *Making handouts*   You, colleagues or learners draw, copy or trace pictures, altering or omitting details as required. (If you are using pictures which may legally be photocopied, details can be changed with Tippex liquid before copying.) Master sheets of drawings can then be duplicated, cut up as necessary and used.

Fresh copies can be made each time the material is used. The advantages are that learners may write or draw on the papers, and keep them in their files as a permanent record of work done; also, there are no storage problems for the teacher. On the other hand, continual copying from masters costs more time and money in the long run; it is impractical with some material (coloured drawings, photographs, etc.); and with other than self-made material or hand-drawn copies, it is usually illegal!

d) *Permanent pictures and sets*   Stick the material on cards with 'magic' sticky tape (the standard sticky tapes dry and peel off) or with transparent plastic film. If you are making several

163

identical sets, mark each one for identification, for example
with differently coloured stripes drawn on the backs of the
papers or cards) and number each card in the set discreetly so
that you and the learners can check if everything is present,
both before and after use.

Cards can then be stored in the classroom or a central area,
in envelopes or folders clearly marked with the names of the
activities, the language items or textbook units, and the levels
for which they can be used. These sets can be used for many
years and in many ways, including use by pairs and groups of
learners at any time as 'fillers' or as alternative work. I mention
this variety of applications, because teachers are too busy to
spend time preparing cards which may be usable just once a
year with one set of learners: in such a case, a master sheet
which can be photocopied when necessary is preferable. (Local
printing companies will often give away off-cuts of card.)

As with drawing pictures, learners and colleagues can help
in preparing visual material for permanent use. Much of it can
be used by all modern and native language teachers, so that
building up a suitable resource centre or library of visual
material can become an inter-departmental project.
Collecting, copying, colouring, labelling, cutting up or
sticking pictures on cards can provide useful projects for
learners at various levels. Parent Teacher Associations can also
be asked to help. Involving learners and parents in this way can
prove particularly motivating: learners like to see material
they have prepared being used in class, and parents like to hear
about it. Learners usually enjoy work with visual handouts or
cards, whether the material is authentic (i.e. not originally
designed for the classroom) or specially prepared by teachers
or fellow-learners.

Booklist 2b lists books and magazines of use to all FL
teachers.

5.3 Visual material

No. 1 *Miscellany*   See 3.2, 3.3, 3.4, 4.6, 5.5, 5.8, 6.4

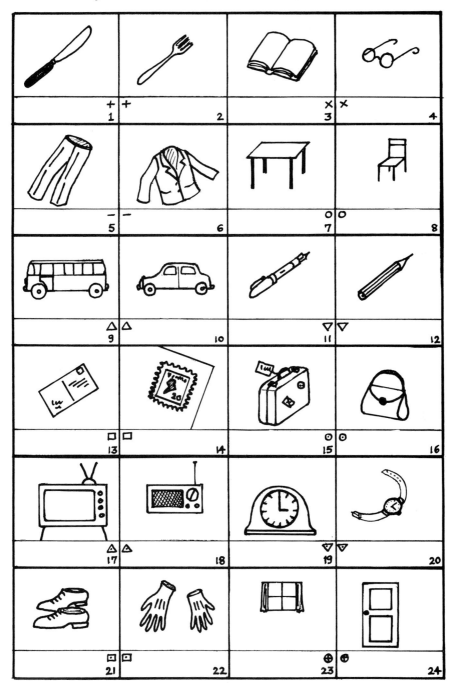

From *Developing Communication Skills* by Pat Pattison
© Cambridge University Press 1987

No. 2 *Families*   See 2.6, 3.6, 4.6, 5.4, 5.5, 5.6, 6.6

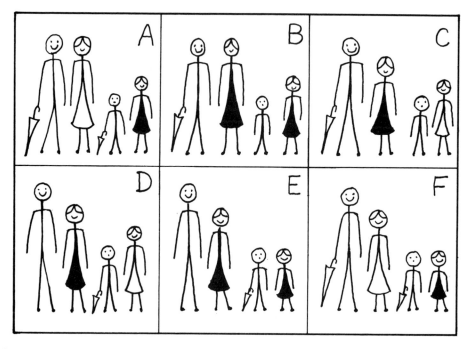

No. 3 *Faces*   See 2.6, 3.6, 4.6, 5.4, 5.5, 5.6, 6.6

No. 4 *Rooms*   See 2.6, 3.6, 4.6, 5.4, 5.5, 5.6, 6.6

No. 5 *Monsters*   See 4.6, 5.5, 5.6, 5.8, 6.6

From *Developing Communication Skills* by Pat Pattison
© Cambridge University Press 1987

No. 6 *The room*   See 4.6, 5.5, 5.6, 6.6

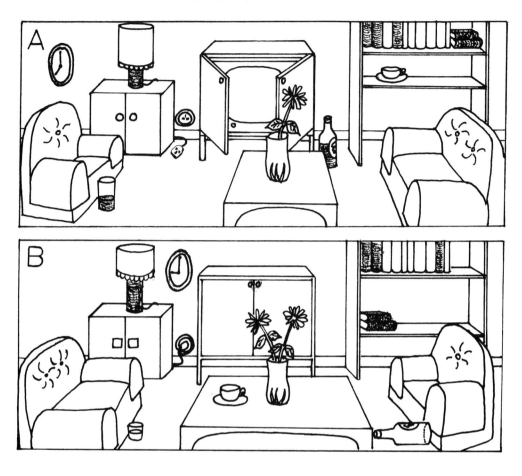

No. 7 *Balconies*   See 2.6, 3.6, 4.6, 5.4, 5.5, 5.6, 5.7, 5.8, 6.6

From *Developing Communication Skills* by Pat Pattison
© Cambridge University Press 1987

No. 8 *Pipe*   See 2.6, 3.6, 4.5, 4.6, 5.4, 5.5, 5.6, 5.7, 5.8, 6.6

No. 9 *Schoolchildren*   See 2.6, 3.6, 4.6, 5.4, 5.5, 5.6, 5.7, 5.8, 6.6

No. 10 *Canary*   See 2.6, 3.6, 4.6, 5.4, 5.5, 5.6, 5.7, 5.8, 6.6

From *Developing Communication Skills* by Pat Pattison
© Cambridge University Press 1987

No. 11   *Bank robbery*   See 2.6, 3.6, 4.5, 4.6, 5.4, 5.5, 5.6, 5.7, 5.8, 6.6

From *Developing Communication Skills* by Pat Pattison
© Cambridge University Press 1987

No. 12 *Mistakes*   See 4.6, 5.5, 5.6, 5.8, 6.6

From *Developing Communication Skills* by Pat Pattison
© Cambridge University Press 1987

No. 13 *Artist*   See 4.6, 5.5, 5.8, 6.6

From *Developing Communication Skills* by Pat Pattison
© Cambridge University Press 1987

No. 14   *Bicycle*   See 2.6, 3.6, 4.6, 5.4, 5.5, 5.6, 5.7, 5.8, 6.6

No. 15   *Wasp*   See 2.6, 3.6, 4.6, 5.4, 5.5, 5.6, 5.7, 5.8, 6.6

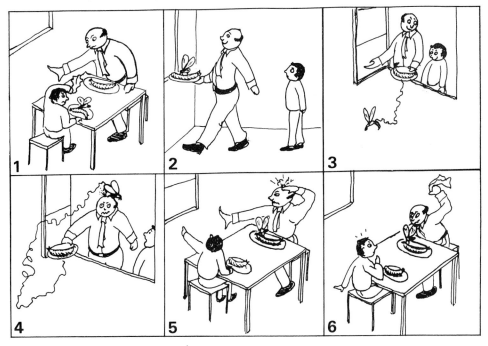

From *Developing Communication Skills* by Pat Pattison
© Cambridge University Press 1987

5.4 Find the picture
Retrouvez l'image
Das richtige Bild finden

Basic gap   Information and observation gap, based on secret choice
Aim   To describe pictures for identification; to identify pictures from a description
Language   Controlled, guided or free, with any communication strategies
Preparation and material   Sets of similar pictures on display or handouts, or in textbook; language frame on display or handouts for controlled practice

Stage 1 E,I (5 minutes)

Team   Describe one of the pictures from the set and ask learners to signal when they recognise it, and then to identify the picture by its number or letter (for purely receptive practice), or by describing its position: *It's the middle picture in the top row*; or by adding more details to your description. They score points if correct; to discourage them from guessing too quickly, take off points for wrong identifications. Learners can act as referees (deciding who signalled first) and scorers. An imaginative introduction adds interest. For example, with No. 3 *Faces* from 5.3, you might say:
One of these men is wanted by the police – listen to the description and then identify him, etc.

Stage 2 E,I (5 minutes)

Team/group/pair   Learners take it in turns to describe pictures for the others to recognise, using the language frame. They should try to organise their descriptions so that the others cannot identify the picture too quickly.

Stage 3 E,I,A (15 minutes)

Team/group/pair   As above, without a language frame. Level I and A learners can use more complicated pictures or photographs. For example, a set of magazine photographs showing the same person displaying different emotions, elicits language like: *He's looking surprised and a little bit worried in this picture*, rather than the simpler: *He has dark hair and glasses.*

Variant 1 Yes/No questions

One person chooses a picture and the others ask *Yes/No* questions to identify it.

Variant 2 Memory test

You or a learner can describe one of the pictures before the set is shown; other learners must retain the information long enough to recognize the picture when they see it.

Variant 3 Find the person

(Without pictures) Learners write down a few facts about themselves: *I've got dark hair, I live in . . ., I like swimming*, etc. The papers are mixed up, redistributed and read out in class to see how many of the writers can be identified.

   See 2.6 *What are we talking about?* and 3.6 *Find your partners* for other practice based on sets of similar material.

Finding and making material

See 5.2 *General notes*. Picture sets can be specifically made for use with a language frame. To make a set of, for example, six similar pictures, list those items to be changed in each picture, as shown below (based on No. 2 *Families*):

1 Girl taller   (boy taller)
2 Woman in black dress   (white dress)
3 Man taller   (woman as tall)
4 Boy with umbrella   (without umbrella)
5 Girl in black dress   (white dress)
6 Man with umbrella   (without umbrella)

and fill these in on the pictures A to F as shown in the grid:

The blank squares have the items listed in brackets above. The number of items, and of pictures, can be extended.

	Picture					
	A	B	C	D	E	F
	1	1	1	1		
		2	2	2	2	
			3	3	3	3
	4			4	4	4
	5	5			5	5
	6	6	6			6

This system helps you to check that you have not produced any identical pictures in the set.

   Picture stories and some magazine advertisements often contain similar picture sets.

175

Teaching material

ENGLISH *Find the picture*

Language frame for No. 2 Families
(*Present continuous;* carry, wear; *Comparatives*)

The man (and) the boy	is / isn't	carrying	an umbrella (umbrellas)
The woman (and) the girl	(are both)	wearing	a black dress (black dresses)

The man / woman	is	taller than	the woman / man
boy / girl	isn't	as tall as	the girl / boy

Description for No. 11 Bank robbery

There are three people in this picture: a woman and two men. The men are holding guns. One of them is a policeman. The other one must be a bank robber because he is holding a bag. He is also holding the woman – she has dropped her bag. (4)

FRANÇAIS *Retrouvez l'image*

Language frame for No. 3 Faces
(*Verbs, affirmative and negative;* pas de; *Direct object pronoun; Past tense can be used:* L'homme que j'ai vu avait . . . *etc.*)

Cet homme	porte	une cravatte blanche/noire
	a	une moustache
	porte	des lunettes
	n'a pas	de moustache
	ne porte pas	de lunettes
(il)	est / n'est pas	chauve
	sourit / ne sourit pas	

Cet homme (il)	nous regarde / ne nous regarde pas

Description for No. 15 Wasp

> Un homme et un petit garçon sont à table. Dans chaque assiette il y a une saucisse et sur l'une des saucisses, il y a une grosse guêpe. L'homme a le bras droit tendu; il a la main gauche sur la tête. (5)

DEUTSCH *Das richtige Bild finden*

Language frame for No. 4 Rooms
(prepositions with dative; accusative)

Die Tür Das Fenster Der Tisch Der Stuhl	ist	rechts neben links neben vor hinter	dem Fenster der Tür dem Tisch
Der Mann	steht		
Die Katze	sitzt	auf	dem Stuhl
Die Uhr	hängt	über	

Die Katze	sitzt	zwischen	dem Tisch und dem Stuhl
Die Uhr	hängt		dem Fenster und der Tür
Der Mann	legt	einen Brief auf	den Tisch

Description for No. 15 Wasp

> Ein Vater und sein Sohn stehen vor einem Fenster. Der Vater hält einen Teller mit einer Wurst in der Hand. Eine Wespe fliegt gerade von der Wurst hoch. Der Vater zeigt zufrieden darauf. (3)

5.5 Memory tests
Epreuves de mémorisation
Gedächtnisübungen

Basic gap	Observation gap, based on information first shared, then split
Aim	To recall as much information as possible
Language	Controlled, guided or free, with any communication strategies
Preparation and material	Minimal – selecting picture from textbook, or putting picture on display or handouts; language frames or model questions on display for controlled or guided practice

Stage 1   E,I,A (5 minutes)

Class/team   Learners study a picture or photograph for a few minutes; then it is removed or concealed and they answer simple *Yes/No* questions (for receptive practice) or *What/where/how many*, etc. questions, about what they have just seen.

Stage 2   E,I,A (10 minutes)

Team   Learners study a picture and ask for any language items they may need (using communication strategies if possible); these items can be added to any guided language on display. Team A prepare questions. The picture is then concealed from the other team(s): for example, they turn over their books or handouts, or turn their backs to the picture; or the picture is handed to team A, or positioned so that only team A can see it. Team A members take turns to ask the other team(s) questions, and points are scored for correct answers.

Stage 3   E,I,A (5 minutes)

Group/pair   Learners study a picture in their textbooks or on handouts, then some cover the picture while their partners ask them questions about it.

Variant 1 Describing things

Learners answer questions from you or classmates about things in the classroom: either behind them or temporarily concealed (or learners close their eyes while answering). Examples:
How many pictures are there on the wall behind you?
(Of objects arranged on the desk and then covered):
Is the ruler on or in the book?

Variant 2 Describing people

One or more learners are observed closely by the others. They then move out of sight, but not hearing, of their classmates (behind blackboard, to back of room, etc.). You or the learners themselves ask questions about their appearance:
Am I wearing a watch?
What colour are John's shoes? etc.
If this is done in groups or pairs, partners simply turn their backs and ask each other questions about their own appearance.

Changing pairs   All or some of the learners move round the class observing each other. At a given signal they stand back to back with the nearest person(s), and describe or answer questions about each other's appearance. If some learners are still seated, they can also ask questions of those who are standing back-to-back.

Variant 3 Describing actions

A group of learners prepare a brief dramatic mime or sketch (e.g. any crime from picking pockets to murder, or based on textbook material, etc.), if necessary as homework. They act it out in class and then move out of sight while their classmates try to recall as much as they can of their appearance, actions and words in answer to questions from you or the actors.

If available, short scenes from videos or films can be used in this way; you or learners ask questions about them.

See 5.4 *Find the picture, Variant 2*, and 5.6 *Spot the differences, Variant 4* for other memory tests. See 4.5 *Silent film* for other practice in describing actions.

Finding and making material

Any pictures with clear details can be used, such as those in 5.3, selected according to level and the language you wish to practise (including pictures with cultural content, like maps of a foreign country or city).

To demonstrate various possibilities, *Teaching material* ENGLISH has examples of questions to be used with any picture, FRANÇAIS has a question frame based on a puzzle picture, and DEUTSCH has a question frame based on a set of picture cards. Material like that in *Teaching material* FRANÇAIS for 4.6 *Picture dictation, Variant 2* can also be used as a memory test (with cultural content).

Variant 3: you can adapt scripts from *Teaching material* in 4.5 *Silent film*.

For more detailed treatment of *Variants 1* and *2*, see Maley and Duff 1978 and 1982, in *Booklist* 2a.

Teaching material

ENGLISH *Memory tests*

Model questions
(*Present tense*, Yes/No *questions*)

Can you see a/any . . . in the picture?
Is/are there a/any . . . in the picture?
Is there anything/anybody in/on . . . *etc.*?
Is the . . . in/on . . ., *etc.* the . . .?
        . . . doing/wearing, *etc.* . . .?
        . . . bigger/smaller, *etc.* than the . . .?

(*Past tense*, Wh- *questions*)

How many . . . did/could you see in the picture?
How many . . . were there in the picture?
What was/were the . . . doing/wearing, *etc.*?
What colour was/were the . . .?
Where was/were the . . .?
Who was/were . . .?
Which . . . was/were in/on, *etc.* . . .?
Which . . . was/were doing/wearing, *etc.* . . .?

FRANÇAIS *Epreuves de mémorisation*

Question frame based on No. 12 Mistakes

Qu'est ce qui ne va pas avec –
la mouche?   le poisson?   l'oiseau?
l'animal devant le téléviseur?   le téléviseur?
les chaussures de l'homme?   le livre?
la cafetière?   le calendrier?   les rideaux?
le tapis devant la fenêtre?   la pendule? *etc.*

DEUTSCH *Gedächtnisübungen*

Question frame, based on any arrangement of pictures from No. 1 Miscellany
(*General vocabulary, prepositions with dative or accusative*)
1 *Dative:* See frame below.
2 *Accusative:* Habe ich den/die/das . . . links/rechts neben, *usw.* den/die/das . . .
gelegt? (*adapt frame below*)

Ist	der Tisch/Stuhl	rechts/links neben	dem Stuhl/Tisch?
	die Gabel/Jacke	über	der Jacke/Gabel?
	das Messer/Buch	unter	dem Buch/Messer?

5.6   Spot the differences
Relevez les différences
Unterschiede finden

Basic gap Observation gap based on shared information
Aim To find all the differences between two pictures
Language Guided and free, with any communication strategies
Preparation and material Minimal if textbook material is used; pairs of similar pictures in textbook, or on display or handouts; skeleton phrases and vocabulary on display or handouts, for guided practice

Stage 1   E,I,A (2 minutes)

Class Name a few differences between the pictures, to demonstrate the language used.

Stage 2   E,I (5 minutes)

Team Teams take it in turns to name differences, with the help of guided language. Allow consultation between team members and encourage them to use communication strategies to acquire any new language items they need.

Examples from practice

1 Level E learners of English, working with pictures from No. 2 *Families* in 5.3. The class had not yet studied comparatives, so were saying: *The boy is big but the girl is small*, etc. until one learner tried borrowing from his mother tongue (very similar to English on this point):
*In the first picture the man is – bigger, but in the second picture, he is – *even big as the woman.*
The teacher wrote *bigger than* and *as big as* on the board and other learners immediately took up the new pattern in describing differences.
2 Level I learners using No. 6 *The room* had named all the most easily expressed differences; they now used paraphrase and gesture to score extra points.
   L: *In the first picture, the lamp is – lighted. In the second pciture, it's not lighted.*
   T: *How do you know?*
   L: *The electricity – in the wall – the electric cable – it's not in the wall – between the television and the cupboard – how do you call that?*

181

T: *What do you call this thing?* (Pointing to picture on display.) *A plug* (Wrote *plug* on board.) *So you mean the lamp isn't plugged in?*

L: *Yes, it isn't plugged in.* (Learner won his point.)

Stage 3   E,I,A (10 minutes)

Team   As above, without guided language.

Group/pair   Learners note all the differences they can, in writing if necessary, within a time limit. Then groups report in turn, those with the shortest lists beginning. The winners are those with differences no one else noticed. Pictures with at least ten differences are needed.

Variant 1 Split pictures

Each half of the class, group or pair is given one of the two pictures on handouts. Without looking at each other's pictures, they must exchange information to find all the differences between them.

Variant 2 Compare and contrast

Half the learners name the differences between two pictures, while the other half name the similarities, to see which group runs out of comments first. Learners sometimes go to extravagant lengths in finding (negative) similarities.

Example from practice

Level A class working in pairs:

L1: *The first woman is blonde, but the other one has black hair.*

L2: *Yes, but neither of them is bald!*

If they cannot see each other's pictures, learners try to find the differences and similarities by exchanging information as in *Variant 1*.

Variant 3 Personal comparisons

In pairs, learners try to find at least three similarities and three differences between them, e.g. in likes and dislikes, habits, hobbies, possessions, etc. and then report these to the class.

See 1.3 *Secret choice I, Variant 1* for simpler practice with given or personal information, and 1.5 *Hunt the answer* or 3.6 *Find your partners, Variant 1* for more extensive practice with personal information.

Variant 4 Spot the changes

With visual material Show two sets of material with a time interval. Examples:
– The first picture is removed or covered before the second is shown.
– Classroom objects, models or picture cards are shown in one arrangement then concealed while items are removed, added, or changed in position.
– The arrangement of the classroom is changed in minor ways between lessons, and learners are warned in advance to look out for all the differences.
– Two or three learners stand in front of the class for a moment then go out and alter details of their appearance – removing or exchanging scarves, jewellery, glasses; changing their hair; even standing in a different position when they return to the class.
– A group mimes a short scene and repeats it with changes (see suggestions in 4.5 *Silent film*).

Learners may now use the past tense in describing the first presentation, and present, perfect or future tenses in describing the second. Examples (based on No. 10 *Canary* in 5.3):
The canary was asleep, now it's awake/it's woken up.
I think the cat's going to eat/will have eaten the canary in the second picture.

Prepare simple language frames, or refer learners to textbook material, to encourage them to use the desired patterns.

With spoken or written material You or learners tell a story or act a dialogue. After an interval of a few minutes or even a whole lesson, depending on level, this is repeated with some changes which other learners or teams can gain points for spotting. Example (based on the story in *Teaching material* FRANÇAIS, *Variant 4*):
Learner 1: *No, she wasn't run over by a bus.* (Wins a point.)
Teacher/story-teller: *Right. Can anyone say what it was?*
Learner 2: *It was a lorry.* (Wins a second point.)
(6.6 *What's wrong?* gives further suggestions for organising this kind of activity.)

See 3.6 *Find your partners* and 5.4 *Find the picture* for simpler practice in describing pictures. 5.5 *Memory tests, Variants 1, 2 and 3* give simpler practice in remembering pictures or actions: 6.6 *What's wrong?* is a more challenging exercise in correcting a narrative.

Finding and making material

Many textbooks contain pictures designed for this activity, or have picture stories or illustrations with dialogues from which two similar pictures can be used. Such pictures can often be used long before or after studying the associated lesson units, since the language and the communication strategies used will be adapted to or reflect the learners' level (see examples in stage 2).

See sources (a) to (f) in 5.2.1 *Finding material*: many newspapers and comics have 'Spot the difference' puzzles (note that these are often too detailed for *Variant 1*). 'Before and after' advertisements are useful. You can also compare and contrast objects or people in the same picture: e.g. two models in a fashion photograph. See also 5.2.2 *Making material*: you or the learners can trace and alter any clear line drawings from a textbook or other source (e.g. cartoons) and use these in association with the original pictures; or you can draw your own pairs of simple pictures. 4.6 *Picture dictation* supplies many such pairs (and see 5.3 No. 5 *Monsters*).

Variant 1: adapt question frames from 5.5 *Memory tests* if required.

Variant 2: only pictures or photographs with a general resemblance are needed: two (groups of) people, two rooms, two street scenes, etc.

Variant 4: for visual material, select any two similar pictures from Nos. 2 to 11 in 5.3, according to the level of the class. For spoken or written material, take stories or dialogues from the textbook or any source or write your own, and change items for the second version. These should be significant, not trivial details, as the learners should concentrate on the main message of the text or dialogue.

Teaching material gives skeleton phrases for the basic activity and *Variant 2*; you can provide other guided language (patterns or lexis), depending on the pictures chosen and the learners' level. FRANÇAIS has a sample text for *Variant 4*, with changes in brackets.

Teaching material

ENGLISH *Spot the differences*

In the first picture, . . . but in the second picture . . .
The . . . in the first picture is/are . . ., but in the second picture he/she/it/they . . .

There's/are . . . in the first picture, but there isn't/aren't in the second; there's/there are only . . . in the second.

Variant 2 Compare and contrast

(*See above for contrasts*)

Both the . . . are (have, *etc.*) . . .
They're both (they've both, *etc.*) . . .
Neither of the . . . is (has, *etc.*) . . .
There's/there are . . . in both the pictures.
There isn't a/any (aren't any) . . . in either of the pictures.

FRANÇAIS *Relevez les différences*

(*Skeleton phrases*)

Sur la première image . . ., mais sur la deuxième . . .
Il y a . . . sur la première image, mais sur la deuxième il n'y en a pas (il n'y a que) . . .
Celui/celle-ci est (a, fait, *etc.*). . . . mais l'autre/celui/celle-là . . .

Variant 2 Comparaisons et contrastes

(*See above for contrasts*)

Les deux sont (ont, font, *etc.*) . . .
Ils/elles sont, *etc.* . . ., tous les deux/toutes les deux.
Il y a un(e)/des . . . sur les deux images.
Il n'y a pas de . . . sur les deux images.
Ni l'un(e) ni l'autre est (a, fait, *etc.*) . . .
Ils/elles ne sont pas (n'ont pas, ne font pas, *etc.*) . . ., ni l'un(e) ni l'autre.

Variant 4 Qu'est-ce qui est changé?

Un jour, dans son petit village, Mme Legrand traverse la rue et est renversée par un camion (un autobus) qui passe. On porte la blessée jusque chez elle (dans un magasin tout près) et on fait venir le médecin qui se met tout de suite à l'examiner (la frotter): d'abord la tête, puis les bras (les yeux) et ensuite les jambes. Pendant tout ce temps, la malade ne bouge pas (crie très fort). Enfin le médecin lève les yeux et dit: – C'est très grave. – Oh, ma pauvre femme (soeur), s'écrie M. Legrand, et il se met à pleurer. – Oui, continue le médecin, – c'est vraiment très grave. Elle est morte (elle va mourir). – Mais à ces mots, Mme Legrand ouvre les yeux et crie: – Mais non, je ne suis pas morte! – Mais tais-toi imbécile, répond son mari, le médecin sait beaucoup mieux que toi (si tu es morte, je ne dois pas payer le médecin).

DEUTSCH *Unterschiede finden*

Auf dem ersten Bild, gibt es (ist) . . ., aber auf dem zweiten gibt es (ist) . . .

Der/die/das . . . auf dem ersten Bild ist/sind . . ., aber der/die/das auf dem zweiten Bild ist/sind . . .

Es gibt . . . auf dem ersten Bild, aber nicht auf dem zweiten; aber auf dem zweiten gibt es nur . . .

Variant 2 Übereinkünfte und Unterschiede

(*See above for contrasts*)

Auf beiden Bildern gibt es . . .

Beide . . . sind (haben, machen, *usw.*) . . .

Beide sind, *usw.* . . .

Die . . . sind, *usw.* beide . . .

Kein(er)(e)(es) von beiden ist, *usw.* . . .

Kein(er)(e)(es) der . . . ist, *usw.* . . .

Auf keinem von beiden Bildern gibt es . . .

Weder . . . noch. . . ist/sind, *usw.* . . .

Weder auf dem ersten noch auf dem zweiten Bild gibt es (ist/sind) . . .

5.7 Split picture stories
Histoires éclatées
Bildergeschichten zusammenstellen

Basic gap	Information, opinion and ideas gap based on split information
Aim	To make up a story based on pictures described by different people
Language	Guided and free, with any communication strategies
Preparation and material	Pictures from picture stories on separate handouts, posters or OHP transparencies; skeleton phrases on display for guided practice

Stage 1   E,I,A (10 minutes)

Class Without showing them, describe frames from a short picture story in the wrong order; it is important to describe each picture as if you cannot see the others in the sequence (see examples in *Teaching material*). Invite learners to ask further questions, and to consult each other before making suggestions about the order of the pictures and the story or stories that could be based on them. For purely receptive practice, learners can do this in their mother tongue. Otherwise, help them with the phrases they need for discussion and write these on the board to be copied and used in stage 2 or 3. Finally, the learners see the original picture story on display, or on a handout (which can be passed round the class) or in their textbooks. If it differs greatly from their own suggestions, they can discuss how and why: did they misunderstand or forget details in the descriptions, or not ask enough questions about them, or were the descriptions themselves faulty? Can the pictures be interpreted in different ways? Which version(s) do they prefer?

Stage 2   E,I,A (10 minutes)

Class Each group is given one frame from a picture story, and they describe their pictures in turn to the rest of the class, following your example in stage 1, and using communicative strategies when necessary. Key words from each description can be written on the board as reminders. After this, the groups ask each other for further information about their pictures, and discuss in what order(s) they might be arranged, before suggesting one or more stories based on the information they have exchanged. Then they see the original picture story, which may lead to further discussion, as in stage 1.

   With advanced classes, have two or three picture stories passed round the class so that learners also have to decide which pictures belong to which story.

Stage 3   I,A (15 minutes)

Group Each member of a group has one or two frames from a picture story and must describe it/them to the other group members. Questions and discussion proceed as in stages 1 and 2. Learners must not show their pictures before the reporting stage. Without this rule, learners tend to look at partners' pictures as soon as they have an idea for a story – after which oral communication stops as they move the pictures round on the desk to find the best order! (Groups who finish before others can start writing down their stories.) When all or most of the groups are ready, they can report their stories to the class, and the pictures can be shown (or passed round the groups). If all groups have the same picture story, the following procedure helps avoid unnecessary repetition:
– Group members still do not show their pictures to each other.

– One group describes the first picture in their story. Any groups who have different interpretations, or who have chosen different first pictures, give their descriptions; groups are encouraged to discuss the differences.

– This continues frame by frame until each group has had at least one chance to speak.

– Finally, each group sees all the pictures; encourage further discussion within and between groups.

Examples from practice

Stories by mixed level French groups, working with No. 14 *Bicycle* in 5.3 (summarised and translated).

1 *A fat man buys a bicycle to lose weight* ('scales' was conveyed by paraphrase and later supplied by the teacher). *But his dog is too small to run with the bicycle. He likes his little dog so he sells the bike.*

2 (Story begins in same way) . . . *but he accidentally runs over his little dog. He gets off the bike and sees the dog lying dead in the road. In the last picture he's sitting with the dead dog on his knee. He's very sad and he wants to sell the bike.*

Variant 1 Missing pictures

Picture stories can be used with one frame missing (usually the last one). Learners exchange as much information as they can, and then exchange ideas about what the story might be and how it might be completed. For example, omit the last frame of No. 11 *Bank robbery*. This variant can be combined with both the basic activity and *Variant 2*, below.

Variant 2 Mixed picture stories

Learners see a picture story in the wrong order (on display or handouts) and exchange ideas, report and discuss various possible versions of the story.

Examples from practice

Level I learners' interpretations of No. 9 *Schoolchildren* (summarised):

1 *Boy and girl go home from school together every day. Boy falls in love with girl, starts carrying her bag. They get married.*

2 (starts as above) . . . *Then they pretend to get married. After that, the boy carries the girl's schoolbag.*

3 *Boy loves girl and carries her schoolbag. They get married. After that, she has to carry her own bag!*

Variant 3 Predicting pictures

If the picture frames can be displayed one by one (e.g. on posters, slides or transparencies), pairs or groups of learners can be asked, with each frame, to describe what they see, to speculate about the situation, and to predict how the picture story may continue. The final frame can be omitted and learners asked to discuss and report their ideas for the full story. (Suitable films or video can also be shown bit by bit for discussion.)

See 5.8 *Strange pictures, Variant 2* for similar practice with single pictures; and 6.5 *Incomplete stories, Variant 1* for similar practice with texts.

Finding and making material

See 5.3 *Visual material* for all the picture stories referred to above. The descriptions of these pictures for stage 1, in *Teaching material* below, have numbers in brackets next to each paragraph: these suggest the order in which you can read the paragraphs for stage 1.

See 5.2.1, sources (a) to (d) and the sources of visual material in *Booklist* 2b; of these, Sempé and *Mad* magazine often have longer picture stories which are suitable for stage 2. For stage 3, it is often possible to omit one or two pictures from a longer story, without affecting its comprehensibility, so that you have enough pictures for groups of four or five learners.

Teaching material

ENGLISH *Split picture stories*

Stage 1 No. 7 Balconies

(1) There's a balcony on the left and a balcony on the right. Between them you can see the sun shining. There's a man on the left-hand balcony. He's looking at a woman on the right-hand balcony. She's got a packet of cigarettes (*or, to elicit more questions:* She's got a small box or packet) in her hands.

(3) There are two balconies, one on the left and one on the right. A man's leaning over the left-hand balcony, and he's stretching out his arm towards a woman who's on the right-hand balcony. I think he's holding something in his hand – it's very small. The woman's holding a cigarette in her mouth and looking at the man.

(2) There's a very tall building on the left, with three balconies, one under the other, and the same on the right.

A woman's sitting on the top balcony on the right. She's smoking a cigarette. A man's falling or diving, head first, between the two buildings – he's near the bottom of the picture.

Stage 2
(*Skeleton phrases*)

In my/this picture, there's/there are/I can see . . . (I think) . . . could/might be . . .
No, it/they can't be . . ., because . . .
I don't think . . ., because . . .

FRANÇAIS *Histoires éclatées*

Stage 1 No. 8 Pipe

(3) Sur cette image on voit le coin d'une maison avec, à gauche, une fenêtre d'où sort beaucoup de fumée. Il y a un homme debout, à droite. Il regarde la fumée et il semble paniqué.

(2) À gauche, on voit la fenêtre d'une maison. On dirait que la maison est en train de brûler. Beaucoup de fumée sort de la fenêtre. Par celle-ci, un homme est en train de jeter de l'eau à l'intérieur de la maison.

(1) Là, je vois un homme à la fenêtre d'une maison. Il est tout mouillé. Il tient une pipe à la main. La pipe fume un peu. Il jette un regard furieux à un homme qui est devant la maison et qui tient un seau à la main.

Stage 2
(*Skeleton phrases*)

Sur mon/cette image, il y a/je vois . . .
Je crois que . . .
Il me semble que . . .
Il se peut que . . .
X pourrait être . . .
Ça doit être . . .
Non, ce n'est pas possible, parce que . . .
Je ne crois pas que (+ *subjunctive*) . . . parce que . . .

DEUTSCH *Bildergeschichten zusammenstellen*

Stage 1 No. 10 Canary

(2) Auf diesem Bild steht ein Vogelkäfig auf einem Tisch. Darin sitzt ein Kanarienvogel. Ich glaube, er schläft. Die Augen sind zu. Rechts vom Käfig, über dem Tischrand, sieht man den Kopf und die zwei Pfoten einer Katze. Sie schaut zum Vogelkäfig.

(1) Ich sehe hier einen Käfig mit einem ängstlichen Kanarienvogel – er flattert im Käfig herum und schaut zur Katze, die vor dem Käfig sitzt und eine Pfote auf die Tür des Käfigs legt.

(3) Auf diesem Bild sehe ich einen großen Vogelkäfig mit einem sehr dicken Vogel. Die Tür des Käfigs ist offen. Der Vogel hat Haare oder so etwas im Schnabel.

Stage 2
(Skeleton phrases)

Auf meinem/diesem Bild ist . . .
Es könnte . . . sein
Nein, das geht nicht, weil . . .
Ich glaube nicht, daß . . ., weil . . .

5.8 Strange pictures
Images étranges
Merkwürdige Bilder

Basic gap Ideas and opinion gap based on shared information
Aim To make up explanations, stories or role-plays based on odd or ambiguous pictures
Language Free, with any communication strategies
Preparation and material Minimal – selecting suitable pictures for display or from textbook; or putting pictures on handouts

Stage 1 E,I,A (5 minutes)

Class Show or pass round a picture and provide an interpretation of it as an example (see *Example from practice* in stage 3).

Stage 2 E,I,A (15 minutes)

Class Invite learners to exchange ideas about a picture in small groups, in response to suitable questions. Examples:
What can you/do you think you can see in the picture? Where is this scene/might this scene be? Who are the people in the picture? What are they doing/saying? How do they feel? Why? What happened before this? What's happening now? What may happen next?
The groups report back and compare their ideas, while you help them with language. Make it clear that the aim is to make use of their own imagination to create a story around the picture, not to guess the – often far more banal – original meaning or context; though you can tell them this after they have given their own ideas.

Stage 3   I,A (15 minutes)

Group/pair   Learners choose one of the displayed pictures or handouts, and make up an explanation, story or sketch expressing their interpretation. Choice is recommended because not everyone is inspired by the same picture; also, the reporting stage is more interesting if all the reports are quite different (though they may still be different even if two or more groups happen to choose the same picture). Finally, groups report back or act out their ideas, showing their picture at whatever point is appropriate. If facilities are available, learners can record their stories or sketches on tape and play these back in class.

Example from practice

'Radio play' on tape by a level A group (summarised):
Once upon a time, there was a planet inhabited by cups, plates, teapots, etc. One day, a plate fell in love with a cup. They got married and had a little flying saucer. One day the saucer ran away from home and travelled all round the galaxy. After many adventures, (and some wonderful sound-effects!) *he landed in John's garden. John caught him, put him in a cage, and took this photograph of him.* (and at this point the group displayed a photograph of a small painted plate in a birdcage; this was from a Wedgwood advertisement claiming that the birds painted on their china were so real you'd want to cage them.)

Variant 1 Combining pictures

Learners can choose two or more pictures and make up stories or sketches combining them, or can base a story on a random selection of pictures.

Example from practice

Story by a level A group (summarised) with pictures of a wine glass, a rose and a passport:
This passport belongs to a man who had to travel and leave the woman he loved. Before he left she gave him this rose. On the anniversary of their parting he always drinks a glass of wine to her memory.
See 3.3 *Duets, Variant 1* for simpler practice in linking items.

Variant 2 Unclear pictures

Use a picture which is incomplete or imperfectly seen: learners guess what it may be, or discuss and report what they think they saw or how they interpret the image. Example:
– Start drawing something line by line on the board and let

learners guess what it is going to be, for vocabulary practice on the lines of: *It's a bird – it's a plane – it's Superman!*

It is a positive advantage in this activity if you are not a very good artist! Learners can also take turns at drawing pictures for others to guess.

Show learners a picture very rapidly, or out of focus. Examples:
– Picture, OHP transparency or slide is shown for a split second (or shown out of focus). The time of exposure (or sharpness of focus) is increased slightly each time the picture is shown (or as the discussion continues).
– Picture, OHP transparency or slide is unmasked bit by bit.

Between each showing of the picture, learners discuss their ideas of what it might be. You or a learner can write key words from these suggestions on the board.

Example from practice

Level A (adult) groups working with OHP transparency shown bit by bit No. 13 *Artist*, in 5.3:
(Section 1 uncovered) *They're schoolboys looking at something in the street. They look happy – the teacher is running into school, late! They're men looking at something in the street – an accident? There is a circus parade, etc. They're people looking into a room; there is a party? A fight? etc.*
(Section 2 uncovered) *They're looking out of a house at the man in the street. He's got something in his hand. Is he a window cleaner? He's got long hair; is he a musician playing a guitar? They're looking into a room where a musician is playing – or singing. The man is an artist, he's painting something. He's teaching somebody to dance.*
(Section 3 uncovered) *They're looking into a room where an artist is painting something funny* – various suggestions including – *he's painting a nude.*
(Section 4 uncovered) *Yes, he's painting a nude.* (One group notes that the canvas is still invisible and suggests that he's painting the onlookers.)
(Section 5 uncovered) They were right!

The above suggestions work best with large cartoons, photographs or slides, and pictures showing unusual or striking situations or angles.

See also the variants to 5.7 *Split picture stories*

Variant 3 Strange sounds

Use tapes of short ambiguous dialogues or series of sound effects – made by yourself or learners – so that learners can discuss and report their interpretations of what they have heard; or use a suitable enigmatic soundtrack from a film or video, if available, without the pictures so that learners must try to reconstruct what is happening.

See 2.6 *What are we talking about?* for simpler practice, and 4.5 *Silent film, Variant 3* for the reversed use of video or film: showing the pictures without the soundtrack for interpretation.

Finding and making material

You can choose pictures which will encourage practice with particular vocabulary or tenses: *What has/may have happened? What's been done to . . .? What's going to/may happen?* Some textbooks have suitable pictures; and see the books mentioned in *Booklist* 2b, the section on visual aids. See also 5.2.1, where source (d) is most useful – magazine advertisements and photographs from photography magazines. Learners will often bring suitable pictures to challenge their classmates.

Variant 1: Besides the above sources, use any combination of pictures from No. 1 *Miscellany*, in 5.3.

Variant 2: See the above sources and pictures in 5.3; take any suitable cartoons, drawings, or photographs of dramatic events, selected according to learners' level.

Variant 3: see Maley and Duff 1975 and 1979 for tapes of sound effects; Maley and Duff 1978, and Mortimer 1985 (all in *Booklist* 2a) have examples of ambiguous dialogues in English, which are brief enough to be quickly translated for other languages.

There are no further examples of teaching material for this activity; model phrases can be adapted from those in *Teaching material* for 5.5 *Memory tests* and 5.7 *Split picture stories*.

See Maley, Duff and Grellet 1980, in *Booklist* 2b for further ideas and examples of work with pictures.

6 Puzzles and problems

6.1 Introduction

In solving the various puzzles and problems in this section, learners have to make guesses, draw on their general knowledge and personal experience, use their imagination, and test their powers of logical reasoning. Different types of learner are therefore likely to find at least one kind of activity in which they can do well.

6.3 *Destination words* offers practice in giving and following directions, with the added motivation that if all the right locations are found, they will spell a word. The language used is clearly relevant to future communicative needs, and the puzzle element permits intensive practice without loss of interest. The incidental spelling and vocabulary practice is also useful!

6.4 *Quizzes* includes various types of guessing games and general knowledge quizzes. A great variety of language items, from prepositions to passive, can be incorporated, as well as knowledge of cultural background and literature. The quiz format gives learners a more convincing reason to speak than a standard school exercise, and the result – whether it is simply finding the right answer, winning 'prizes', or winning points for oneself or one's team – also seems to give more personal satisfaction than the more school-bound result of the teacher's saying *Correct* or giving a mark. See 6.2 below, for general notes on organising quizzes.

In 6.5 *Incomplete stories*, learners try to reconstruct a whole story from the parts they hear. There is both an information and an ideas or opinion gap as learners express their own interpretations of what they heard. This leads to further discussion, and provides more challenging communication practice (both in listening and speaking) than simply asking learners to re-tell a complete story.

In 6.6 *What's wrong?* learners concentrate on finding errors in communication, based on stories or descriptions with deliberate mistakes. This provides welcome opportunities for them to correct the teacher; and also allows the natural liars in the class to demonstrate their talents!

In 6.7 *Logic problems*, each learner is given only part of the information needed to solve the problem, so that everyone can and must contribute the information they hold, and listen to what the others have to say, in order to reach a solution. This is very helpful in dealing both with those learners who are reluctant to speak, and those who are all too ready to dominate the conversation. This activity is based on material used to train discussion skills – listening, turn-taking, etc. – rather than specifically FL skills. However, the relevance to developing communication skills in any language is obvious. Preliminary training in solving logic problems and in discussion techniques can be given in stages 1 and 2. Learners appreciate the chance to learn and practise such skills in and through the FL, instead of simply practising the language in and for itself.

The brief descriptions in 6.8 *What's it all about?* require learners to draw on personal experience to suggest explanations, and to provide further stories for discussion; the variants require imagination and lateral thinking.

See *Booklist* 2c for further ideas and material.

6.2   Quiz organisation

As with so many communication activities, quizzes are most effective when run almost entirely by the learners, acting as question-masters, scorers, time-keepers and referees – while teachers represent the final Court of Appeal. Team work promotes collaboration and co-operation within the group, instead of competition between individual learners. (See p. 28 *Team* for more details.)

The suggestions below increase the chance that all learners will participate in the quiz and co-operate with each other:
– Teams answer strictly in turn, and the question-master decides who has the next turn to answer from each team.
– In large classes, learners who have had a turn or given a correct answer do not get another turn; but they may continue to help other team members with their answers.
– There is a time limit on responses, after which another learner takes a turn.
In over-enthusiastic or unruly classes, you can explain in advance that if the rules are broken or the quiz otherwise disrupted, points will be deducted from the score of the team responsible. I have found this effective when it is regarded by everyone concerned as simply one of the rules of the game, like a penalty in football, and the referee (or teacher) deducts points without stopping the quiz to make any further critical comment. The teams, in fact, usually impose discipline on themselves in such circumstances.

If you wish to stress accurate language use, you can give two points for an answer, one for content, and one for linguistic accuracy. The points may be split between teams. Example:

Shakespeare *is born in 1564 gains one point, and the other team gains the second point for correcting this to *was born.*

In quizzes where learners ask questions, a wrongly-phrased question may mean missing a turn if it cannot be corrected by the speaker or a fellow team member.

Quiz formats   Learners enjoy quizzes based on the format of familiar media shows in their own country – this can go so far as using a bell or buzzer to signal right or wrong answers, *Time's up*, etc., or an elaborate scoring system. Magazine photographs of washing machines, stereos, holidays in the sun, etc. can be given as prizes (or foreign stamps, postcards or brochures if these are available). Example:

Criss cross quiz

A numbered noughts and crosses (tic tac toe) grid is put on the board. Learners from the O and X teams take it in turns to choose a numbered box and to answer a question. If the answer is correct, their symbol goes in that box; if not, it is left blank. Each team aims to fill a complete vertical, horizontal or diagonal line with their own symbol, and to block their opponents.

1	2	3
4	5	6
7	8	9

6.3 Destination words
Mots – objectifs
Zielwörter

Basic gap	Information gap based on secret choice
Aim	To give and follow directions to letters which will spell words
Language	Controlled, guided or free
Preparation and material	Map with letters on display or handout; language frame on display or handouts, or in textbook, for controlled practice

Stage 1   E,I (5 minutes)

Class/team   Give the learners a series of directions to letters on a map, beginning from *Start* each time. If they find and write down these letters correctly, they will spell a word. All the vowels are placed at *Start*, and learners are told when to pick them up

(see examples in *Teaching material*). Points are scored for
identifying the words.

Stage 2 E,I (5 minutes)

Class/team/
group/pair
Learners, preferably working in pairs, choose a word and give
directions to spell it, using a language frame. You can set a
minimum and maximum length for the words, such as three
to six letters.

Stage 3 E,I,A (5 minutes)

Class/team/
group/pair
As in stage 2, without using the language frame.

Variant 1 Alphabet practice

Instead of placing vowels at *Start*, place a group of letters
which cause difficulty: depending on learners' mother tongue
and the FL, these may include A E G H I J R Y, etc. Learners
now have to pronounce and understand the problem letters
correctly, since they cannot discover them simply from their
location.

Variant 2 Anagrams

Directions are given in mixed order, so that learners end up
with letters forming an anagram – TCA instead of CAT. This
has the advantage that learners cannot usually guess the word
in advance, so they have to listen to all the directions very
carefully.

Variant 3 Word-building

Learners do not prepare words in advance. One learner gives
directions from *Start* to a letter. Following learners, each
beginning from *Start*, give directions to a letter which can
continue from those already given, to spell a word. Learners
can challenge each other if they think the letter just given will
not make a word. Example:
The first letters are P H, and the following learner gives directions to
D. The next learner challenges this. Would you accept the challenged
learner's claim that Ph.D. is an acceptable word?
A traditional game has the rule that anyone giving the final

letter of a word must drop out, so learners do their best to think of very long words. Example:
A learner continuing from SECON by adding D tells the next learner to continue; she challenges him, and he wins a point by naming the word SECONDARY – not SECONDS, as plurals are not allowed. SCHOOL would not be allowed either, since this is a separate word.

Speakers of Germanic languages often try to build up combination words like 'secondaryschool', and you may need a good dictionary to check which are possible! Conversely, speakers of other languages can learn to use word-building in German: a learner continuing from REA by adding L has not necessarily completed a word, since SCHULE or POLITIK, etc. can be added.

As this variant requires some thinking ahead, let learners take turns in order, rather than at random.

See 2.5 *Finding the way* for more realistic practice with maps.

Finding and making material

The basic map should be simple, since many people have difficulty following left/right directions even in their mother tongue! The map in *Teaching material* has letters to indicate L(eft) and R(ight). It also has traffic signs which can be used as points of reference: alternatively, add a few named buildings in order to practise *Turn left at the cathedral*, etc. If the textbook has a map with enough buildings or other points of reference, you can ask learners to write letters at each of these points, with extra letters at the starting point, so that directions will be something like:
Take the second road on the right and then take the road between the station and the art gallery. From there take the third road on your right, and take the letter outside the building on your left.

Language frames A, B and C in *Teaching material* can be used together or as alternatives, according to the level. The final sentences are used with all the frames.

Teaching material

Map for Destination words

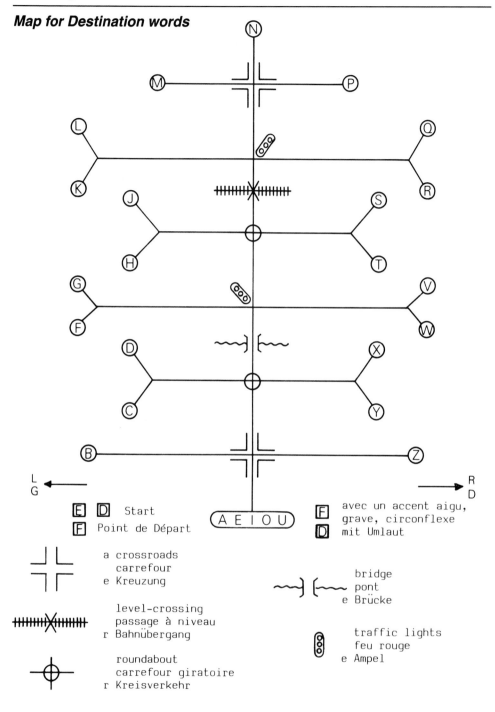

From *Developing Communication Skills* by Pat Pattison
© Cambridge University Press 1987

ENGLISH *Destination words*

(Directions – beginning from START each time)

1 Take the second left and then the first left.   (C)
   Go back to Start and take the letter A.
   Take the fourth right, and then turn right again.   (T)
2 Turn left at the crossroads.   (B)
   Go back to Start and take the letter O.
   Turn right at the first roundabout just before the bridge, and
   then take the first left.   (X)

Language frames

A Take the | first | right | and then turn | left
              | second | left | | right
              | *etc.* |

B Turn | right | at the | first | crossroads | and then | left
          | | | | | take the |
          | left | | second | roundabout | first | right
          | | | | traffic lights | |
          | | | | *etc.* |

C Cross the | level crossing | and then | first | right | and | left
               | | take the | | | turn |
               | bridge | | second | left | | right

+ Go straight on . . .
  Go back to Start and take the letter . . .

From *Developing Communication Skills* by Pat Pattison

FRANÇAIS   *Objectif – mot*

Directions – toujours à partir du POINT DE DÉPART

1 Prenez la première rue à gauche.   (B)
Revenez au Point de départ et prenez la lettre A.
Prenez la quatrième rue à droite, et puis tournez à gauche.   (S)

2 Vous tournez à gauche au premier carrefour giratoire, et puis encore à gauche.   (C)
Revenez au Point de départ et prenez la lettre O.
Vous allez tout droit: vous traversez le passage à niveau et puis vous allez à droite au feu rouge. Prenez ensuite la première rue à gauche.   (Q)

Language frames

A Prenez

la première	rue	à droite	et puis tournez	à gauche
la deuxième		à gauche		à droite
etc.				

B Tournez

à gauche	au premier	carrefour	et puis prenez la	à gauche
à droite	au deuxième	carrefour giratoire feu rouge *etc.*	première rue	à droite

C Traversez

le passage à niveau,	prenez	la première	rue	à gauche,
		la deuxième		à droite,
le pont,				

	et puis tournez	à droite
		à gauche

+ Allez tout droit . . .
Revenez au Point de départ et prenez la lettre . . .

DEUTSCH *Zielwörter*

Anweisungen- immer vom START *aus*

1 Nehmen Sie den Buchstaben U.
Gehen (fahren) Sie immer geradeaus, bis zum Ende der Straße. (N)
(Zurück zum Start) Nehmen Sie die vierte Straße rechts, und dann die erste Straße links. (S)

2 Sie biegen beim ersten Kreisverkehr links ab und nehmen die erste Straße rechts. (D)
Sie gehen (fahren) zurück zum Start und nehmen den Buchstaben A.
Sie gehen (fahren) immer geradeaus. Dabei kommen Sie erst an eine Kreuzung, dann an einen Kreisverkehr, und dann überqueren Sie eine Brücke. Bei der Ampel biegen Sie links ab und gleich danach rechts. (G)

Language frames

A Nehmen Sie

die erste	Straße	rechts,	und dann biegen	rechts ab
die zweite *usw.*		links,	Sie nach	links ab

B Biegen Sie

beim	ersten	Kreisverkehr	links ab,	und dann biegen	rechts ab
bei der	zweiten	Kreuzung Ampel	rechts ab,	Sie nach	links ab

C Überqueren Sie

den Bahnübergang,	nehmen Sie	die erste	Straße
die Brücke,		die zweite	

rechts,	und dann biegen	rechts ab
links,	Sie nach	links ab

+ Gehen (fahren) Sie immer geradeaus . . .
zurück zum Start und nehmen Sie den Buchstaben . . .

From *Developing Communication Skills* by Pat Pattison
© Cambridge University Press 1987

6.4 Quizzes
Quiz
Quiz

Basic gap   Information gap based on secret choice or split information
Aim   To guess the right answer
Language   Guided or free, with any communication strategies
Preparation and material   Minimal – choosing items to be guessed; model questions and replies on display or handouts for guided practice

Stage 1   E,I,A (5 minutes)

Class   Ask learners to choose an object (freely or from a list) and to hold it up or write it on the board, behind you. Ask the class *Yes/No* questions (to demonstrate the kind of language used) until you discover the object – or give up! You can write a few phrases on the board to cover occasions when a simple *Yes/No* answer is inappropriate. Examples:
I can't answer that question – Can you re-phrase that question? – That's not relevant, etc.
Learners can be asked to tell the questioner(s):
You're warm (cold); getting warmer (colder), etc.
Extra elements can be added:
– At level E, you can work with an object in the classroom or in a picture or list: *Here's a picture of a zoo. Which animal am I?*
– At levels I and A, the object need not be visible, and you must be told if it is *abstract* or *concrete*; *animal, vegetable* or *mineral* or some combination of these.
– The answers can be exclusively things (*What is it?*), people (*Who is it?*), places (*Where is it?*) or jobs (*What's my job?*), etc.
– There may be a time limit, or a maximum of twenty questions. Recapitulation questions do not count:
Did you say it was yellow? etc.

Stage 2   E,I (5 minutes)

Class/team/ group/pair   A learner or pair chooses or is given an item to be guessed and classmates or partners try to discover it, with the help of model questions on display. Individuals or teams score points for correct guesses. Those who guessed correctly can choose the next object. Learners sometimes turn this into a vocabulary-listing exercise: *Is it a pen? a book? / Are you a penguin? a giraffe?* To avoid this, you can add a rule that at least

X general questions must be asked before direct guesses are made: *Is it on your desk? / Have you got four legs?* etc. or that points are lost for a direct guess which is wrong. Encourage learners to use communication strategies to acquire the language they need to express their ideas (there are *Examples from practice* in 4.1).

Stage 3   E,I,A (5 minutes)

Class/team/ group/pair   As above, without guided language.

Variant 1 General knowledge quizzes

Collect or make up suitable questions on any topics for yourself or learners to ask. You can choose questions according to the language patterns to be practised, and ask learners to repeat the pattern in their answers. This is unnatural in normal communication, but less so when it is part of the quiz format. At level E or with young learners, *either/or* questions are useful. Examples:

[E] (Passive) *Was Shakespeare born in 1564 or 1864?*
(He was born in) 1564.

[D] (Reflexive verbs) *Setzen wir uns auf einen Tisch oder auf einen Stuhl?*
(Wir setzen uns) auf einen Stuhl.

Questions about dead or living people, past or future events naturally lead to use of past, present or future tenses, and may be combined with the passive. Examples:

Where/when was President Kennedy assassinated?
How many Rocky films have been made?
Where/when will the next Olympic Games be held?

There are further examples in *Finding and making material*.

Variant 2 Language quizzes

Some media quiz games are based on spelling, sorting out scrambled words, idioms or proverbs, completing sentences appropriately, giving or recognising correct definitions, etc., all of which are useful in the language classroom. The quiz format gives such practice more communicative force (in terms of the purpose and result of speech) than when it is presented purely as a language exercise.

See section 1 *Questions and answers* for controlled practice which can form a useful preparation for quizzes. See 2.7 *Interviews, Variant 1, 3.3 Duets, Variant 2,* and 4.2 *Guess the word* for other types of quiz.

205

Finding and making material

You or learners can prepare papers with objects, names, jobs, places, etc. to be guessed. Model questions can be selected according to the learners' level and the kind of language you wish to practise. In *Who is it?* or *What's my job?* quizzes, learners can use the second or third person: *Are you/Do you . . .?* or *Is/Does (this person) . . .? Where is it?* quizzes can be based on a map or picture, the classroom itself, or general knowledge. For level E, objects or picture cards (see 5.3 No. 1 *Miscellany*) can be hidden in the classroom or somewhere near the teacher's desk and can actually be looked for by you or learners in response to guesses, to reinforce the meaning of what is said. If you are using a displayed picture or map, you or a learner can point to the places named. The quiz may concern destinations: *Where is he going/coming from?*; and can be carried out with totally controlled language.

Model questions or language frames for the various types of quiz are divided between the languages in *Teaching material*.

Variant 1: General knowledge quizzes can be adapted to the language and information level of the learners, and based on knowledge of the foreign country and its culture: *Who lives in the White House? What is the capital of Austria?* as well as more general questions: *What is the date of Christmas?* and those concerning the learners' immediate environment: *What song is top in the* (native country) *charts this week? Which street is the town hall in?* etc.

Give the learners a few suggestions like this and ask them to write down possible questions, in the mother tongue if necessary, to give you an idea of the kind of information they possess and which interests them – and to provide a greater selection of material than one person alone can make!

Other sources are quiz and puzzle books, or games and quizzes which are familiar to the learners from the radio or television in their own country (see *Variant 2*, above).

Teaching material

ENGLISH *Quizzes*

What is it?

The tape recorder, my left eyebrow, a helicopter, *etc.*
(*Model questions*)

Is it in this room? Is it (*adjective*)? Is it (*comparative*) than X? Is it made of (*substance*)? Can/could we touch, break, see, hear, drink, eat it, *etc.*? Are there many of these things? Have I/you

got one of these? Would you like to have one? *etc.*
Recapitulation: Did you say there were many of these things?

Who is it?

Gandhi, Princess Diana, Mickey Mouse, myself, *etc.*
(*Model questions*)

> Is this person a man or a woman? Is she alive or dead? Is he a
> character from a book, film, TV programme, *etc.*? Is/was she
> (*nationality*)? Is/was he connected with sport, politics, show
> business, television, the theatre, the cinema, music, literature,
> *etc.*? Does/did she live/work in . . .? Does/did he appear on
> TV, in films, in the theatre/write books, *etc.* Have you/I ever
> met him/seen her in person? *etc.*
> *Recapitulation:* Did you say she was Australian?

Where is it?

Model questions: see FRANÇAIS or DEUTSCH

What's my job?

Shop asistant, lion tamer, Member of Parliament, pop star, teacher, *etc.* (*Mime
some action typical of the job.*)
(*Model questions*)

> Is your job unusual/interesting/well-paid/dangerous? Can
> this job be done by a man or a woman? Do you work indoors?
> Do you work with other people? Do you meet the public in
> your job? Do you need special training for this job? Do you
> make something in this job? Do you help people in your work?
> Do you get a regular salary for this job? Could I do this job?
> Could you do this work for me?
> *Recapitulation:* Did you say you wore a uniform?

FRANÇAIS *Quiz*

(*Réponses*)

> Il se peut; c'est possible; pas précisement; pas tout à fait;
> quelquefois; ce n'est pas important; il faut poser la question
> autrement; *etc.*
> C'est chaud; ça brûle! C'est froid; c'est gelé!

Qu'est-ce que c'est?

(*Model questions*)

> C'est un mot avec le? C'est dans la classe? C'est blanc(he),
> lourd(e), *etc.*? C'est plus grand(e) que . . .? Est-ce qu'on peut
> le/la voir, toucher, casser, manger, boire, *etc.*? Il y en a
> plusieurs? Est-ce que j'en ai un(e)? Est-ce que j'aimerais
> avoir/ça me ferait plaisir d'avoir une de ces choses/cette chose?
> *etc.*
> *Récapitulation:* Vous avez dit qu'il n'y en avait qu'un(e)?

Qui est-ce?

Marie Antoinette, Pierre Trudeau, Jacques Brel, Astérix, moi-même, *etc.*
Model questions: see ENGLISH

Où est-ce?

Language frames based on map in 2.5 Finding the way
1 (Sortir de; *present or perfect tenses*)

> Un espion a déposé une bombe dans un de ces bâtiments. Il faut découvrir d'où il sort (est sorti) pour pouvoir trouver la bombe. On a X minutes avant qu'elle n'explose!

Est-ce qu'il sort (est sorti)	du restaurant de la banque de l'hôpital, *etc.*

2 (Aller à; *present or future tenses*)

> Un espion va déposer une bombe dans un de ces bâtiments (demain). Il faut trouver où il va (ira), *etc.*

Est-ce qu'il va (ira)	au café à la gare à l'agence de voyages, *etc.*

Quel est mon travail?

Model questions: see ENGLISH

DEUTSCH *Quiz*

(*Antworten*)

> Ich kann diese Frage nicht beantworten. Können Sie diese Frage anders stellen? Das ist nicht wichtig.
> Warm/kalt; wärmer/kälter.

Was ist es?

(*Model questions*)

> Ist es ein Wort mit der/die/das? Ist es im Klassenzimmer? Ist es klein, *usw.*? Ist es größer als . . .? Ist es aus Holz, Glas, *usw.*? Kann man es berühren, sehen, essen, trinken, *usw.*? Gibt es mehrere? Habe ich/haben Sie ein(e)(en)/so etwas? Würde ich (würden Sie) gerne sowas haben?
> *Rekapitulation:* Sie haben gesagt, es gibt nur eins von diesen Dingen?

Wer ist es?

Goethe, Natassja Kinski, Adenauer, Günther Grass
Model questions: see ENGLISH

Wo ist es?

Language frames based on No. 6 The Room in 5.3.
(*Prepositions with genitive or dative; present tense; perfect*)

Choose suitable locations from list below:

1 Ein Mikrofilm/der unsichtbare Mann ist in diesem Zimmer verborgen.
2 Ein Geheimagent hat einen Mikrofilm/eine Bombe in diesem Zimmer versteckt.

Ihr habt X Minuten, um ihn/es zu finden!

F1: Ist es . . . verborgen?
F2: Hat er es . . . versteckt?
Liste (adapt for accusative)
. . . in der Nähe des Fernsehens, Sofas/der Vase/der Bücher, *usw.*?
. . . in, auf, unter, hinter, vor dem Tisch, *usw.* im Glas, im Schrank?
. . . in der Vase, Tasse/in dem Regal/in den Büchern, Blumen, *usw.*?

Was ist mein Beruf?

Model questions: see ENGLISH

6.5 Incomplete stories
Histoires incomplètes
Unvollendete Geschichten

Basic gap	Information, ideas and opinion gap based on incomplete information
Aim	To reconstruct a complete story from the parts heard
Language	Guided or free, with any communication strategies
Preparation and material	Minimal – selecting and marking a suitable story or anecdote

Stage 1   E,I,A (10 minutes)

Class   Explain that you are going to read a story with some omissions (see details in *Finding and making material*). Indicate the gaps by a pause, cough or other signal. Learners can make notes while you are speaking. They then compare notes briefly in pairs or small groups, before reporting their ideas about what the complete story might be. The whole class thus gradually reconstructs a story or stories which will fit the extracts they heard. This can be done in the mother tongue for purely receptive practice.

    When the class has agreed on a story or stories, read out the missing lines and let the discussion continue as learners put the new information together with the parts they heard before, to reconstruct the original story completely. (If you are short of

time, omit this step and read out the whole story after the first
discussion.) Learners are often surprised at how well they can
reconstruct the whole story after hearing only 75% or even
50%; this helps to build confidence in their ability to grasp the
gist of a message in the FL even if they do not hear or
understand every word.

Stage 2   I,A (10 minutes)

Class   As above, now exclusively in the FL, and with your help when
required. You can make a note of the learners' suggestions on
the board, including any new language items they acquire in
order to express their ideas.

Stage 3   I,A (15 minutes)

Group   Tell a story with gaps to the whole class and let them discuss it
in groups until they are satisfied with their own reconstruction
of it. These stories can then be reported back (or written) and
compared in the whole class.

Variant 1 Predicting stories

Read out a story section by section, as dramatically as possible
(and preferably paraphrased in your own words). Stop at
intriguing points (suggested by X in *Teaching material*) so that
the learners can discuss what they think might happen next.
You or a learner can note their ideas on the board. As the story
continues, they can decide which of these suggestions they
will retain or reject, or what new suggestions must be made.
Encourage learners to discuss each other's ideas, as in the main
activity. The last paragraph can be omitted and learners asked
to write an ending to the story or to prepare a role-play to
express their ideas, for comparison and discussion in a later
lesson.

Examples from practice

These three endings to a story were written by teenage level I
learners of English, working in pairs. I have shortened but not
corrected them.
1 *Mr Smith was lying on the bed, and around him an enormous
   amount of food . . . gallons of porridge . . . steaks and goulash . . .
   everything you could think of, it was a terrible mess. Just before he
   fainted of all the food he had eaten, . . . he said, mumbling 'I never
   liked your dinners.'*

2 *The curtains were closed and it was almost dark in the room. Some candles were shining on the nightstand near the bed. The bed was very disorderly . . . and what saw Mrs Smith with her pupils wide open. On the bed was lying, with his eyes closed, her husband – with the housemaid.*

3 *Mrs Smith said, 'Oh, now I remember what I did with that hammer this morning.'* (Compare this ending with the original in *Teaching material* under FRANÇAIS.)

See 5.7 *Split picture stories, Variants 1 and 3* for similar practice with picture stories or video.

Finding and making material

Choose a brief story with a strong narrative line and not too much dialogue, and mark the lines to be omitted. Examples:
Level E – read three or four lines, omit one.
Level I – read three or four lines, omit two.
Level A – read three lines, omit three.
Learners always need to hear the first few lines of the story, and I sometimes read them the concluding sentence also, even if it breaks the pattern of omissions. In the main body of the text, however, it is better to stick strictly to this pattern, not giving key words or the first or last words of a sentence, for example, if they happen to fall on a line to be omitted. This leads to far more communication between learners and exploration of logical or linguistic possibilities.

Variant 1: Use any story or anecdote with an unpredictable ending. For many years I used shortened versions of Roald Dahl's stories (available in various FL editions) for levels I and A; now, partly via television, they are becoming too widely known. There are similar stories with surprise endings in (mystery) magazines, and in some collections of short stories and anecdotes for FL teaching.

The stories in *Teaching material* are for levels I or A. The language can be adapted – or simpler stories chosen – for level E. (X) indicates pauses for *Variant 1*.

Teaching material

ENGLISH *Incomplete stories*

The castle (or *The shortest ghost story in the world*)
It was midnight and the wind was howling as the weary traveller approached the castle. He knocked at the door but

there was no answer. He pushed the door and it swung slowly open (X). He entered the castle and found a lighted candle burning on a table in the hall. He cried 'Is anyone there?' There was no answer; but somewhere, in the distance, music was playing softly. He picked up the candle and went slowly through the rooms: they were all empty. Finally he came to a bedroom where he saw (X) a large four poster bed. He was so exhausted he got into the bed, blew out the candle and immediately fell into a deep sleep. Then suddenly he woke up. He did not know what had woken him but somehow, although he could see and hear nothing (X), he knew that he was no longer alone in the room. He remembered the candle – but how could he light it again? He stretched out his hand to find it. Silently, from the darkness (X), a box of matches was placed in his hand.

FRANÇAIS *Histoires incomplètes*

M Durand est en retard

Mme Durand était en train de préparer le dîner, lorsque son jeune fils est entré. Il pleurait parce qu'une des roues de son train était cassée et il voulait que sa mère la répare. – J'ai besoin du marteau, dit Mme Durand. Elle a cherché mais elle ne l'a pas trouvé. – C'est étrange, dit-elle, je me suis servi du marteau ce matin, mais je ne me souviens pas de ce que j'en ai fait. Puis elle a regardé la pendule. Il était six heures moins le quart et le dîner n'était pas prêt! (X) Mme Durand était inquiète. Son mari se mettait toujours en colère lorsque le dîner n'était pas prêt à temps. Son fils pleurait toujours et Mme Durand avait envie de pleurer, elle aussi. La pendule sonnait six heures. M Durand était en retard! (X) D'abord, Mme Durand a été contente car cela lui donnait plus de temps. Mais à sept heures, elle a commencé à s'inquiéter. Elle a fait manger son fils et l'a mis au lit. À huit heures quelqu'un a frappé à la porte (X), mais ce n'était pas son mari, c'était M Martin, son patron – Je suis désolé de vous déranger, dit-il, mais je voulais vous demander si votre mari était malade. Il n'était pas à son travail aujourd'hui (X). Mme Durand était très étonnée. – Mais mon mari n'est pas là, dit-elle. – À quelle heure est-il parti ce matin? a demandé M Martin. – Je ne l'ai pas vu partir, dit Mme Durand, J'ai conduit mon fils à l'école. – Si vous ne l'avez pas vu partir, dit-il, vous ne savez pas s'il avait quelque chose avec lui, une valise par exemple? (X) Peut-être votre mari avait-il besoin de quelques jours de vacances. Peut-être a-t-il emmené, ce matin, une valise avec des vêtements de rechange. – Non, non, dit Mme Durand. Il ne partirait pas sans me prévenir. – Je vous en prie, madame, dit M Martin, pourriez-vous jeter un coup d'oeil dans sa chambre pour voir si certains de ses vêtements manquent? C'est très urgent pour moi, car j'avais confié à votre mari des papiers très importants. Il faut que je sache où il est. (X) Mme Durand était tellement choquée qu'elle ne pouvait pas réagir. Alors M Martin est allé voir lui-même. Mme Durand l'a entendu monter l'escalier et ouvrir la porte de la chambre. Puis elle l'a entendu crier – Ah mon Dieu! (X) Elle s'est precipitée vers l'escalier. Le visage de M Martin était tout blanc. – Ne regardez pas! lui dit-il. Mais c'était trop tard. Mme Durand avait déjà aperçu ce qu'il y avait dans la chambre. (X) – Ah, mais oui! s'est-elle écriée, voilà ce que j'avais fait du marteau ce matin!

DEUTSCH *Unvollendete Geschichten*

Das Malheur
Eine Ärztin wurde eines Morgens sehr früh angerufen: ein gewisser Herr Schmidt war am Telefon. 'Kommen Sie bitte so schnell wie möglich! Meiner Frau ist etwas Schreckliches passiert (X). Sie schläft mit offenem Mund, und nun ist heute früh eine Maus über die Bettdecke gelaufen und meiner Frau in den Mund gekrochen!' Die Ärztin erschrak natürlich sehr. Sie wollte sofort mit dem Auto kommen, riet Herrn Schmidt aber (X), solange seiner Frau ein Stück Käse vor den Mund zu halten. Dann würde die Maus vielleicht herauskriechen. Als die Ärztin nach zehn Minuten endlich das Haus der Familie Schmidt erreicht hatte, fand sie Herrn Schmidt neben dem Bett seiner Frau, während er mit einem Fisch vor ihrem offenen Mund herumwedelte (X). 'Was machen Sie denn da?' rief die Ärztin entsetzt. 'Ich habe doch gesagt, daß Sie der Maus Käse vorhalten sollen!' 'Die Sache ist inzwischen viel ernster geworden,' antwortete Herr Schmidt (X). 'Ich muß jetzt die Katze hervorlocken!'

6.6 What's wrong?
Qu'est-ce qui ne va pas?
Was stimmt nicht?

Basic gap	Observation gap based on shared information
Aim	To tell a story with deliberate mistakes; to find all the mistakes
Language	Guided or free, with any communication strategies
Preparation and material	Preparing suitable texts; model phrases on display for guided practice

Stage 1   E,I,A (5 minutes)

Class/team   Tell a story (see examples in *Teaching material*) with deliberate mistakes. Learners who spot the mistakes win a point for doing do. Appoint learners as referees to decide whose hand was raised first or who first called *Stop!* and to keep score. Let a second learner, or, if you work with teams, someone from another team gain a second point for correcting the mistake. This prevents the quicker learners from dominating the activity, because you choose the second speaker.

For purely receptive practice, all learner responses can be in the mother tongue. At other levels, provide model phrases for correcting the speaker (learners enjoy the opportunity to catch you making mistakes!) and encourage learners to argue whether or not something is necessarily a mistake.

Example from practice

German level A class (translated):
Story-teller:. . . *and then I went to see an exhibition of Beethoven's paintings* . . . Team A claimed this was a mistake. Team B (not wanting to lose a point) protested that perhaps this was Beethoven's younger brother – the obscure artist Wolfgang van Beethoven!

Stage 2   E,I,A (5 minutes)

Class/team   Learners or pairs prepare a story or account with deliberate mistakes (if necessary as homework) – or you can give them a script. They re-tell their story while other learners try to spot mistakes, or argue about them, as in stage 1. You can help them with language, and act as referee. Learners may notice and challenge each other's involuntary linguistic errors (deliberate errors of this kind should not be included in the stories); I find it better to 'score' these separately, if at all, and to ignore mistakes which do not affect comprehensibility.

Stage 3   I,A (5 minutes)

Group   Learners tell their stories in groups, proceeding as in stage 2, and then report what mistakes were found. If any group misses some of the mistakes, the story-tellers can re-tell their story in the whole class, to see if they can do better.

Variant 1 Mistaken description

Learners describe something or someone everyone can see, such as a picture or picture story from their textbooks, making deliberate errors for their partners or classmates to spot.

Variant 2 True or false?

Learners tell personal anecdotes or describe people, places or things unknown to, or pictures which cannot be seen by, their partners or classmates. The latter ask detailed questions before deciding whether the anecdote or description is based on fact or is purely imaginary – giving reasons for their decision.

Variant 3 Mistaken pictures

Learners, working in teams or pairs, try to name all the deliberate mistakes they can find in a picture.

See 5.6 *Spot the differences*, and variants, for similar practice in noting and describing changes in stories or pictures.

Finding and making material

The mistakes may be introduced into well-known stories such as Cinderella:
She had three ugly sisters . . . she lost her glove at the ball, etc.
or any story which the whole class knows (e.g. from their textbooks or other reading). Alternatively, you or learners can make up stories containing impossibilities, illogicalities, or inner contradictions:
Jack Jones is a bachelor . . . yesterday I saw him and his wife . . ., etc.
or plain errors of fact, based on general knowledge or cultural and literary knowledge of the foreign country:
President Richard Reagan has just met the President of France, Madame Marguerite de Gaulle . . .
The helicopter landed on the wide flat roof of Sydney's famous opera house . . . (See the example under FRANÇAIS in *Teaching material*.)

Variant 1: do not make the mistakes too predictable, for example by placing them at too regular intervals, or always at the end of a sentence, etc.

Variant 3: some textbooks have pictures with deliberate mistakes, or pictures which can be adapted in this way (see 5.2.2 Sources (b) and (c)); you can also find this sort of picture in sources (a), (b) and (c) from 5.2.1, or in *Booklist* 2c; or you and the learners can make your own. See No. 12 *Mistakes* in 5.3 *Visual material* for an example.

Teaching material

ENGLISH *What's wrong?*

(Mistakes indicated by (X))

Yesterday morning I woke up very late and had to run to catch my train. I was a bit late for work as we got stuck in a traffic jam in Oxford Street (X). I work for BBC Television and I have to travel a lot for my work, so I always carry my bright red British passport (X – *dark blue*) with me. My boss told me that I was to fly to India with a camera team that day.

'You'll be flying by the most direct route,' he told me, 'from Heathrow to Leonardo da Vinci Airport in Rome, from there to JFK Airport in New York, and then to Bombay (X – *not direct*). I want you to make a film about Indian tigers and elephants.'

Unfortunately, when we got to India there weren't any tigers and elephants to be seen, but we did see a flock of the very rare and beautiful Indian penguins (X). We were very excited and set up our cameras immediately. But just as we were ready to film them, they all flew away (X).

(X – *this could not all have taken place in one day; see beginning of story*)

Variant 1 *Mistaken description*

Based on No. 13 Artist in 5.3.

This is a picture of an artist's studio. There is a table with some brushes and paints. The artist and her (X) model are in the studio, and outside there is a crowd of men. They are looking through the door (X) at the model, who is only wearing a green hat (X). The artist is painting her (X) but the men do not know this. They think he is painting them (X).

(*Model phrases*)

No, that's wrong/that's not right/that's impossible/that must be a mistake/I think you've made a mistake . . . you said (that) . . ., *etc.*

FRANÇAIS *Qu'est-ce qui ne va pas?*

(Mistakes indicated by (X))

Une courte histoire de la littérature française

Au temps de Louis XIV, trois grands auteurs écrivent pour le théâtre: Racine, Molière et bien sûr Corneille avec sa comédie (X) la plus connue, *Le Cid*. C'est une pièce qu'il a écrite pour la plus grande actrice de l'époque, Madame de Sévigné (X).

Nous passons maintenant au XIXe siècle – c'est un siècle riche en romans tels que *Le Rouge et le Noir* de Balzac (X), *Le Comte de Monte Cristo* d'Alexandre Dumas, et *Les Misérables* de Victor Hugo. Au XXe siècle, enfin, Georges Simenon est très apprécié pour ses romans policiers: il est devenu célèbre par le commissaire-détective, Hercule Poirot (X). N'oublions pas de mentionner quelques livres pour enfants, commes les *Fables* de Lafayette (X). De nos jours, nous avons le roman de St Éxupéry, *Le Petit Prince,* et on peut apprendre l'histoire de France du temps des Romains avec les bandes dessinées du célèbre parisien (X) Astérix.

(Model phrases)

Non, ce n'est pas juste/ce n'est pas vrai/c'est faux/c'est impossible/vous vous trompez, je crois . . . vous avez dit que . . . *etc.*

DEUTSCH *Was stimmt nicht?*

(Mistakes indicated by (X))

Der Einkaufsbummel

Gestern fuhr ich mit dem Bus zum Einkaufen in die Stadt. Ich wollte eine Menge kaufen, darum nahm ich eine kleine (X) Einkaufstasche mit. Zuerst wollte ich eine Tischdecke für das Badezimmer kaufen (X), und dann ein paar Laken für das Schlafzimmer. Das Kaufhaus war so voll, daß ich Kopfschmerzen bekam und zur Apotheke ging, wo ich Aspirin kaufte. Danach beschloß ich, etwas essen zu gehen, weil ich nicht sehr hungrig war (X). Also ging ich in ein vegetarisches Restaurant und bestellte einen Käsesalat. Zufällig sah ich dort einen alten Bekannten, der mir von einer Ausstellung von Beethovens Gemälden (X) in der Kunstgalerie erzählte. Nachdem er sein Schinkenbrötchen (X) aufgegessen hatte, gingen wir beide zur Ausstellung. Hinterher holte ich mein Auto im Parkhaus ab (X) und fuhr wieder nach Hause.

Variant 1 Falsche Beschreibung

Based on No. 11 Bank robbery

(Mistakes indicated by (X))

Dieses hier ist die Geschichte eines Bankraubs. Eines Tages kam eine sehr schöne junge Dame (X) in eine Bank. Während sie bei der Kasse stand, kamen ihre zwei (X) Komplizen in die Bank. Der eine überwaltigte den Polizisten, der in der Nähe stand (X), während der andere mit einer Waffe Geld vom Kassierer verlangte. Danach geiselte er die alte Dame, sodaß der Polizist nicht zu schießen wagte. Dann ließ er die Dame los (X) und ging mit dem Geld zur Tür hinaus, wo ein großes schwarzes (X) Auto auf ihn wartete. Er erschoß den Polizisten, (X) und dann fuhren er und die Dame weg. Die Räuber fuhren schließlich auf die Bahamas, wo sie sich unter den Palmen (X) zu viert (X) das Geld teilten.

(Model phrases)

Nein, das stimmt nicht/das geht nicht/das muß ein Irrtum sein/das ist völlig unmöglich/ich glaube, Sie irren sich . . . Sie haben gesagt, daß . . . *usw.*

6.7   Logic problems
Problèmes de logique
Logische Probleme

Basic gap	Information gap based on split information
Aim	To solve a logic problem
Language	Guided or free, with any communication strategies
Preparation and material	Clues to solve a logic problem split between handouts; logic grid and model phrases on display or handouts

Stage 1   E,I,A (10 minutes)

Class   Demonstrate the use of the grid to solve logic problems, and the language used in solving them: you or a learner can read the question and clues one by one, leaving time between each clue to discuss what information can be deduced from it. You or any learner familiar with logic problems should fill in the grid according to the class's deductions. Example:

Question: *What is the name of each cat?*

Clue 1: *The cats' names are MIC, MAC and MEC.*

Write the names on the grid in any order. (These were chosen to reinforce correct pronunciation, but other names can be used.)

mic	1	2	3
mac	4	5	6
mec	7	8	9

Clue 2: *MIC is larger than MAC.*

So MIC can't be the smallest cat. Put a cross in the grid to show this (1). And MAC can't be the largest. Put another cross in the grid (6).

mic	1 X	2	3
mac	4	5	6 X
mec	7	8	9

218

Clue 3: *MEC is not the smallest.*
Put a cross in the grid (7). If MIC and
MEC are not the smallest, then
MAC must be the smallest cat. Put a
tick in the grid (4). And if MAC is
the smallest, he can't be the middle
cat. Put a cross in the grid (5).

	♿	♿	♿
mic	1 X	2	3
mac	4 ✓	5 X	6 X
mec	7 X	8	9

(Learners often overlook the possibility of putting the tick in 4
and the cross in 5: point this out later if so.)

Clue 4: *MIC is not as large as MEC.*
So MIC can't be the largest. Put a
cross in the grid (3). So MIC must be
the middle cat. Put a tick in the grid
(2) – and you can put a cross in the
grid (8) to show that therefore MEC
cannot be the middle cat. So MEC
must be the largest cat: put a tick in
the grid (9).
Problem solved!

	♿	♿	♿
mic	1 X	2 ✓	3 X
mac	4 ✓	5 X	6 X
mec	7 X	8 X	9 ✓

Stage 2 E,I,A (15 minutes)

Class Hand out the questions and clues, so that each learner or group
has a paper. One or two learners stand at the front of the class
and fill in the grid according to their classmates' deductions
and instructions: they can also join in the discussion. No one
else should make notes (learners stop listening to each other if
they are all busy writing). Learners share the questions and
clues with each other, listening carefully to what is said to see
what can be deduced from it; and using any of the phrases on
display for their discussion. Intervene only when necessary:
for example, if learners ask for help, if they start speaking their
mother tongue, or if everyone tries to talk at once. In practice,
the learners who are filling in the grid are usually the first to
protest if their classmates all call out at the same time!

When the class has agreed on a solution, or at the time limit,
tell them if their solution is correct. If it is not, discuss what
problems they had (in the mother tongue if necessary). These
are sometimes linguistic: they misunderstood words or
mispronounced them so that their classmates misunderstood
(e.g. a girl who said *He was shot in the tie* instead of *thigh*, so that
classmates thought the man was shot in the chest and killed).
The problems are more often because some learners did not
read out relevant clues at the appropriate moment (an extreme
example was a girl who did not read out the question until the

discussion was almost ended – the class having meanwhile invented a question of their own); or they failed to make all possible deductions from a clue (see clue 3 in stage 1 above); or learners did not listen to each other carefully and missed relevant information; or those who had a fixed idea of the correct answer refused to listen to other people's clues or conclusions (those who assumed a man was killed by a gun refused to consider other evidence proving he was killed by a knife – see the *Murder* problem in *Teaching material*). If you point out these mistakes immediately, learners may stop trying to solve the problem themselves and start addressing all their remarks to you. Let them run into difficulties and afterwards discuss why this happened and how they can avoid it next time (in the mother tongue if necessary). If the class have no such difficulties, they are to be congratulated on their discussion skills, as well as their grasp of language and logic!

Stage 3   E,I,A (20 minutes)

Group   The group appoints one member as secretary. The secretaries deal out the paper as equally as possible, and may include themselves; they also make all notes for the group and fill in the grid. The rules of discussion are:
– The problem is to be solved in the FL.
– No one makes notes except the secretary.
– No looking at each other's papers at any time; everyone can look at the secretary's notes, the grid and extra material such as maps.
– Groups call you when they think they have the answer. You do not accept an answer that is incorrect in any detail: the group must go on trying!
  It is better to start near the beginning of the lesson and not impose a time limit, as learners can become deeply involved in their problem-solving. Groups who finish early can be asked to write a story based on their solution, if appropriate (e.g. *Murder*), or to start making their own logic problem (see guidelines in *Finding and making material*); or be given any 'filler' activity (see the *General index*). If they have written stories they can read these out or display them, and logic problems they have written may be used in further sessions.

Finding and making material

You or the learners can make up simple problems, following these guidelines:

1 Decide on the topic and fill in the solution on a grid.
2 Devise the question(s):
   How many horses took part in the race?
   Which horse was first? etc.
3 Split information so that one clue is only useful when combined with others:
   There were more than five horses in the race.
   There were fewer than seven horses in the race.
4 If appropriate, use general knowledge in the clues:
   The winning horse was named after a man with six wives.
5 Fill in the grid with crosses or ticks as you write the clues: sometimes only one square on a line is left blank so there is no need to write a clue for it, as it is the only possible answer (see clues 3 and 4 in stage 1). Whenever you can fill in a tick, all the boxes to the left and right, and above and below that box are automatically crossed out, so you need no clues for them.
6 If you need a larger number of clues, you can write a few 'empty' or negative items:
   Henry VIII wasn't the slowest horse in the race.
7 Try reading the clues in any order and checking the grid to see if the whole problem can be solved by using only a few clues. If so, rewrite them! (Writing problems for stage 1 is much easier because you can decide in what order they are to be read out.) With problems for level E groups, or those based on general knowledge or cultural background, you can be less strict and write extra clues to confirm or expand information given in other terms (see the *Holiday* problems in *Teaching material*).
8 Split up the clues and questions between four or five papers (for group work); make a blank grid and a copy of any other material required, such as a map. If possible, test the problem with another group to be sure that it is not too easy or too difficult.
9 Fold the papers with the writing inside, except those with the grid, maps, etc. which the whole group may see. See further notes on preparing sets of material in 5.2.2 (d).

Holidays in America and *Ferien in der BRD* are based on material written by level I and level A groups respectively (the learners of English were all keen followers of *Dallas* and *Dynasty*!).

Logic puzzles can be found in special puzzle magazines for children and adults, and the puzzle pages in magazines and newspapers (see 5.2.1 (a) to (d)). Many of these need simplification and extra clues before being used in the FL class. Extra clues which can be given to young level E learners are included in *Teaching material* where appropriate.

The questions and clues in *Teaching material* can be written on separate cards (by you or learners) for class work, or photocopied and cut up along the dotted lines for group work.

Model phrases which may be used in solving the problems are placed at the beginning of *Teaching material*, in ENGLISH, FRANÇAIS, DEUTSCH. The *Murder* and *Holiday* problems are placed at the end, in all three languages. They are suitable for level I and A learners; the latter will need less time to solve them.

Teaching material

ENGLISH *Logic problems*

(*Model phrases*)

If X . . ., then Y . . . must be/can't be . . .
X must/can't be . . ., because . . .
I think (that) / Do you think (that) . . .?
No, that can't be right because . . .
It says here . . . / I have . . .
Has anybody got any information about . . .?
Does anybody know if/when/where . . . *etc.*?
Did you say (that) . . . / Didn't somebody say (that) . . .?
Wait a minute! / Could you repeat that slowly?

FRANÇAIS *Problèmes de logique*

(*Model phrases*)

Si X . . ., alors Y doit être . . ./ne peut pas être . . .
X doit être/ne peut pas être . . ., parce que . . .
Non, ce n'est pas possible, parce que . . .
Moi, je crois que . . . / Il me semble que . . .
Sur mon papier, il est écrit que . . .
Ici, c'est écrit que . . . / Moi, j'ai que . . .
Qui sait quelque chose sur . . .?
Est-ce que quelqu'un sait qui/quand/où . . .?
A-t-on des renseignements sur . . .?
A-t-on parlé de . . .?
Un moment! Un instant!
Tu peux répéter cela, s'il te plaît?

DEUTSCH *Logische Probleme*

(*Model phrases*)

> Wenn X . . . (ist), dann muß Y . . . (sein).
> Nein, das kann nicht stimmen, weil . . .
> Ich denke/meine/glaube, daß . . .
> Meinst du, daß . . .?
> Hier heißt es, daß . . .
> Ich habe eine Information über . . .
> Wer hat eine Information über . . .?
> Weiß jemand, wer/wo/wann . . .?
> Hat einer gesagt, daß . . .?
> Moment bitte. Moment mal.
> Kannst du das noch mal langsam wiederholen?

ENGLISH

The family

(*18/19 clues, grid with pictures*)

Solution: 1 Chris, boy, six months old
2 Cal, girl, five
3 Jo, girl, ten
4 Ellen, girl, sixteen
5 Sid, boy, seventeen

(*See next page*)

The family

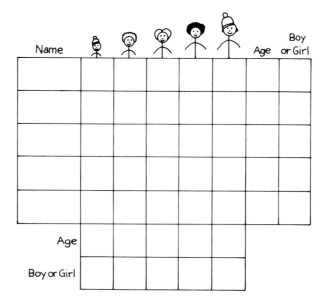

Name						Age	Boy or Girl

Age					
Boy or Girl					

✂- -

Question 1: What are the children's names?
The older the child, the taller he or she is.
The youngest child is a boy.
Ellen is not the tallest.
The eldest child is seventeen years old.

✂- -

Question 2: What is the name of each child?
Jo has a sister who is five years younger than she is.
The baby is six months old.
One of the girls is sixteen.

✂- -

Question 3: How old is each child?
Cal is smaller than Jo.
'Jo' 'Chris' and 'Cal' are names for boys or girls.
Sid is older than Chris.

✂- -

Question 4: Which children are boys and which are girls?
Ellen is taller than Jo.
Jo is ten.
Cal is not the youngest.
Chris and Sid are wearing caps.

✂- -

(*Extra clue*) Chris is the baby.

FRANÇAIS

La course hippique

(15/17 indices)

Solution: 1 Arlequin
2 Lune de Miel
3 Henri II
4 Tonnerre
5 Stella Artois
6 Truc
7 Astérix

(Learners draw their own grid, when they discover the number of horses in the race.)

✂---

Question 1: Combien de chevaux ont participé à la course?
Le favori n'a pas gagné.
Henri II n'a pas obtenu la deuxième place.
Les chevaux avec la lettre T dans leur nom ont pris les dernières
places.

✂---

Question 2: Quels sont les noms des chevaux?
Lune de Miel était le favori.
Il y avait deux chevaux entre Tonnerre et Arlequin.
Truc n'a pas été le cheval le plus rapide.

✂---

Question 3: Quel était l'ordre d'arrivée des chevaux?
Plus de six chevaux ont participé à la course.
Le cheval qui avait le nom le plus long a terminé devant le
cheval qui avait le nom le plus court.

✂---

Henri II a terminé devant Tonnerre.
Astérix a été le cheval le plus lent.
Tonnerre a terminé devant Stella Artois.
Moins de huit chevaux ont participé à la course.

✂---

(Information supplémentaire)
Un cheval dont le nom commence avec la lettre A a gagné.
Les chevaux avec la lettre N dans leur nom ont pris les
premières quatre places.

✂---

From *Developing Communication Skills* by Pat Pattison
© Cambridge University Press 1987

DEUTSCH

Die Häuser

(*9 Hinweise, Schema mit Bild*)

Lösung: Cleo ↓   Bob ↓   Ali ↓   Di ↓

✂--

Die Häuser

Namen

✂--

Frage 1: Wie heißen die Leute, die in diesen Häusern
wohnen?
Di wohnt in einem Haus mit einer weißen Tür.

✂--

Das Haus von Ali hat eine weiße Tür.
Das Haus von Bob hat keine weiße Tür.

✂--

Frage 2: Wer wohnt in welchem Haus?
Das Haus von Cleo hat ein Fenster über der Tür.
Das Haus von Ali hat kein Fenster über der Tür.

✂--

Die Tür von Di steht zwischen zwei Fenstern.
Die Tür von Bob steht nicht zwischen zwei Fenstern.

✂--

From *Developing Communication Skills* by Pat Pattison
© Cambridge University Press 1987

ENGLISH   FRANÇAIS   DEUTSCH

Solution and grid for Holidays in USA   Les vacances d'été
Ferien in der BRD

E *Holidays in USA*

(20 clues, grid and map)

Solution:	Home town	Name	Holiday resort
	Chicago	Leo	New York
	Los Angeles	Dennis	Washington
	Dallas	William	Chicago
	New York	Krystle	Los Angeles
	Washington	Nancy	Dallas

F *Les vacances d'été*

(21 indices, schéma et carte)

Solution:	Habite à . . .	Noms	Va en vacances à . . .
	Strasbourg	Gaston	Bordeaux
	Grenoble	Marcel	Paris
	Bordeaux	Stéphane	Marseille
	Paris	Bernard	Grenoble
	Marseille	Pierre	Strasbourg

D *Ferien in der Bundesrepublik*

(23/24 Hinweise, Schema und Landkarte)

Lösung:	Wohnstadt	Name	Urlaubsstadt
	Berlin	Franz	München
	München	Johann	Frankfurt
	Hamburg	Berthold	Köln
	Bonn	Dieter	Berlin
	Bremen	Christoph	Bonn
	Frankfurt	Manfred	Hamburg
	Köln	Hans	Bremen

227

Grid/Schéma

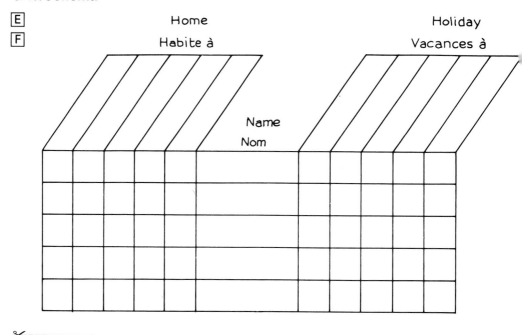

E
F

Home   Holiday
Habite à   Vacances à

Name
Nom

✂ -

D

Wohnstadt   Urlaubstadt

Name

From *Developing Communication Skills* by Pat Pattison
© Cambridge University Press 1987

ENGLISH

✂--

Holidays in USA

✂--

Question 1: What are these people's names?
Hollywood is part of one of these towns.
All the home towns are also holiday resorts.
William is a big oil man.
Leo wants to go shopping on 5th Avenue during his holidays.

✂--

Question 2: Where do these people live?
Nancy lives near the White House.
Krystle is an actress on Broadway.
Leo doesn't want to visit the South on his holidays.
The Ewing family lives in one of the towns.

✂--

Question 3: Where will these people go on holidays?
Nancy wants to visit Southfork.
Krystle lives in a town near the sea.
Dennis wants to meet the President during his holidays.
Al Capone used to live in one of these towns.
One of the towns is the capital of the United States.

✂--

Krystle has the longest journey to go to her holiday resort.
Dennis lives near Disneyland.
Leo doesn't live in the South.
William wants to go sailing during his holidays.

✂--

From *Developing Communication Skills* by Pat Pattison
© Cambridge University Press 1987

FRANÇAIS

✂---

Les vacances d'été

From *Developing Communication Skills* by Pat Pattison
© Cambridge University Press 1987

✂--

Question 1: Quels sont les noms des cinq jeunes Français dont il s'agit?
Bernard n'aime pas les grandes villes bruyantes et animées.
Gaston parle couramment allemand.
C'est Bernard qui habite le plus près de l'Angleterre.
Gaston aime le vin rouge.
Deux des cinq villes sont Marseille et Grenoble.

✂--

Pierre habite une maison qui donne sur la mer.
Bernard aime le calme des montagnes.
Marcel est moniteur de ski pendant l'hiver.
Trois des cinq villes sont Bordeaux, Paris et Strasbourg.
Personne n'habite une ville dont le nom commence par la même lettre que son propre nom. Par exemple, Marcel n'habite pas à Marseille.

✂--

Question 2: Le problème à résoudre est le suivant: où habite chaque jeune homme et dans quelle ville va-t-il passer ses vacances d'été?
Stéphane préfère passer ses vacances dans le Midi.
Marcel préfère prendre ses vacances dans une ville où il y a beaucoup de choses à faire et à voir.
Stéphane passera ses vacances dans la ville où habite Pierre.
Pierre n'a jamais vu Strasbourg.

✂--

Personne n'ira en vacances dans une ville dont le nom commence par la même lettre que son propre nom. Par exemple, Pierre n'ira pas à Paris.
Gaston et Marcel habitent dans l'est de la France.
Bernard et Marcel vont parcourir la même distance pour se rendre sur leur lieu de vacances.
Stéphane ira nager tous les jours dans la Méditerranée pendant ses vacances.
Gaston est allé à Marseille l'année dernière et il n'a pas aimé cette ville.

✂--

DEUTSCH

✂--

Ferien in der Bundesrepublik

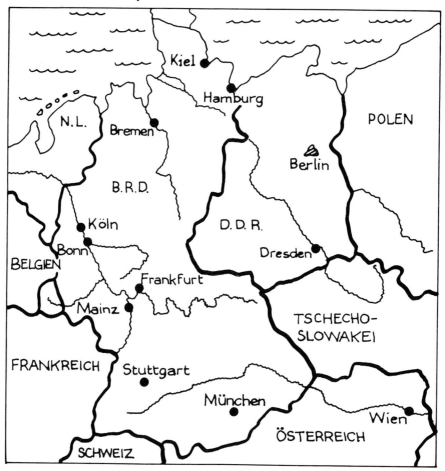

✂--

Frage 1: Wie heißen diese jungen Männer?

Niemand wohnt in einer Stadt, deren Name denselben Anfangsbuchstaben trägt wie sein eigener Name.

Manfred will das Eros-Center in Sankt Pauli besuchen.

Berthold will im Urlaub eine Rheinreise machen. Er fährt dann mit dem Rheindampfer von seinem Urlaubsort bis nach Mainz.

Jeder fährt in den Ferien in eine Stadt, in der einer der anderen wohnt.

Dieter wohnt in der Regierungshauptstadt von West-Deutschland.

✂--

Frage 2: In welchen deutschen Städten wohnen diese jungen
Männer?
Berthold fährt im Urlaub von einer Stadt an der Elbe in eine
Stadt am Rhein.
Christoph will von seinem Urlaubsort aus eine kurze Reise ins
Siebengebirge unternehmen.
Franz trinkt auch im Urlaub gern Bier. Er will zum
Oktoberfest fahren.
Johann will in den Ferien das Geburtshaus seines
Lieblingsdichters Goethe besuchen.
Hans arbeitet für die Firma '4711'.

✂---

Frage 3: In welchen deutschen Städten wollen die jungen
Männer ihren Urlaub verbringen?
Berthold ist Hafenarbeiter in Westdeutschlands größtem
Seehafen.
Berthold beginnt seinen Urlaub in der Stadt mit dem höchsten
Dom von West-Deutschland.
Dieter will im Urlaub ein Foto vom Brandenburger Tor
machen.
Franz arbeitet als Kellner in einem Restaurant auf dem
Ku'damm.
Niemand verbringt seinen Urlaub in einer Stadt, deren Name
denselben Anfangsbuchstaben hat wie sein eigener Name.

✂---

Franz und Dieter müssen ihren Paß bei sich haben, wenn sie in
die Ferien fahren wollen.
Christoph hat seine Heimatstadt 1962 verlassen, als die Mauer
gebaut wurde. Er will nie wieder dorthin fahren.
Manfred wohnt in einem Hochhaus, von wo aus er einen
wunderschönen Ausblick auf den Main hat.
Hans verbringt seine Ferien in derselben Stadt, in der
Christoph wohnt.
Johann wohnt in der bayerischen Landeshauptstadt.

✂---

Zusatzinformation: Die sieben Städte sind Berlin, Bonn,
Bremen, Frankfurt, Hamburg, Köln und München.

✂---

	ENGLISH	FRANÇAIS	DEUTSCH
	Murder	***Le meurtre***	***Der Mord***

(*22 clues and plan*)

Solution:

	Victim	Murderer	Weapon	Time	Place
E	Brown	Smith	Knife	12.30 a.m.	Smith's apartment
F	Duval	Gaillard	Couteau	0.30	L'appartement de Gaillard
D	Braun	Schmidt	Messer	0.30	Schmidts Wohnung

Plan

		Park/Jardin public →
E Brown F Duval D Braun	Entrance Entrée Eingang	Jones Clavier Jonas
E Smith F Gaillard D Schmidt	Hall porter Concierge Hausmeister	Neighbour Voisine Nachbarin

(There is no grid for this activity: learners find it easier to write relevant information on the plan itself. This simple plan can be copied from the blackboard.)

From *Developing Communication Skills* by Pat Pattison
© Cambridge University Press 1987

ENGLISH

Murder

✂--

Question: Who was killed, by whom, with what, when and where?
The hall porter saw Mr Brown going into Mr Smith's apartment at 12.25 a.m.
Mr Smith's fingerprints were on the knife which was found in the entrance of the apartment block.
The police couldn't find Mr Smith after the murder.
Mr Jones said he had fired at an intruder in his flat at midnight.

✂--

Mr Brown's bloodstains were found in Mr Smith's car.
Only one bullet had been fired from Mr Jones's gun.
When the hall porter saw Mr Brown, he was bleeding slightly but he didn't seem to be seriously hurt.
The hall porter went off duty at 12.30 a.m.
A knife with Mr Brown's bloodstains was found in the entrance of the apartment block.
Mr Brown had been dead for an hour when he was found.

✂--

At 11.55 p.m. a neighbour saw Mr Brown going into Mr Jones's apartment.
Mr Jones, Mr Brown and Mr Smith all lived in the same apartment block in Chicago.
Mr Brown's body was found at 1.30 a.m.
The hall porter told the police that he had seen Mr Brown at 12.15 a.m.
When Mr Brown was found, he had two wounds: a bullet wound in his thigh and knife wound in his back.

✂--

Mr Brown's bloodstains were found in the hall of Mr Jones's apartment.
The bullet in Mr Brown's leg was from Mr Jones's gun.
When the police went to look for Mr Jones, he had disappeared.
From the state of Mr Brown's body, it was clear that it had been dragged for several metres.
Mr Brown's body was found in the park.

✂--

FRANÇAIS

Le meurtre

✄---

Question: Qui a été tué, par qui, avec quoi, quand, et où?

La concierge avait vu M Duval se rendre chez M Gaillard, à 00.25.

Il y avait des empreintes de M Gaillard sur le couteau qu'on on a trouvé dans l'entrée de l'immeuble.

La police n'a pas pu trouver M Gaillard après le crime.

M Clavier a déclaré: À minuit, j'ai tiré sur un inconnu, qui s'était introduit dans mon appartement.

✄---

On a trouvé des traces de sang de M Duval dans la voiture de M Gaillard.

Une seule balle avait été tirée avec le pistolet de M Clavier.

Quand la concierge a vu M Duval, celui-ci saignait un peu. Pourtant, il n'avait pas l'air grièvement blessé.

La concierge avait quitté son service à 00.30.

On a trouvé un couteau, qui portait des traces de sang de M Duval, dans l'entrée de l'immeuble.

Quand on a trouvé M Duval, celui-ci était mort depuis une heure.

✄---

A 11.55, une voisine a vu M Duval se rendre chez M Clavier.

Messieurs Clavier, Duval et Gaillard habitaient tous dans le même immeuble, à Marseille.

On a trouvé le corps de M Duval à 1.30.

La concierge a expliqué à la police qu'elle avait vu M Duval à 00.15.

Quand M Duval a été trouvé mort, il avait deux blessures: une dans la jambe, causée par un coup de feu, et une dans le dos, causée par un coup de couteau.

✄---

Sur le tapis de l'appartement de M Clavier, on a trouvé les traces de sang de M Duval.

La balle, qui se trouvait dans la jambe de M Duval, provenait du pistolet de M Clavier.

Au moment où la police est partie à la recherche de M Clavier, elle a constaté qu'il avait disparu.

A en juger par l'état du corps de M Duval, il est évident qu'il a été traîné sur plusieurs mètres.

On a trouvé le corps de M Duval dans le jardin public.

✄---

From *Developing Communication Skills* by Pat Pattison
© Cambridge University Press 1987

DEUTSCH

Der Mord

✂--

Frage: Wer wurde ermordet, von wem, womit, wo und wann?

Der Hausmeister sah, daß Herr Braun um 00.25 zu Herrn Schmidts Wohnung ging.

Das Messer, das man in der Eingangshalle fand, wies Fingerabdrücke von Herrn Schmidt auf.

Der Polizei gelang es nicht, Herrn Schmidts Aufenthaltsort nach dem Mord festzustellen.

Herr Jonas schoß um Mitternacht in seiner Wohnung auf einen Eindringling.

✂--

Spuren von Herrn Brauns Blut wurden in Herrn Schmidts Wagen gefunden.

Nur eine Kugel wurde aus Herrn Jonas Pistole abgefeuert.

Als der Hausmeister Herrn Braun sah, blutete dieser leicht, aber er schien nicht schwer verwundet zu sein.

Der Hausmeister beendete seinen Dienst um 00.30 Uhr.

Ein Messer mit Blutspuren von Herrn Braun wurde in der Eingangshalle des Hochhauses gefunden.

Herr Braun war seit einer Stunde tot, als man ihn fand.

✂--

Eine Nachbarin sah Herrn Braun um 23.55 Uhr zur Wohnung von Herrn Jonas gehen.

Die Herren Braun, Jonas und Schmidt wohnten in demselben Hochhaus in Berlin.

Herr Brauns Leiche wurde um 01.30 Uhr gefunden.

Der Hausmeister berichtete der Polizei, daß er Herrn Braun um 00.15 Uhr gesehen hatte.

Als Herr Braun tot gefunden wurde, hatte er eine Schußwunde im Bein und eine Messerwunde im Rücken.

✂--

Spuren von Herrn Brauns Blut fand man auf dem Teppich in der Halle von Herrn Jonas Wohnung.

Die Kugel in Herrn Brauns Bein stammte aus Herrn Jonas Pistole.

Als die Polizei versuchte, Herrn Jonas nach dem Mord ausfindig zu machen, merkte sie, daß er verschwunden war.

Am Zustand von Herrn Brauns Körper war deutlich zu erkennen, daß er über einen langen Abstand geschleift worden war.

Herr Brauns Leiche wurde im Park gefunden.

✂--

From *Developing Communication Skills* by Pat Pattison

6.8 What's it all about?
De quoi s'agit-il?
Was hat das zu bedeuten?

Basic gap   Ideas or opinion gap based on incomplete information
Aim   To discover or invent an explanation for an incomplete and
puzzling story
Language   Guided and free, with any communication strategies
Preparation and   Minimal – selecting, inventing or remembering suitable
material   anecdotes; on handouts for stage 3 (optional)

Stage 1   E,I,A (10 minutes)

Class   Tell the learners part of an anecdote. Example:
*I was once sitting in a bar in Tahiti when a man I didn't recognise came
up to me and said, 'You must let me buy you a drink. If it wasn't for
you I wouldn't be here today.'*
Invite the learners to ask questions and make suggestions
which will lead them to the full story. Let them discuss their
ideas in small groups, and invite groups to make suggestions
or ask questions in turn, so that the more fluent and
imaginative speakers do not dominate. Help learners with
language where necessary, and guide them with remarks like
That's not relevant or *You're getting closer*, etc. until they have
discovered the whole story.
    Alternatively, let the class develop an explanation by
accepting questions or suggestions which may lead in
promising directions. For example, if you accept a learner's
suggestion that you travelled by air, and that something went
wrong during the flight, the class may develop a story about
your saving all the passengers on a plane by taking over the
controls when the pilot fell ill. You can also tell the story in the
third person, to give even more scope to the learners'
imagination, as they try to find the narrator's identity and role,
as well as build up the complete story. Stories built up in this
way are often far more exciting than the truth, which in this
case is:
*The man and I had both flown from Paris to Tahiti two weeks before.
He had had problems with his ticket in Paris and I had helped by
translating.*

Stage 2   E,I,A (10 minutes)

Class   Ask learners to prepare similar anecdotes, based on personal
experience or any other source; or give them partial stories on

handouts, with or without explanations. These learners tell the partial story and respond to questions and suggestions, following your example in stage 1. You can offer help to both sides when required; if you do not know the story, you can also join in the questioning.

Stage 3   E,I,A (10 minutes)

Group   As above, with one learner in each group telling a partial story. At the time limit, groups report to the whole class. If they all had the same story but were free to develop any explanation, they can compare and discuss their versions.

Variant 1   Puzzle stories

Use puzzle stories of this type:
A man is lying on the ground. He died a violent death. A half-open package is lying beside him.
There are usually some learners who know the solution. They can lead the discussion, and if their classmates are having difficulties they can provide clues to help them. Example:
The man was not dead until he touched the ground.
Explaining these situations does not depend simply on commonsense or experience: it requires more lateral thinking, and a wider vocabulary to express more unusual ideas in order to arrive at the solution, which in this case is:
The man was a parachutist whose parachute had failed to open.
   Some learners are fanatically keen puzzle solvers, but some do not enjoy them even in their mother tongue, and some object to the often tricky solutions.

Example from practice

An ex-airman in an adult group objected strongly to the above solution on the grounds that one always carries a reserve 'chute!
   For these reasons, I use puzzle stories most for level I or A groups who are enthusiastic 'puzzlers', while others work with stories based on personal experience, or an alternative activity.

Finding and making material

You or the learners can refer to personal experiences or adapt any suitable anecdotes. You can collect a fund of suitable material from the learners in the course of the activity itself;

this is the source of most of the teaching material below.

Variant 1: there will usually be at least one or two learners in any group who know several puzzle stories, which you can help them to translate and put on handouts, with suitable clues. Other sources are specialist puzzle magazines, or the puzzle pages of magazines and newspapers.

Teaching material

ENGLISH *What's it all about?*

I was once given a bunch of flowers by some people I didn't know, and who didn't know me either.
(The flowers were given to me by my new neighbours when I moved into the house I'd just bought: I found them on the table when I moved in.)

Variant 1 Puzzle stories

1   A man and his son were crossing the road when they were knocked down by a bus. The man was killed and the boy was rushed to hospital for an operation. However, the surgeon refused to operate saying 'I cannot operate on my own son.' What's it all about?
Clue: Are all nurses women?
Answer: The surgeon was the boy's mother.

2   Very early one morning in autumn the police found two cars on a narrow country road. They were about a hundred yards apart and facing in opposite directions. The window beside the driver was open in each car and each driver was dead. What's it all about?
Clue: What kind of weather do you often have on early mornings in autumn?
or: It was a very foggy morning.
Answer: It was foggy so the drivers had stuck their heads out of their car windows to see the way more clearly. As the cars passed each other, the drivers hit their heads and were killed.

From *Developing Communication Skills* by Pat Pattison
© Cambridge University Press 1987

FRANÇAIS   *De quoi s'agit-il?*

Une nuit je me suis réveillé(e) en sursaut: il y avait quelque chose de froid et de mouillé qui touchait mon visage.

Indice: Il y avait un ruisseau pas loin de mon bungalow.

Solution: C'était en été et je dormais la fenêtre ouverte. Mon chat apportait toujours sa proie à la maison. La plupart du temps, c'était une souris ou un oiseau: cette fois, c'était un poisson qu'il avait pêché!

Variant 1   Histoires énigmatiques

1   Un jour, en rentrant à la maison, les enfants ont trouvé une carotte, deux morceaux de charbon et une pipe dans le jardin, et ils ont beaucoup pleuré. De quoi s'agit-il?

Indice: C'était en hiver.

Solution: Les enfants avaient fait un bonhomme de neige qui avait fondu.

2   Jeannot et Pierre sont étendus sur le sol, morts. Ils sont entourés d'eau et de verre brisé. De quoi s'agit-il?

Indice: Jeannot et Pierre ne sont pas des personnes.

Solution: Ce sont des poissons rouges. Leur aquarium s'est cassé.

From *Developing Communication Skills* by Pat Pattison
© Cambridge University Press 1987

DEUTSCH *Was hat das zu bedeuten?*

Eines Abends ging ich am Meer spazieren und bewunderte den Sonnenuntergang. Es war ein wunderschöner Abend, aber ich verließ den Strand beinahe weinend.

Antwort: Ich hatte einen ertrunkenen Hund im Wasser gesehen. Man hatte ihm die Beine zusammen gebunden und ihn ins Wasser geworfen.

Variant 1 *Rätselgeschichte*

1 Ein Mann geht in eine Bar und bittet um ein Glas Wasser. Der Kellner zieht ein Gewehr hervor und feuert es über dem Kopf des Mannes ab. Der Mann geht hinaus und fühlt sich schon sehr viel besser. Was hat das zu bedeuten?

Tip: Warum könnte ein Mann um ein Glas Wasser bitten?

Antwort: Der Mann hatte Schluckauf. Der Kellner wußte, daß in einem solchen Fall auch ein Schock hilft. Darum feuerte er das Gewehr ab. Dadurch wurde der Mann von seinem Schluckauf geheilt.

2 Ein Mann verläßt jeden Morgen seine Wohnung im siebzehnten Stock, nimmt den Lift nach unten und geht zur Arbeit. Abends fährt er mit dem Lift zum fünften Stock und geht dann die restlichen zwölf Stockwerke zu Fuß hinauf. Was hat das zu bedeuten?

Tip: Denke an die Anordnung der Knöpfe im Lift.

Antwort: Der Mann ist ein Zwerg. Er kann im Lift nur bis zum fünften Knopf hinaufreichen.

7 Discussions and decisions

7.1 Introduction

The problems of class discussions or conversation lessons are well known:

1 Organised discussion is often artificial and doubly so in the FL. (*Class 6B will discuss 'International sport' or 'Nuclear disarmament' from 3 p.m. till 3.30 on Monday afternoon – in French.*)
2 Large groups make normal exchanges of views and comments very difficult.
3 Not everyone has something to say on the given topic.
4 Not everyone is willing and able to speak spontaneously in the FL (or even in their own!).

One source of these problems is that free conversation or discussion in the classroom often lacks almost all characteristics of natural communication in the FL. The activities in this section are therefore based on introducing such characteristics, as described on pp. 7–8, List 2. Since there are innumerable possible topics of discussion, I have concentrated on various ways of organising discussions. The topics given as examples here are supplemented by references to other topics in other sections of the book.

WHAT: *Content of communication*
The topic can be provided by material in the FL (7.2 *Order of preference*, 7.4 *Holiday plans*), or suggestions by learners themselves in a brainstorming session (7.3 *Choices*, 7.5 *Planning*). These sessions can be useful vocabulary building exercises as learners look for words to express their ideas.

  This helps with problems 3 and 4; learners have something to say and some words with which to say it.

WHY 1: *Reason for communication*
The basis of communication in these activities is an information, opinion or ideas gap. Wherever possible, the topic should be one which there is some reason to discuss in the FL. This may mean using FL texts or authentic material (7.2, 7.4), or having the discussion take place in an imagined situation. You can change familiar topics such as *What would you take to a desert island?* or *Who would you throw off a sinking balloon?* in ways which give learners the chance to express ideas and opinions of more apparent relevance for the FL (7.3). In both 7.3 and 7.4, learners may practise talking about their own land and culture in the FL (something they may well have to do in contact with foreign speakers). Some discussions can be

conducted with role-play, which helps many learners to overcome their inhibitions in speaking (see 2.1 *Introduction* to *Dialogues and role-plays*).

This helps with problems 1 and 4: reducing the artificiality or irrelevance of some classroom FL discussions, and the learners' inhibitions about speaking.

WHY 2:   *Result of communication*
The result of all these activities is a decision or series of decisions by the class or group, and the discussion is not therefore concluded simply by time. You can of course announce time limits for reaching a decision, and for group reports. You may decide to use (parts of) a series of lessons to complete the discussions and reports – this will depend to some extent on the learners' own interest and involvement in the topic.

This helps to solve problem 1: learners now talk with a definite end in view.

WHO: *Participants in communication*
The most natural discussions take place in small, face to face groups, as in stage 3 of all these activities. At levels E and I you may use more stage 2 activities – class discussions in which everyone can express an opinion or choice, however simply, and with your help (learners may speak more readily if given time to exchange ideas in pairs or groups first). This class discussion shows if and when level I learners are ready to proceed to stage 3; level A learners may proceed immediately from the introduction in stage 1 to group work.

This helps with problem 2: there is more communication in small groups.

HOW: *Means of communication*
No model phrases are suggested for these activities. In my experience, learners feel hampered in expressing their opinions by the need to use prescribed formulae, if they are not ready to use them naturally.

Most of the activities in this section are designed for free communication practice with any communication strategies, in which you can offer maximum help to the learners in stages 1 and 2 (see 4.1 *Introduction* to *Communication strategies*). With this help from you and their classmates, learners can develop both skill and confidence in communicating their ideas and opinions in the FL.

This helps to solve problem 4: learners are less inhibited when the emphasis is on the content rather than the form of their message.

Other activities in the book offer opportunities to practise phrases for suggesting, agreeing and disagreeing in more controlled situations and with more controlled language: see 5.7 *Split picture stories* and most activities in Section 6 *Puzzles and problems*. 2.4 *Shopping, Variant 3*, and 3.4 *People and things* also give opportunities for group discussions.

See p. 29 for notes on group work, and p. 30 for details of the jury panel which is mentioned in many of these activities.

Penny Ur 1981, in *Booklist* 2a, is the best single source of ideas for discussion practice, for all ages and levels.

7.2   Order of preference
Par ordre de préférence
Einstufung

Basic gap   Opinion gap based on shared information
Aim   To agree on an order of preference
Language   Free, with any communication strategies
Preparation and material   Selecting stories; (optional: stories on handouts for stage 3)

Stage 1   E,I (10 minutes)

Class   Tell a story and write the names of the main characters on the board. Ask the learners to decide their order of preference for these people (see examples in *Teaching material*). Collect the votes and write the results in a grid on the board: *X people put A first, X put him second* etc.; *X people put B first, X put her second*, etc. Where the choices are very different, ask a few learners for their reasons. For purely receptive practice, they can reply in the mother tongue.

Stage 2   E,I (15 minutes)

Class   Tell a story as in stage 1. Learners discuss their preferences briefly in small groups and then report which characters they would put first, second, third, etc., giving reasons. Help them as required with language, and encourage discussion between learners and groups who make different choices. The class may finally be able to agree on an order of preference.

Stage 3   I,A (20 minutes)

Group   Groups hear or read a story on handouts and then try to reach an order of preference for the whole group. At the time limit,

245

groups report and compare their results. If groups can persuade each other, it may be possible for the class to reach a unanimous order. However, the main interest of the activity is finding out each other's different points of view and interpretations of the story.

Example from practice

Level A adult class working with *The shipwreck* (*Teaching material* FRANÇAIS):
Some put the young sailor low on their list because he blackmailed the girl, while some put him high because he made a bargain with her and stuck to it. Some put the fiancé high on the list for his moral standards; some put him at the bottom for being a male chauvinist pig! After lively discussion within and between groups, some learners revised their opinions and others agreed to differ.

Variant 1 Discover the order

A story can be split between a number of handouts so that learners have to reconstruct the story by summarising or reading out (not showing) their sections to each other, and establishing the correct order. Learners then discuss their order of preference for the characters.

See 5.7 *Split picture stories* and 6.7 *Logic problems* for similar practice with split information and discussion.

Variant 2 Best order

This is based on the competitions found in many advertisements which ask readers to put objects in order of importance for a particular context or purpose; or the opinion polls which report general preferences. Groups discuss and report their opinions, to end with a class decision or a (jury panel) vote on the best list. Example:
The ideal partner should be: attractive – faithful – intelligent – kind – rich; have a good job – good manners – good taste – a sense of humour, etc.
Given a context, such as *The ideal holiday hotel* or *The ideal school*, learners can suggest their own list of features, and discuss the final order of preference.

1.6 *Questionnaires* gives guided practice in collecting and discussing information and opinions. See 3.4 *People and things* for similar discussion at a simpler level and 7.5 *Planning* for more elaborate discussions.

Finding and making material

Use stories with at least three characters whose behaviour can be evaluated differently (these are underlined in *Teaching material*). They can be adapted from any of the following sources:
– Newspaper reports (ENGLISH *The accident*).
– Personal experiences of yourself or the learners (DEUTSCH, *The bicycle*).
– Stories from 'personality tests' to discover people's preferences and values (FRANÇAIS *The Shipwreck* – bracketed phrases can be used with adult learners).
– Stories or anecdotes in magazines or collections.
Simple pictures help learners to follow the stories.

Teaching material

ENGLISH *Order of preference*

The accident

A driver came along a country road at midnight, driving too fast. He knocked down a man and his wife, injuring them very badly, but drove on without stopping. A witness took the number of his car and called an ambulance. The driver later appeared in court; the man and wife were too badly hurt to attend. The witness reported that they were gypsies from a local camp who had been walking in the middle of the road. The judge said that gypsies were trouble makers who should all be removed from the area, and dismissed the driver with a £10 fine.

Put the characters in order of who behaved most/least badly in your opinion.

From *Developing Communication Skills* by Pat Pattison
© Cambridge University Press 1987

FRANÇAIS *Par ordre de préférence*

Le naufrage

Un bateau a fait naufrage entre deux petites îles. Il n'y a eu que
cinq survivants: un vieux marin, un jeune marin, une jeune
femme, son fiancé, et un autre jeune homme, l'ami du fiancé.
Ils ont tous nagé vers une des îles. Le vieux marin, le jeune
marin et la femme sont arrivés sur une île avec des rochers, sur
lesquels le vieux marin s'est gravement blessé. Le fiancé et son
ami sont arrivés sur l'autre île, où il n'y avait que des buissons.

La jeune femme était très triste sans son fiancé et l'autre île
était trop loin pour pouvoir y arriver à la nage. Alors, elle a
demandé au jeune marin: Voudriez-vous bien couper un arbre
et me construire un petit canoë? Le marin lui a répondu: Je le
ferai si vous m'embrassez (couchez avec moi ce soir). La jeune
femme ne savait pas quoi faire, alors elle est allée voir le vieux
marin pour lui demander conseil. Il a écouté son histoire et il
lui a dit: Tu dois écouter la voix de ton coeur. La jeune femme
a réfléchi quelques temps et puis elle a dit au jeune marin:
Construisez le canoë!

Il a travaillé toute la journée, et quand le canoë était prêt, la
jeune femme l'a embrassé (à couché avec lui). Ensuite, elle est
montée dans le canoë et est allée vers l'autre île. Son fiancé et
son ami l'ont vue arriver, et l'ami s'est éloigné pour les laisser
seuls. Son fiancé lui a demandé comment elle avait pu
construire le canoë et la jeune femme lui a raconté ce qui s'était
passé. Son fiancé était horrifié. Comment as-tu pu faire cela!
s'est-il écrié. Il l'a quittée, la laissant en pleurs sur la plage. Un
peu plus tard, l'ami est revenu sur la plage et il a vu la jeune
femme, qui pleurait toujours. Il lui a demandé ce qu'elle avait
et, son histoire terminée, il lui a dit: ne pleurez pas, laissez-moi
vous consoler. Il a mis son bras autour de ses épaules et ils sont
partis ainsi tous les deux, dans l'ombre des buissons.

*Décidez d'une hiérarchie dans les caractères; partez du plus
sympathique pour arriver au moins sympathique.*

From *Developing Communication Skills* by Pat Pattison
© Cambridge University Press 1987

DEUTSCH *Einstufung*

Das Rad

Ein fünfzehnjähriger Junge bekam von seinen Eltern ein
Fahrrad. Sie baten ihn, das Rad nachts im Schuppen
einzuschließen, da in der Umgebung schon oft Räder
gestohlen worden waren. Aber der Junge ließ das Fahrrad
meistens auf dem Bürgersteig vor dem Haus stehen. Drei
Wochen lang stellten die Eltern selbst das Rad nachts in den
Schuppen. Dann entschlossen sie sich, ihrem Sohn einen
Denkzettel zu verpassen. Eines Abends, als der Junge wieder
das Rad vor dem Haus hatte stehen lassen, gingen die Eltern zu
ihrem Nachbarn und baten ihn, das Rad in seiner Garage zu
verstecken, so daß der Sohn denken würde, es sei gestohlen
worden. Der Nachbar war einverstanden und versprach, die
Garagentür abzuschließen, aber er vergaß es. Und in dieser
Nacht hat ein Dieb wirklich das Fahrrad aus seiner Garage
gestohlen.

*Wer war deiner Meinung nach für den Diebstahl am meisten/am
wenigsten verantwortlich? Stelle eine Reihenfolge auf.*

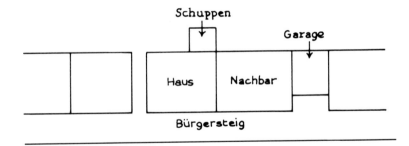

7.3 Choices
Choix
Wählen

Basic gap	Opinion gap based on shared information
Aim	To agree on the most essential items for a particular purpose
Language	Free, with any communication strategies
Preparation and material	Minimal – lists on display or handouts (optional)

Stage 1 E,I,A (5 minutes)

Class Announce a context, such as a holiday in the foreign country, and have a brainstorming session with the whole class (including yourself), deciding what items you want to take. Learners use any communication strategies to express their ideas. You or learners can write all suggestions and new vocabulary on the board, to be used in stages 2 or 3.

Stage 2 E,I (10 minutes)

Class Tell the learners they can only take X% of the items on the list. They discuss their choices briefly in pairs or small groups and then make suggestions about which items to take/leave behind, with reasons, and with your help when required. The class discuss the suggestions and finally vote or reach a unanimous decision.

Stage 3 I,A (15 minutes)

Group Groups discuss how and why they would shorten the given lists, as above; or they make up their own lists of not more than X items. At the time limit, groups write their lists on the board side by side, for comparison and further discussion. A jury panel may decide on the best lists.
See 2.7 *Interviews, Variant 2* for more individual choices.

Variant 1 Charter flight

A more detailed context leads to more detailed discussion: for example, learners can imagine they are taking a charter flight to their holiday destination for a week's stay. The plane is overloaded: Each group of four or five tourists can take only one suitcase between them, which will hold X% of the list, or

X items. So the learners must decide what each person will need individually (this includes the clothes they are wearing) and what items they can leave behind or share, to save space in the suitcase. They can also decide to buy some things at their destination, but must remember that they have only limited spending money. Examples:
Will they share the suntan oil? Do they need suntan oil? Should they all take raincoats or can they share one umbrella? Does it rain much where they are going? Will there be soap and towels in the hotel? Are films expensive at their destination? etc.
You or group leaders can act as tourist guides who give them the information they need about the climate or facilities at their destination (information can come from guidebooks, brochures, personal knowledge or personal invention!). The tourists must speak the FL, as this is the only language the tourist guide can understand.

Variant 2 Desert island

Learners decide what are the absolutely essential items for a stay on a desert island. You or group leaders add details to make the discussion more precise:
Is there fruit on the desert island? Any wild animals? Are they shipwrecked or just camping? etc.

Variant 3 Mme Tussaud's

This context allows discussion based on knowledge of the foreign and native countries. Mme Tussaud's in the foreign capital has to get rid of X% of the figures on display. Learners can suggest or be given names of famous people in various categories: historical, political, famous contemporaries, the arts, show business, sports, etc.; further divided into groups from the country(ies) where the FL is spoken, and the native country.

Learners or pairs choose people from the lists and if necessary look up information and prepare their arguments in advance. The learners then defend their choices in a discussion as to which one or two figures from each category should be retained. They may point out the figures' historical or artistic importance, etc., or the reasons why they will attract tourists to the exhibition. Learners may pretend to be or simply argue on behalf of the chosen person:
(I'm) Kiri te Kanawa/Sir Edmund Hillary, etc. *(and I) must represent New Zealand in Mme Tussaud's because . . .*
The discussion may take place in groups, each taking one set of names and reporting results; or it may be in the form of a

debate in the whole class which can be spread over several lessons, with different learners arguing on behalf of political figures one week, show business the next, etc. with a class discussion and vote each time. Example:

Who would your or your group choose to represent:

E *The American presidency: Washington, Lincoln, Kennedy, the present incumbent?*

F *L'Histoire française: Jeanne D'Arc, Louis XIV, Napoléon, De Gaulle?*

D *Die österreichische Musik: Mozart, Johann Strauss, Karajan, Maria von Trapp* (heroine of *The Sound of Music*)? etc.

After hearing all the arguments, the final decision is made by a class vote or a jury panel.

Variant 4 Balloon or raft debate

Learners choose roles and then argue about why they are so important to society that they must not be thrown off a sinking balloon or raft in order to save the rest. Examples: *Pacifist, policeman, politician, pop star, priest, punk,* etc.

See 2.7 *Interviews, Variant 2,* for similar practice.

Finding and making material

You can provide lists or let the learners make their own, with help from you or dictionaries. Learners can suggest contexts for similar discussions.

Teaching material

ENGLISH *Choices*

Variant 2 Desert island

bottles   plastic bags   tent   axe   spade   knife
gun   rope   radio   batteries   matches   paper
pens   watch   compass   telescope   fishing rod
sleeping bags   salt tablets   vegetable seeds
medicine chest, *etc.*

FRANÇAIS *Choix*

> *Vacances à St Tropez*
>
> un appareil photo   une pellicule   un T-shirt
> des chaussures   des sandales   des sandales de plage
> des lunettes de soleil   de l'huile à bronzer
> un chapeau de soleil   du shampooing   un ciré
> un parasol   un réveil   un matelas pneumatique
> un maillot/slip de bain   des livres de poche
> un dictionnaire, *etc.*

DEUTSCH *Wählen*

> *Ferien im Schwarzwald*
>
> e Schuhe   e Regenjacke   r Regenmantel aus Plastik
> e Jeans   s T-shirt   e Jacke   r Badeanzug
> s Mückenspray   r Reiseführer   s Transistorradio, *usw.*

7.4   Holiday plans
Projets de vacances
Ferienpläne

Basic gap   Information and/or opinion gap based on split or shared information

Aim   To plan a holiday in the foreign country

Language   Free, with any communication strategies

Preparation and material   Collecting holiday brochures or advertisements

Stage 1   E,I (5 minutes)

Class   Show or give some travel posters or brochures to the learners and invite them to make comments or ask questions about the places shown, the language or symbols used, etc. Those who have visited any of the places shown can talk about their visit. For receptive practice, learners may respond in the mother tongue. Mention some holidays you would or would not like to take and given reasons, as a model for stages 2 or 3.

Stage 2 E,I,A (10 minutes)

Class Pairs or groups are given holiday brochures or advertisements in the FL, whose contents they describe to the rest of the class, using communication strategies where necessary, while you help them to express their ideas. Learners discuss the contents of the brochures, and say which holiday they would like to take and why. The decisions may be individual or agreed by the whole class.

Stage 3 I,A (Time to be decided with class)

Group Shared information: Each group has a set of brochures, advertisements, etc. and members have to agree on which holiday they will take together and why.

Split information: each group member has different holiday information, so they must exchange (not show) their information before they can come to a decision about their holiday. Groups then report on the holidays they have chosen and why, and display their material.

See 2.7 *Interviews* for guided practice on a similar topic.

Variant 1 Sightseeing

With the aid of town plans and tourist guides, groups can plan a programme for a day or weekend visit to a foreign city, including:
How they will move about the city, where and what they will eat, where they will stay, what sights they will see, what they will buy, what they will do in the evening, if it rains, etc.
Groups report their plans and a jury panel may decide which is the best.

Variant 2 Television

With the aid of pages from FL television guides, groups plan an evening's or a week's television viewing, then report and compare their results.

Variant 3 Role-play

Learners can make up roles for any of these discussions, either in terms of simple labels or detailed descriptions. Such descriptions can be written by and then exchanged between learners. Examples:
A grandmother, a hippy, an intellectual, a vegetarian, a monk/nun, etc.

You are a non-smoking, non-drinking person who likes the open air and all sports, especially sailing. You hate crowded places and loud music.
Some learners speak more freely when wearing a mask in this way: others prefer to speak as themselves. If possible, let learners form groups according to these preferences.

Finding and making material

See 5.2.1, sources (d), (f) and (g). The destinations may be international, so long as the information is in the FL. English and French are the first or second languages of many exotic holiday destinations, from Polynesia to the Seychelles. Material may include advertisements or brochures for cruises, touring holidays, package holidays, holiday camps such as the Club Méditerranée (brochures in all FLs available). In newspapers and holiday magazines there are notices of specialist holidays: riding, sailing, golf, tennis, sketching, etc. Write for or collect material concerning particular holiday resorts, local or national or international festivals (examples for German: *Bayreuth, Salzburg, Oberammergau, das Oktoberfest in München*), or, on a different scale, brochures for hotels, villas, cottages, caravan and camp sites.

Variant 1: besides the material mentioned above, use the entertainments pages from FL national newspapers, or pages from the weekly guides: *This week in London/Paris/New York*, etc.; or travel brochures for *A weekend in* (city), etc. These need not be absolutely up to date. English teachers: see Birt and Fletcher 1981, 'Night out' in *Booklist* 2a.

7.5 **Planning**
Projets
Planen

Basic gap	Ideas and opinion gap based on personal ideas
Aim	To design plans
Language	Free, with any communication strategies
Preparation and material	Minimal – list of suggestions (optional)

Stage 1   E,I,A (5 minutes)

Class   Announce a contest such as designing a holiday villa or village in the foreign country; decide the location (country, mountains, seaside, near any big town, etc.). Have a brainstorming session in which everyone suggests what this place should contain (see *Teaching material* for examples), using any communication strategies. You or learners can write the suggestions on the board; learners can copy them for use in stage 2 or 3.

Stage 2   E,I,A (20 minutes)

Class   You or learners draw a basic ground plan for the villa or village on the board, which is then filled in more precisely according to suggestions from the class, using ideas from the brainstorming session in stage 1. Encourage discussion until the whole class agrees on the final plan.

Stage 3   I,A (Time to be decided with class)

Group   Groups make up their own plans: for example, they may design a villa, or a holiday camp, with facilities to suit each member of the group; or, on a larger scale, an ideal village or town. They can use the list of suggestions from stages 1 or 2, or start from scratch. Finally the groups display their labelled plans for comparison and discussion. A jury panel can select the best plan(s).

Alternatively, the report stage can be organised as a press conference or public meeting (role-play). Two members of each group, acting as architects or planners, present their plans to the rest of the class, who act as reporters or interested members of the public and question them closely about the advantages and failings of their work:

The kitchen is facing south – it will get too hot.
Why isn't there an infirmary or hospital in the town?
When all the projects have been examined in this way, there can be a class vote on the best one.

See 7.2 *Order of preference* for simpler practice on these lines.

Variant 1 Difficult decisions

You or learners can devise plans which make more detailed discussion and compromise necessary. Examples:
Holiday villa: the rooms differ in size and amenities: some are single, some double; some have a bathroom or shower, some have not; some have a balcony and sea view, others have not, etc. The group decides who will take each room and how they will share the cost of renting the villa.
Town plan: learners each live in a different quarter of the town and must decide where the most and the least desirable locations – from golf course to gasworks – shall be located.

Finding and making material

Learners use their own ideas and experience; they can also gain ideas – and vocabulary – from previous work with 7.4 *Holiday plans* and the variants if this has included advertisements for holiday villas, resorts, etc. in the FL. 'Foreign country' includes any land where the FL is spoken. Learners may suggest further planning projects.

Examples of lists are divided between the languages in *Teaching material*. For *Variant 1*, there is a list for each language and a sample map.

Teaching material

ENGLISH *Planning*

Holiday villa:
Terrace, patio – garden – pool – bar – balconies – barbecue – bath, shower, jacuzzi – TV, stereo, video – various rooms, maid's room – (double) garage with car(s) – stable for horse(s) – private beach, *etc.*

Variant 1 Difficult decisions

Airport – rubbish dump – soap factory – prison – nuclear power station – football stadium, *etc.*

FRANÇAIS *Projets*

Village/ville:
le café – le centre commercial (l'ensemble de magasins) – le
commissariat – l'école – l'église – la gare – l'hôpital – l'hôtel de
ville – le bureau de poste – la piscine – le casino – le court de
tennis – la bibliothèque – la discothèque – l'hôtel – le restaurant
– l'aéroport – la maison des jeunes, *etc.*

Variant 1 **Décisions difficiles**

l'aéroport – le dépôt d'ordures – l'usine de savon – la centrale
nucléaire – la prison – le stade (de football), *etc.*

DEUTSCH *Planen*

Ferienlager:
s Hotel oder (r) Bungalows – s (Garten)Restaurant – e Bar –
r Nachtclub – e Diskothek – s Spielkasino – s Schwimmbad –
r Schwimmunterricht – (r) Tennisplätze – r Tennisunterricht –
s Segeln – s Tiefseetauchen – (s) Pferde – e Reitschule – s Golf
– s Yoga – (s) Mietboote – s Rollschuhlaufen
(Schlittschuhlaufen) – Skilaufen – e Bibliothek – Kunst und
Handwerk – r Bridge Club – Aerobic, *usw.*

Variant 1 **Schwierige Entscheidungen**

r Flughafen – e Mülldeponie – e Seifenfabrik – s Gefängnis –
s Atomkraftwerk – s Fußballstadion, *usw.*

ENGLISH   FRANÇAIS   DEUTSCH

Map for Variant 1

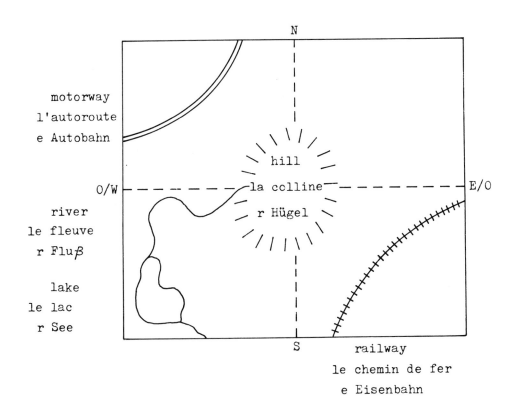

From *Developing Communication Skills* by Pat Pattison
© Cambridge University Press 1987

Villa plan for Variant 1

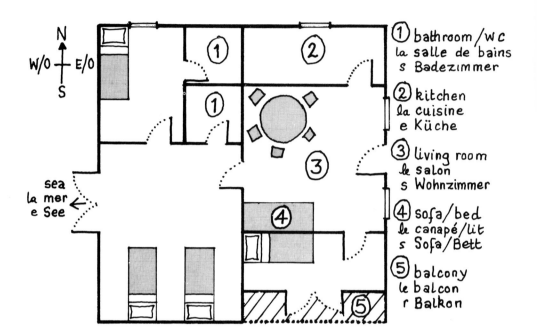

From *Developing Communication Skills* by Pat Pattison
© Cambridge University Press 1987

Booklists

1 Textbooks consulted

These books are listed alphabetically by title, under
ENGLISH, FRANÇAIS and DEUTSCH. Since many form a
series published over a number of years, and often in revised
editions at different times and in different countries, only the
country and the decade of first publication are given, so far as
these can be ascertained. Where no country is given, the books
were originally published in the United Kingdom.

ENGLISH

Access to English. Oxford University Press (1970s)
Channel 6, 5, etc. (France): Belin (1980s)
English Visa. Oxford University Press (1980s)
Imagine You're English. (France): Belin (1970s)
Learning English: Modern Course. (W. Germany): Klett (1970s)
Mainstream. (Sweden): Skolforlaget Gävle (1970s)
New Concept English. Longman (1960s)
New Present Day English. Hodder and Stoughton (1970s)
Quartet. Oxford University Press (1980s)
Strategies. Longman (1970s)
Streamline. Oxford University Press (1970s)
Success with English. Penguin (1960s)

FRANÇAIS

Action. Nelson (1980s)
Archipel. (France): Didier (1980s)
Bleu, Blanc, Rouge. (Sweden): Almqvist & Wiksell (1970s)
Carrefour. (Netherlands): Educaboek (1970s)
Cartes sur Table. (France): Hachette (1980s)
Communications. Oxford University Press (1980s)
En Avant. E. J. Arnold (1967–79)
Etudes françaises. (W. Germany): Klett (1970s)
Hexagone. Oxford University Press (1980s)
Nos Amis (U.S.A.): Harcourt Brace Jovanovich (1970s)
On parle français. (Sweden): Almqvist & Wiksell (1960s)
On y va. (Sweden): Skolforlaget Gävle (1970s)
Salut! (Eire): The Educational Company (1980s) and Cambridge
  University Press (1980s)
Sans Frontières. (France): Clé International (1980s)
Tricolore. Arnold-Wheaton (1980s)
Vive le français. (Sweden): Glurup (1970s)
Vive le français. (Canada and U.S.A.): Addison-Wesley (1980s)

DEUTSCH

Aufbau. Oliver and Boyd (1970s)
Deutsch Aktiv. (W. Germany): Langenscheidt (1970s)
Deutsch Heute. Nelson (1980s)
Deutsch Konkret. (W. Germany): Langenscheidt (1980s)
Die Deutschstunde. (Sweden): Esselte Studium (1970s)
Kapiert. Oxford University Press (1980s)
Kennzeichen D. (Netherlands): Wolters Noordhoff (1970s)
Themen. (W. Germany): Hueber (1980s)
Unsere Freunde. (U.S.A.): Harcourt Brace Jovanovich (1970s)
Vorwärts. E. J. Arnold (1970s)
Wer? Wie? Was? (Vorwärts International). E. J. Arnold (1980s)

2a Sources of communicative activities and material

These books all include useful ideas and material which can be
adapted for any language. Their contents are not exclusively
directed to oral communication practice. There are references
to them in Sections 1 to 7.

Birt, D. and M. Fletcher (1981). *Activity Pack Elementary.* London:
  Edward Arnold. (see 2.4 and 7.4)
Byrne, D. and S. Rixon (1979). *ELT Guide 1: Communication games.*
  Slough: NFER Publishing Company.
Carrier, M. (1980). *Take 5: Games and activities for the language learner.*
  Walton-on-Thames: Nelson-Harrap.
Chamberlin, A. and K. Stenberg (1976) *Play and Practise.* London:
  John Murray.
Christion, A. M. and S. Bassano (1982). *Look Who's Talking!*
  Oxford: Pergamon.
Frank, C. and M. Rinvolucri (1983). *Grammar in action.* Oxford:
  Pergamon.
Klippel, F. (1985). *Keep talking: Communicative fluency activities for
  language teaching.* Cambridge University Press.
Hadfield, J. (1984). *Communication Games: A collection of games and
  activities for elementary students of English.* Walton-on-Thames:
  Nelson-Harrap.
Lee, W. R. (1965, 1979 new edn). *Language Teaching Games and
  Contests.* Oxford University Press.
Lohfert, W. (1983). *Kommunikative Spiele für Deutsch als
  Fremdsprache.* Munich: Hueber.
Maley, A. and A. Duff (1975). *Sounds Interesting.* Cambridge
  University Press (see 5.8).
Maley, A. and A. Duff (1979). *Sounds Intriguing.* Cambridge
  University Press. (see 5.8)
Maley, A. and A. Duff (1978). *Variations on a Theme.* Cambridge
  University Press. (see 2.6 and 5.8)
Maley, A. and A. Duff (1978, 1982 new edn). *Drama Techniques in*

*Language Learning: A resource book of communication activities for
language learners.* Cambridge University Press. (see 5.5 and 6.4)
(German edition: *Szenisches Spiel und freies Sprechen im Fremd-
sprachenunterricht: Grundlagen und Modelle für die Unterrichtspraxis.*
Munich: Hueber Verlag.)
Mortimer, C. (1985). 'Stress time', *Elements of Pronunciation.*
Cambridge University Press. (see 5.8)
Moskowitz, G. (1978). *Caring and Sharing in the Foreign Language
Class.* Rowley, Mass.: Newbury House. (see 1.1)
Mundschau, H. (1974). *Lernspiele für den neusprachlichen Unterricht*
(Englisch/Französisch). Munich: Manz Verlag.
Olsen, J. E. W-B. (1982). *Communication Starters: Techniques for the
language classroom.* Oxford: Pergamon.
Page, B. (ed.) (1982–4). *Communication in French* series. Cambridge
University Press.
Ur, P. (1981) *Discussions that Work: Task-centred fluency practice.*
Cambridge University Press. (see 7.1)
Weiss, F. (1983). *Jeux et Activités Communicatives dans la Classe de
Langue.* Paris: Hachette.
Wright, A., D. Betteridge and M. Buckby (1979, 1984 new edn).
Games for language learning. Cambridge University Press. (see 2.3)

2b   Sources for pictures and picture stories

Further sources of pictures and picture stories which can be
used or adapted for communication practice in any language
(see Section 5).

Byrne, D. and A. Wright (1974). *What's it All About?* London:
Longman.
Heaton, J. B. (1966). *Composition Through Pictures.* London:
Longman.
Kossatz, H. (1972). *So ein Dackel.* Stuttgart: Ernst Klett Verlag.
MacAlpin, J. 1980. *The Magazine Picture Library.* London: Allen and
Unwin. (ideas on collecting and using magazine pictures)
Mad Magazine, in FL editions. (see 5.7)
Maley, A., A. Duff and F. Grellet (1980). *The Mind's Eye.*
Cambridge University Press. (see 5.8)
Plauen, E. O. (1964). *Vater und Sohn.* Constance: Otto Maier
Verlag. (with teaching texts in German by F. Eppert: 1971 and
1975. Munich: Hueber.)
Sempé (various FL editions of his cartoons and cartoon stories; in
France, many paperback editions published by Denoël in 1950s
and 1960s.)
Timms, W. W. (1977). *International Picture Stories.* London: Hodder
and Stoughton. (with vocabulary in English, French, German and
Spanish)
Wright, A. (1984). *1000 Pictures for Teachers to Copy.* London and
Glasgow: Collins.

2c Sources for puzzles

Most of these books are in and for English, but teachers who have time to translate or adapt the basic material will find they provide a rich and stimulating source of communicative practice with all language skills.

Frank, C., M. Rinvolucri and M. Berer (1982). *Challenge to Think*. Oxford University Press.

Jones, L. (1980). *Graded English Puzzles 1, 2 and 3*. London and Glasgow: Collins.

Maley, A. and F. Grellet (1981). *Mind matters*. Cambridge University Press.

Porter Ladousse, G. (1983). *Speaking Personally: Quizzes and questionnaires for fluency practice*. Cambridge University Press.

Ziegesar, M. and D. van (1978 and 1980). *Practice with Puzzles 1 and 2*. Oxford University Press.

3 Background reading

I have chosen books with useful things to say on the theory and practice of communicative language teaching which teachers may find most directly relevant to their classroom practice.

Brumfit, C. J. and K. Johnson (1979). *The Communicative Approach to Language Teaching*. Oxford University Press.

Hawkins, E. (1981). *Modern Languages in the Curriculum*. Cambridge University Press.

Holden, S. (ed.) (1983). *Focus on the Learner: 1983 Bologna Conference*. Oxford: Modern English Publications.

Holden, S., (ed.). *Teaching and the Teacher: 1984 Bologna Conference*. Oxford: Modern English Publications.

Lunt, H. N. (ed.) (1982). *Communication Skills in Modern Languages: At school and in higher education*. London: C.I.L.T. (Centre for Information on Language Teaching and research).

Littlewood, W. (1981). *Communicative Language Teaching: An introduction*. Cambridge University Press.

Littlewood, W. (1984). *Foreign and Second Language Learning: Language acquisition research and its implications for the classroom*. Cambridge University Press.

Rivers, W. M. (1983). *Communicating Naturally in a Second Language: Theory and practice in language teaching*. Cambridge University Press.

Savignon, S. J. and M. S. Berns (eds.) (1984). *Initiatives in Communicative Language Teaching*. Reading, Mass.: Addison-Wesley.

Stevick, E. W. (1982). *Teaching and Learning Languages*. Cambridge University Press.

Language indexes

1 Structures

The following activities can be used for controlled practice with various grammatical structures: for example 1.3, 1.4, 2.6, 3.5, 6.4. Examples cited below are mostly in *Teaching Material*: some, particularly for English, are in the main text of the activity or variants. Most examples can be adapted for any level or language.

	1					2						3						4					5					6						7			
	2	3	4	5	6	2	3	4	5	6	7	2	3	4	5	6	7	2	3	4	5	6	4	5	6	7	8	3	4	5	6	7	8	2	3	4	5
Verbs: all tenses	✓	✓	✓	✓	✓							✓	✓	✓	✓	✓	✓		✓	✓	✓	✓	✓	✓	✓	✓	✓	✓	✓	✓	✓	✓	✓				
conditionals		✓	✓	✓	✓								✓				✓					✓		✓	✓	✓			✓	✓	✓	✓			✓	✓	
passives			✓		✓		✓						✓				✓							✓	✓	✓	✓		✓	✓	✓	✓	✓				
can, must, need		✓	✓		✓										✓		✓			✓										✓							
reflexives		✓	✓		✓			✓						✓						✓		✓				✓			✓	✓							
with *être/sein*	✓			✓																✓									✓	✓							
Adjectives		✓	✓	✓	✓								✓		✓	✓			✓	✓		✓	✓	✓	✓	✓	✓		✓		✓						
comparative, superlative		✓	✓	✓	✓								✓		✓	✓			✓	✓		✓	✓	✓	✓	✓			✓			✓	✓		✓	✓	
Adverbs		✓	✓	✓	✓											✓					✓																
Indirect speech		✓			✓		✓							✓			✓												✓	✓							
Pronouns, ind. possessives		✓					✓							✓		✓					✓								✓	✓							
Prepositions	✓						✓								✓					✓			✓	✓	✓	✓		✓	✓								
some, any/du, en/kein		✓				✓	✓													✓									✓								
Who? when? etc. questions		✓	✓	✓	✓		✓						✓		✓				✓			✓			✓				✓			✓		✓	✓		
cases (Deutsch)		✓	✓	✓					✓							✓				✓		✓			✓				✓		✓						

2 Functions

The following activities can be used for controlled practice with various language functions: 1.3, 1.4, 2.6, 3.5. Examples cited below are in *Teaching material*, and in all languages unless otherwise stated (some English examples are in the main text of the given activity).

	1					2						3						4								5					6						7			
	2	3	4	5	6	2	3	4	5	6	7	2	3	4	5	6	7	1	2	3	4	5	6	7	8	4	5	6	7	8	3	4	5	6	7	8	2	3	4	5
Asking for/giving personal information	✓	✓									F					F	✓								✓	✓				✓										
general information	✓	✓					✓	✓	✓		✓		E	F	✓	✓	✓						✓	✓	✓		✓	✓	✓		✓	✓	✓				✓	✓	✓	✓
opinions		D	F					✓					F		F		✓						✓	✓						E			✓	✓	✓	✓	✓	✓	✓	✓
(dis)likes, preferences	E	E D	F												✓														✓								✓	✓	✓	✓
feedback over language																			✓	E E		E																		
Suggesting, (dis)agreeing, contradicting														E	E	E	E								E	E	E	E	E								✓	✓	✓	✓
Requesting, offering, inviting, etc.	F D									D										✓		✓	✓																	
Discussing							✓		✓						✓		✓										✓	✓				✓								✓
Describing											E F															✓	✓	✓	✓	✓		✓	✓	✓	✓	✓				✓
Narrating														✓																		✓								
Language used in games																																								

3 Situations and topic areas

The following activities can be set in various situations: 1.3, 1.4, 2.6, 2.7, 3.5, 4.4, 4.5. You can also use 1.5, 1.6, Sections 3, 4, 5, 6 and 7.2 for various topic areas. The following examples for [E]nglish, [F]rançais, [D]eutsch (✓ = all) in text or *Teaching material* can be adapted for all languages and for most levels.

The table lists the following topic areas with cross-references to sections 1–7:

- Buildings, towns, finding the way
- Clothes, appearance
- Customs (douane)
- Family
- Food and drink: restaurants
- Furniture, rooms
- Health
- Holidays, hotels, tourism
- Money
- Pets, animals

Shops, shopping

Sports and hobbies

Time

Travel: car, train, etc.

Weather

Alphabet

Numbers

General index

			Can be used or adapted for:			Can be used with:						
		Minimal preparation	receptive practice (stage 1)	reading and writing	computer programme	cultural content	literary content	film or video	personal imagination and ideas	personal information or values	Ice-breaking activities	Filler activities (stage 3)
1	2	✓			✓							
	3	✓		✓	✓					✓		✓
	4	✓	✓	✓	✓					✓		
	5			✓								
	6	✓		✓		✓	✓			✓	✓	
2	2	✓	✓		✓	✓					✓	✓
	3	✓	✓	✓	✓	✓	✓				✓	✓
	4	✓		✓	✓	✓						
	5		variant 1	✓	✓							
	6		✓	✓	✓	✓			variant 3		✓	✓
	7								✓	variant 2		variant 1
3	2	✓	✓		✓							✓

		C1	C2	C3	C4	C5	C6	C7	C8	C9	C10
3	3	✓	variant 2	variants	✓	✓	✓		variant 1	variants	✓
	4	✓	✓	variant 5	✓	✓	✓	✓	✓		
	5		✓	variant 1	✓	✓	✓				✓
	6		✓		✓	variants	variants	✓	variant 1		✓
4	2	✓	✓	variant 1	✓	variant 2	variant 2				✓
	3	✓	✓	variant 1	✓	·				variant 1	
	4	✓			✓		✓	✓			
	5		✓		✓	variant 2	✓	✓	✓	✓	✓
	6		✓		✓	variant 2		✓		✓	
5	4	✓	✓		✓				variant 3	variant 3	
	5		✓		✓		variant 3				
	6		✓		✓				variant 3	variant 3	variant 3
	7							variant 3	✓		
	8		✓		✓			✓	✓		
6	3	✓	✓	variant 1	✓	✓		✓			
	4	✓	✓		✓	✓			variant 1		✓
	5	✓	✓			✓		✓			✓

(continued)

	Minimal preparation	receptive practice (stage 1)	reading and writing	computer programme	cultural content	literary content	film or video	personal imagination and ideas	personal information or values	Ice-breaking activities	Filler activities (stage 3)
		Can be used or adapted for:						Can be used with:			
6		✓	✓		✓	✓		variant 2			✓
7			✓	✓	✓	✓					✓
8	✓		✓					✓	✓		✓
7 2	✓	✓	✓						✓		✓
3	✓		✓		✓	✓			✓		✓
4		✓	✓		✓				✓		
5	✓		✓					✓	✓		